OUTLAW MACHINE

ALSO BY BROCK YATES

Sunday Driver

The Decline and Fall of the American Auto Industry

Enzo Ferrari: The Man and the Machine

The Critical Path

OUTLAW MACHINE

Harley-Davidson and the Search for the American Soul

BROCK YATES

BROADWAY BOOKS   New York

Designed by Melodie Wertelet

Library of Congress Cataloging-in-Publication Data
Yates, Brock W.
Outlaw Machine: Harley-Davidson and the search for the American soul /
Brock Yates.—1st Broadway Books trade paperback ed.
p. cm.
Originally published: Boston: Little, Brown, and Co., 1999.
1. Harley-Davidson motorcycle—History.   2. Popular culture—United States.
3. Harley-Davidson Incorporated—History.   I. Title.
TL448.H3 Y38 2000
629.227′5′0973—dc21   00-020018

ISBN 0-7679-0516-4

00 01 02 03 04 10 9 8 7 6 5 4 3 2

To my beautiful wife, Pamela.
It was her idea, and she rode with me
from the beginning to the end.

CONTENTS

ACKNOWLEDGMENTS

Many fine writers have recorded the ups and downs of the Harley-Davidson saga. Their efforts, in various books and magazines, supplied invaluable background for this effort, which pales in comparison to the detailed data produced by them. Much is owed to writers like Peter Eagan, Clement Salvatori, Alan Girdler, David K. Wright, Tod Rafferty, Harry V. Sucher, Jerry Smith, Peter C. Reid, Timothy Remus, Malcolm Birkitt, Shaun Barrington, Hugo Wilson, Tim Paulson, Frederic Winkowski, John Carroll, Randy Leffingwell, and Tom Bolfert. Without them and other devoted scholars, much of the history and heritage of this unique American machine would have been lost.

Special thanks to the following:

DAVID ABRAHAMSON, a former editor and associate at *Car and Driver*, who, as an associate professor of journalism at Northwestern University, offered valuable historical and social insights.

BOB BITCHIN, publisher, editor, novelist, and former hard-core biker, for his observations about the outlaw biker lifestyle and ethic.

MONTY BOLFERT, of Harley-Davidson public relations staff, for her enthusiastic help throughout the project.

JEFF BLEUSTEIN, for his prescient comments on the company's business philosophy.

JOHN BRAY, a serious Harley enthusiast and a fair-minded and perceptive observer of the scene.

BUZZ BUZZELLI, editor of *American Rider,* one of the most articulate and clearheaded magazines devoted to Harley-Davidsons.

WILLIE G. DAVIDSON, the man who more than anyone else exemplifies the unique spirit and aesthetics of Harley-Davidson.

PAUL DEAN, editor and writer of *Cycle World* and *Big Twin,* who truly understands the breadth and scope of the Harley-Davidson mystique.

WILLIE HOPKINS, advertising guru, who aided in background research on the subject.

YASHUSHI ISHIWATARI, *Car and Driver*'s Japanese correspondent, who did the navigating through the streets of Tokyo.

MARK LANGELLO, for his vivid photography of the Harley-Davidson scene.

STEFAN PETROUTKA, manager of Bobo's Chopper Corner in Munich, for his insights into the European Harley business.

STEVE PIEHL, Harley-Davidson public relations director, for his help and cooperation.

MARTIN JACK ROSENBLUM, the poetic company historian, for his probing analysis of the company's past and its future.

SEVERAL HELLS ANGELS, who, for obvious reasons, choose to remain anonymous, but whose penetrating insights were invaluable.

JOHN SCHOUTEN and his associate, JAMES MCALEXANDER, for their deeply perceptive and detailed demographic study of the entire Harley-Davidson mind-set.

JERRY SMITH, for his background detail and helpful analysis of the pivotal Hollister riot.

BUDDY STUBBS, for finding my Heritage Softail on short notice when none were supposed to be available.

VINCE VITO, the Nice, France, dealer who provided interesting detail on the influence of Harley-Davidson on the French motorcycle industry and the economy as a whole.

GISA WAGNER, our friend in Singapore, for her constant updates from that part of the world.

JIM WILLIAMS, longtime friend and arm's-length observer of the project.

INTRODUCTION

Like most journalists, I consider myself an outsider, a standoffish observer of scenes, uncommitted, independent, unwilling (or unable) to immerse myself in any single mind-set, devoted, in a broad sense, to the wisdom of Marcel Proust, who counseled, "Embrace those who seek the truth; beware of those who find it." This was the case with the Harley-Davidson phenomenon, which seemed from a distance to embody a zealous, near cultlike involvement with a machine. It is a tiresome canard that Americans maintain a love affair with their automobiles. That is nonsense. By and large they view their cars as necessary appliances to haul the supine body from pillar to post. To find true love of the automobile, one must travel to Germany, Italy, or Great Britain, where affection levels far exceed those to be found in the United States. But the Harley-Davidson is different. Its owners truly cherish the thing, preening it like a pet horse and espousing mystical theories about it and its quasi-human traits. Viewed by an outsider, the Harley-Davidson demanded examination.

Once long ago, I owned a Harley. It was a well-used 1959 XLCH Sportster that I banged around on in the midsixties until impatience with its crankiness and its oil leaks prompted a trade for a Japanese-made Suzuki. The Sportster weighed 480 pounds and made about forty-five horsepower when it was occasionally in proper tune. It offered a heart-stopping top speed of 115 miles per hour, if dealer claims were to be believed, although with a broken speedometer and sufficient vibration to blur vision at any velocity past sixty, speed became an abstraction useful only for impressing the uninitiated. The Sportster's tiny 1.9-gallon gas tank offered limited range, which, thanks to the absence of a fuel gauge, produced a guessing game during short, noisy blasts between service stations.

When I sold the Sportster, there was no mystique attached to it. Harleys had a lousy reputation for reliability and quality, and the trendies found them laughable arks when compared to the new superbikes from Japan. Those who rode Harley-Davidsons fell into three groups: carbohydrate-overloaded slobs who puttered around on their bojangled Electra Glides, greasy punks emulating those rare and exotic California barbarians known as the outlaw bikers, and the outlaws themselves. All operated on the fringes of society; one group the source of condescending amusement, the other two observed warily from a respectable distance.

Then, as the depressing and unfocused seventies opened into the bright and brash eighties, Harley-Davidsons came into prominence. Men who ten years earlier would have resorted to public transportation before buying one of the Milwaukee-built nightmares began lining up like fevered new converts to buy Harleys. My first inkling of the new trend came when a friend, a prominent Porsche dealer, announced that he had purchased a new Harley. It made no sense. Here was a trend surfer of the first magnitude, a man whose social props were the best — Gucci loafers, Rolex Oysters, Vuitton luggage, Porsche 911s, Porsche Design sunglasses, BMW motorcycles — bragging about his newest possession, a monster 665-pound, metallic silver Harley Fat Boy, hauled off his dealer's floor, after a sufficient wait, for $11,000. Clearly, something was going on, and it wasn't happening in the grimy warrens of blue-collar neighborhoods where regular Harleys lived. The bad old machine had come uptown, and my curiosity was piqued.

Somehow the Harley-Davidson seemed connected to the angst that permeated the nation, the pathological fears that consumed the citizenry even as they lived through the most peaceful and prosperous period in recorded history. Was it a subliminal sense that men and women were losing control? That Orwell was right and that Big Brother, in the form of a computerized, centralized nanny state, was seizing personal independence and freedom of action and thought in fiendishly subtle and imperceptible ways? Was the attraction of this aged motorcycle a reaction to the brave new world, much as were the fascinations with traditional architectural forms, natural fabric clothing fashions, antiques of all kinds, older music with discernible lyrics, etc.? Were its roguish image and faint aura of danger a counterbalance to the stifling aspects of political correctness and the rigid codes of gender androgyny?

To probe these questions, I returned to the world of Harley-Davidson. In 1995, the machines were at peak demand. One did not simply walk into a dealership and choose one out of stock. Most popular models required a year or more wait for delivery, and at

premium prices. Thankfully, old friend and longtime dealer Buddy
Stubbs was able to help. A top-level motorcycle racer in his youth,
Stubbs's father had been a Harley-Davidson dealer since the late
1930s, and Buddy's sparkling new store on the north side of
Phoenix was the latest expression of his lifelong involvement with
the brand. Somehow, Stubbs was able to shake loose an all-black
Heritage Softail for me, and on a sunny Arizona afternoon I was re-
united with the legend.

I chose the Softail because it was the most traditional and authentic Harley-Davidson of them all, a throwback machine that retained most of the elemental qualities that make Harleys so special.
An old-fashioned carburetor supplied gasoline to its traditional
forty-five-degree, air-cooled, eighty-cubic-inch V-twin engine, as opposed to the more contemporary fuel-injection setups on other
models. Its engine was solidly mounted to the frame, while other
big cruiser bikes had advanced rubber mounts to reduce vibration.
Its fringed and bechromed leather saddlebags dated to the 1930s.
Its chunky, sculptured power plant and attendant exhaust pipes, its
teardrop-shaped gas tank and the flawless pinstriping formed kinetic sculpture that was more visually riveting than fun to ride. After yanking off the plastic windscreen and installing lower and
sportier handlebars in place of the sprawling buck-horn versions, I
still found that the Harley was truly antediluvian. There being no
tachometer, upshifts were signaled when the foot-pad vibrations
became intolerable. At over seven hundred pounds, the machine
was ungainly and demanded full attention while cornering, even at
modest speeds. Once in fifth gear and cruising between fifty and
sixty miles per hour, the Softail was a pleasant, if docile, motorcycle. At higher velocities, the engine vibration signaled discomfort
both for the rider and power plant. By all contemporary standards,
I was riding a spanking new antique.

Yet there was a haunting quality about the machine, a built-in patina that was impossible to ignore. Yes, on many rides I wished for more power, less eyeball-juddering vibration, better handling, and a reduced sensation of sheer bulk. But counterbalancing that was the innate sensation that this was a Harley-Davidson and that I, in some small way, was linked to nearly a hundred years of American frontier classicism. It also served as an entrée into a special, uniquely American tribalism. Somehow, I felt among the anointed when on the Harley, even as quicker Japanese bikes scooted by on the open road. I was probing into the mind-set that offered a different perception of life, a call to live by the slogan on my custom air cleaner that read, "Live to ride. Ride to live."

That had to be resisted if I was to retain an outsider's view. As I delved into the culture in such diverse locales and hangouts as South Dakota's Sturgis, Florida's Daytona Beach, New Hampshire's Laconia, California's Rock Store restaurant, Tokyo's Roppongi district, Singapore's Orchard Road, Munich's Schwabing district, the Côte d'Azur, central Paris, and London, I tried to stand back, dealing with the subject not as one of the true believers but as a detached observer and reporter.

This was not easy, because the lifestyle surrounding the Harley-Davidson is an intense aphrodisiac, at least for tradition-bound males like myself. There is something so elemental, so lusty, so purely and classically American about the machine that it is hard to resist. Its very flaws, its very unfashionableness, its creaky technology, mark it as uncompromising and unfailingly honest and real. The Heritage Softail was and is part of the American mythology that seems threatened by so many ominous technical and cultural developments as we head into the third millennium. Great turmoil is ahead, and facing that uncertainty, many of us seem to be looking backward, seeking bedrock traditions, especially as they relate to the freedom and independence embodied in the great western frontier. It is in many ways a futile effort, a nostalgic distraction from the smooth-edged, computer-driven, mass-culture realities of the day. But as people embrace aged icons like the Harley-Davidson, the struggle to link the verities of the past with the amorphous threats of the new millennium seems to gain intensity. It is that struggle that makes the Harley-Davidson such a unique and powerful talisman and one that, for nearly three years, led me to ride the trail of the true believers.

BROCK YATES
Wyoming, New York

PART ONE · THE BEAST AWAKENS

1 · FIRST CONTACT

The noise. The god-awful death rattle issuing from the bow-
els of his infernal machine. He had been a quiet kid, one of those
bashful back-markers in elementary school, a pasty-faced runt lost
in the playground stampedes and the adolescent classroom chatter.
Now, suddenly, as a junior in high school, he had reinvented himself, a transmogrification of quasi-lethal intensity.

Among the brush-cut and bobby-soxed hierarchy of 1950s
teenage life, he cut a wide swath, swooping among the Goody Two-
shoes aboard his black-and-chrome monster. Wrapped in a wide-
collared leather jacket studded with chrome, he was someone to be
reckoned with, a stern-faced stud on a bad-ass motorcycle.

His classmates watched him in a confused state of part scorn,
part envy, from the vantage point of establishment tools: teenagers
operating in the mainstream of conventional lusts over fast cars

and faster women. But the notion of a motorcycle — no, make that a Harley-Davidson motorcycle — was beyond the pale, drifting into the lurid red-light districts occupied by the devil drug, marijuana, and the white-slave trade. Other guys tried the zooter gig, fashioning themselves in duck's-ass haircuts and peg pants in open defiance of the conventions of khaki and gray flannel — the Fonzi-like prototypes later to be immortalized in *Grease* and other fifties flashbacks. But the over-the-top gesture, the ultimate fuck-you to the straight arrows and suck-ups of the day was that motherhumper Harley from hell.

"Wheels" of any kind beyond a Schwinn was the ultimate guy fantasy. Decades would pass before the booming middle class could afford to outfit its high-schoolers with automobiles, much less anything as exotic as motorcycles. The periodicals of the early 1950s swooned over the alleged menace of "hot-rodders," a California manifestation involving youths aboard chopped and channeled flathead Fords who engaged in such sociopathic madness as "drag racing" and death-defying games of "chicken." These exotic little home-built machines, hacksawed out of prewar Fords, were viewed as a motorized expression of the newly discovered teenage species known as "juvenile delinquents." This alleged rabble, sporting T-shirts with Camel packs rolled into the sleeves, represented a new surge of Visigoths marauding through the nation's streets. The dreaded hot rods (a contraction of "hot roadster") would be chronicled in countless hysterical magazine and newspaper stories of the day, culminating in the 1955 cult film *Rebel Without a Cause*, starring that paradigm of 1950s punkdom, James Dean. Drag racing, as portrayed in the film's deadly duel, shook moms and pops out of their Barcaloungers from coast to coast. Images of every kid in America behind the wheel of a hopped-up Ford or, God forbid, a thundering Harley slashing through the suburbs at suicidal speeds, seared their suburbanite brains. Hot rods. Motorcycles. Leather jackets, and in the distance the fearsome tribal drumbeats of rock 'n' roll. The fall of Rome was upon them.

Among the foot-sloggers, the kid on the Harley-Davidson enjoyed an automatic status reserved for those with "wheels" of all types, but in his case they belonged to a mysterious, exotic and faintly ominous, flame-belching motorcycle. A scrubbed classmate from the suburbs was also among the anointed, but purely as a midget leaguer. Somehow he had talked his father into letting him buy a used, clapped-out motor scooter, a lumpy Cushman powered by a one-lung lawnmower engine. On days when he rode it to school, he parked it near the Harley, a dinghy moored in the shadow of that battleship, unworthy of notice by the ship's owner.

The Harley guy would leave class, cloaked in his leather armor on even the warmest days, and stride past the Cushman in total disdain. Legging over the Harley, he fiddled briefly with the fuel valve and the choke before commencing his ritual attack on the kick starter, leaping and cursing as his booted foot rocked up and down on the chromium lever. The monster would fart and grumble, fitfully barking in protest against the intrusion by its master. Finally, after minutes of refusal, the mighty engine would awaken, spewing clouds of raw gas and fire from its twin pipes, rattling windows and sending decent folk scurrying, their ears covered against the din. Once satisfied that the beast was awake, he would settle into its saddle and, rolling his gloved right hand on the handlebar throttle, rev the engine until the plugs cleared and the last living creature within earshot had been intimidated. Then, with his left hand he would reach for the shifter, jam the thing into gear, and roar away, weaving and yawing in a shower of gravel. To the witless squares who knew no such power, it was like witnessing a moon shot almost twenty years hence.

Properly costumed, he had become a member of a tiny, exclusive clique headquartered in a grease-stained warren on the edge of town. There a strange, lanky man ran a dealership for Harley-Davidson motorcycles. It was off-limits to decent folk, a corral for outriders and bandits, bikers and weirdos who rode motorcycles, more a collection of shacks than a real building. The floors were soaked black with motor oil and littered with shards of piston rings, broken chains, shattered cylinder heads, and bent forks — the effluvia of a thousand haphazard repairs. Outside leaned a rabble of old motorcycles, bare-boned frames, piles of shredded tires, and broken engines, a graveyard of outlaw machinery tended by the gaunt man who knew all and was all regarding motorcycles — the high priest in the smoky Harley temple.

One day the suburbanite ventured into the forbidden place, naively searching for a part for his Cushman. This was akin to asking the gunnery officer on the USS *Missouri* for a box of BBs. A Cushman motor scooter in a Harley-Davidson store? Send in the clowns! What's that pie-faced twit doing intruding with that puny, gutless slug among real men's machines? The dealer slouched inside, appearing nearly as filthy as the soot-stained walls. He grunted a response to the kid's question, barely deigning to deal with a noncultist. Other men lurked against the workbenches. They wore grimy denims and sported heavy engineer's boots gleaming with caked motor oil. They smoked heavily, filling the morbid room with gray clouds that mingled with the belching and backfiring of the Harley they were attempting to tune with large screwdrivers. The outlander had clearly stifled conversation, and it would remain so until he departed, leaving them to stand in silent witness to the

rattle-bone thud of the big machine under the dealer's crude ministrations. The kid never returned. Nor did anyone he knew who was
considered a member of decent society ever enter those dreaded
precincts.

Who were those men? The term "biker" would not become part
of the national slang for another decade, and they were therefore
nameless outriders — supplicants to a small but true faith centered
around a brutish machine that fit between their legs. Most rode
Harley-Davidsons, but others traveled on giant Indians — a similar
large American-made motorcycle that remained a steadfast rival,
albeit with sagging sales and loyalties. While hard-edged motorcycle gangs were at the time forming in California, the notion of outlaw organizations coalescing around Harleys and Indians in dinky
cities was unthinkable. Motorcycle gangs might exist in sybaritic
California, where debauched movie stars and other bohemians
played their evil games, but not in the great heartland, where motorcycles sputtered on the dark and mysterious perimeter. For
most Americans banditry as defined by such strange and frightful
cults as the Hells Angels was still beyond their ken in the early
1950s.

The men who hung around the little motorcycle shop were for
the most part lost souls: disoriented and disillusioned WWII veterans, functioning alcoholics, unemployed factory workers, and a
few rebellious teenagers, all of whom found solace in the radiated
strength of the big bikes. Power was available at the kick of the leg
and the flick of the wrist. Equality came at the end of an exhaust
pipe, and every Buick-driving Babbitt better know it. Still, the riders were marginalized, meaningless and essentially ignored, crack-
pots who dressed strangely and hung out in sleazy bars and rode
noisy motorcycles. Fringe players in the grand American scheme

whose sullen expressions of independence seemed harmless and irrelevant. Beyond the noise and bluster of their blowsy motorcycles, who cared about them, save for a few addled teenagers who retained a fearful fascination for their monster machines?

The suburbanite fitfully tried to keep up with his Harley-rider classmate, wrestling as he could against middle-class conventions but lacking the money, much less the social chutzpah, to make the leap aboard a Harley — which, truth be known, he and his peers viewed with a combination of fear and lurid fascination. He managed to marshal sufficient funds by selling the Cushman to obtain a tiny Czechoslovakian CZ-125, with a cylinder barely as large as a Harley carburetor but still a legitimate motorcycle. It would be a source of considerable pride for him to later learn that in fact James Dean himself had entered the world of bikes on a sister unit, rising then into fast British twins before killing himself behind the wheel of a Porsche 550 Spyder sports-racing car. Still, it was not enough. The Harley-Davidsons — with their seventy-four-cubic-inch "Knucklehead" engines — larger than the sixty-seven-cubic-inch power plants of the Volkswagen Beetles that were beginning to arrive on these shores — remained alone; the baddest, grumpiest, surliest motorcycles on earth.

So what if any number of Brit bikes, BSAs, Triumphs, Nortons, et al., could wax a Harley in a head-to-head race? So what if Harleys leaked oil like sieves and burned valves and warped their cylinder heads? So what if their tub-thumping exhausts infuriated proper folk? So what if only the lower orders rode and coveted them? So what if Harley-Davidson was not a nice machine? So what if the people who rode them scared the wee-wee out of the good burghers? Wasn't that the point?

His CZ-125 was eventually traded for a collection of used

sports cars and the rigors of family raising and career chasing. So too for his classmate on the Harley, who gave up his leathers for white perma-press shirts — complete with plastic mechanical pencil holders — and an engineering career in that paradigm of establishmentarianism, General Motors.

His short-lived rebellion was over, and his old Harley had no doubt ended up on the rubble pile behind the shop, now long since demolished and replaced by a miniature golf course and driving range. But his statement had been made, and it would play a minuscule role in the expanding legend of Harley-Davidson, which was about to become one of those precious few machines elevated beyond mere function to the apotheosis of a globe-spanning lifestyle. Its role is a curious one, a duality of good and evil, of raffish innocence and snarling pugnacity. No other icon of the machine age, be it a Ferrari or a Porsche automobile, a rare WWII fighter plane, or a megapriced, English-built Vincent Black Shadow motorcycle, possesses this ambiguity of purpose.

Harley-Davidson prospers worldwide, thanks to its lofty status. It has a patina of history and tradition that cannot be created even by the canniest and most creative of advertising wizards. It is hardly the most technologically advanced or best performing of its breed. Quite to the contrary. The current Harley-Davidson is in essence an antique. Its basic design dates back to 1936 and, in a broad engineering sense, to a French twin-cylinder concept developed at the end of the nineteenth century. It is the perfect flintlock rifle. The world's most refined sundial. But with that antiquity comes tradition and a storied continuity that defies imitation. The Japanese — long masters of the art of creating high-performance engines and capable of making vastly superior motorcycles of all kinds — are frantically dumbing down their product lines in slavish attempts to build faux Harley-Davidsons. The results are perfect replications of the venerable Milwaukee original, but hopeless and hollow gestures. They bring nothing to the table to counter Harley's near century-old aura.

Within that essentially hundred-year saga lies a series of stops and starts and the elements of both success and failure. Contradictions abound, and in a broad sense this grand old machine's persona broadly represents that of the nation that created it — and that radiates its personality around the globe. Rooted in Milwaukee, Harley-Davidson symbolizes the best and the worst of a nation whose growth has been fitful, rebellious, disjointed, and cursed by raging crosscurrents and blurred imagery. If perception equals reality, the source of the Harley mystique begins not with the founding of the company in 1903 by the brothers Davidson, Arthur, William, and Walter, and their friend William Harley, but rather in a steamy farming town in Northern California on Independence Day, 1947.

2 · BIRTH OF THE TERROR

Americans gaped in shock at the photograph on page 31 of the July 21, 1947, issue of *Life* magazine. Peering at the citizenry in boozy defiance and waving a beer bottle at the camera was a pudgy man on a motorcycle. Dozens of empties were littered on the pavement around the drunken rider's jackbooted feet. The caption, written in knife-edge *Life* style, enhanced the outrage:

> On the Fourth of July weekend 4,000 members of a motorcycle club roared into Hollister, California, for a three-day convention. They quickly tired of ordinary motorcycle thrills and turned to more exciting stunts. Racing their vehicles down Main Street and through traffic lights, they rammed into restaurants and bars, breaking furniture and mirrors. Some rested on the curb (above). Others hardly paused. Police arrested many for drunkenness and indecent exposure but could

not restore order. Finally, after two days, the cyclists left with a brazen explanation. "We like to show off. It's just a lot of fun." But Hollister's police chief took a different view. Wailed he, "It's just one hell of a mess."

Lock up your daughters! The Huns are on the roll! Your town may be next. The fat man on the Harley became riveted in the skulls of millions of decent, law-abiding, God-fearing Americans as an alcohol-soaked harbinger of anarchy spreading across the nation.

With that single black-and-white photograph in America's most popular and respected newsmagazine, the images of motorcycling and of Harley-Davidson were altered forever. From that moment on, motorcycles would be tinged with evil: predatory machines ridden by raging barbarians. This legend would be enhanced in years hence by magazine stories, songs, and a spate of motion pictures. Despite the horror generated by the photograph and its ensuing alteration of the image of motorcycles — most specifically Harley-Davidsons — recent research by cooler heads reveals that *Life* was involved — perhaps unwittingly — in the age-old game of yellow journalism, wherein a routine incident is cynically sensationalized.

The Gypsy Tour, a relaxed weekend jaunt, at Hollister had been organized by the Salinas (California) Ramblers Motorcycle Club and the Hollister Veterans' Memorial Park Association as a weekend of motorcycle racing, touring, and recreation. It was but one of dozens of such events, all part of the American Motorcycle Association's schedule of competitions across the nation. The races at the little city's ⅓-mile dirt track in Bolado Park attracted expert riders from all over the West Coast, who traveled to the garlic truck-farming center set in the gravelly brown foothills of the Diablo and Gabilan mountains forty-five miles south of San Jose. They began drifting into town on July 2. They rolled in, lone riders and clusters of three and four, streaming across the dusty flats from tough, working-class Bay area towns like Oakland and San Jose. Others had trekked north from Los Angeles and San Pedro, from San Bernardino and Fontana, splay-legged on chuffing Knuckleheads and aged Indians and a few English Nortons and BSAs. Most had sleeping bags wrapped over their back fenders in preparation for a weekend of camping in the clear, chilly desert nights. Some old-sters came on hulking twins with their women huddled in sidecars, the ultimate luxury transportation. Into Hollister they powered, en-gines rumbling ahead of long brown swirls of desert grit, ready for action. By Friday evening, their numbers had swelled to perhaps two thousand. While no official count was ever made, best esti-mates place the peak crowd at about four thousand by the time the little city returned to normal.

Motorcycle clubs had existed in one form or another since the early 1920s. Most were benign, involved in touring and several forms of motor sports like track racing and hill climbing. But a tiny percentage had assumed a darker image. Embittered and disil-lusioned by the American dream during the Depression, gangs formed up, mainly in the grungy industrial districts of Southern California, to ride and drink together, subsisting on menial jobs and dealing in stolen motorcycle parts. Because Harley-Davidson was the most abundant and popular motorcycle, it was obvious that it would be the brand of choice, both as a possession and a source of stolen income.

Following World War II, thousands of veterans spilled out of the armed forces, disoriented and disenfranchised. Although the GI

Bill of Rights offered the most liberal safety net for ex-soldiers in history, inevitably some drifted toward the fringes of society, unable to make the transition from the intensity of warfare to the comparatively pallid pace of civilian life. They, like the men who had returned from the Civil War and headed toward the great western frontier, or the World War I veterans who formed the so-called Lost Generation, were altered forever, inured to violence and incapable of coping with the strictures of organized society.

Worse yet, peace had not come easily to the late 1940s world. While the United States had not suffered greatly in the war compared to other nations (no physical damage to its cities, 323,000 deaths out of an estimated 50 million worldwide), its ascension to the position of most powerful nation on earth brought great burdens. The bellicose Soviet Union had seized all of Europe east of the Elbe River and, in the words of Winston Churchill, cut it off from the west with an "Iron Curtain." To strengthen the non-Communist European nations, the American government instituted the Marshall Plan and other aid programs to stimulate the recovery of their war-ravaged economies. This shift of funding away from the domestic infrastructure had caused violent strikes in the American coal and rail industries and created deep pockets of unemployment. Added to that was paranoia about the threat of Communist infiltration at the very highest levels of government and in the military. The nation remained strangely unsettled during a period when the tranquillity of peacetime should have pervaded the landscape.

Oozing around the edges were the rebels, for the most part veterans still in their early twenties who were not only restless but possessed of a new knowledge of and fascination with machinery. The war had exposed many of them to all manner of technical exotica — airplanes, tanks, trucks, weapons, power plants, electronic devices, etc., that had been unknown prior to the fighting. This newfound interest had led many into the hot rod and sports car movements and would prompt an explosion in automotive enthusiasm and a major market shift toward small high-performance cars in the decades to come. This was for the most part innocent fun — despite a short-lived media fascination with the perils of "hot-rodding" and "drag racing." But motorcycles produced a harder-edged group of devotees. These veterans, feeling cast out of normal society, embraced the motorcycle not only as a recreational diversion but as a weapon against the established order, a raucous, fire-breathing barbarian of a contraption, the exhaust rattle of which was not unlike that of a .50-caliber machine gun. As weapons for wreaking havoc among the citizenry, unmuffled Harley-Davidsons were adopted by hundreds of restless young men flung into the ennui of the postwar world. This phenomenon was most visible in the Los Angeles basin, which had become a locus of the displaced and the disconnected during the vast Dust Bowl migrations of the 1930s. From this ruck rose the first outlaw motorcycle clubs (never, to this day, do they refer to themselves as "gangs"). It was at Hollister that they made their national debut. Riding into the heat-ravaged town in company with multitudes of workaday motorcycle enthusiasts came hard-edged young riders from clubs with names like the Booze Fighters, the Pissed Off Bastards of Bloomington (POBOBs), the Winos, Satan's Sinners, the Galloping Ghosts, and the Market Street Commandos. There was a nihilistic element to their names, as opposed to those of the hot rod clubs that had formed up at the same time. These carried simple, innocent names like the Road Runners, and the Glendale Stokers and Sidewinders, and while their members engaged in reckless street races on occa-

sion, they operated with a boyish enthusiasm. This was harmless
playtime compared to the violence-prone anarchy of the new-style
motorcycle clubs.

They came to Hollister to raise hell. While a vast majority of the
weekend's riders quietly encamped on the edge of Hollister and
caused no trouble to the city's four thousand residents, a nucleus of
perhaps five hundred bikers, led by the Booze Fighters and the
POBOBs, congregated on Friday night in a few saloons lining San
Benito Street in the center of town. The action spilled outside, and
soon a two-block war zone was established between Fourth and
Sixth Streets. Motorcycles were ridden on the sidewalks and thundered into the barrooms. Various riders attempted stunts for the
drunken throng. Several failed miserably. A youth from Tulare
broke his leg in two places; an Oakland biker fractured his skull;
and one of the more senior rioters, a 45-year-old reveler from
Chico, nearly severed his foot when his bike crashed. Brawls were
unrelenting, and Hollister's five-man police force was quickly overwhelmed.

Motors roared, beer bottles shattered on the pavement, and
drunken shouts pierced the still night. The party thundered on
throughout Saturday as the cops attempted to restore order. Several of the worst offenders were tossed in the small jail behind city
hall on nearby Fifth Street. Armed with crowbars, other bikers defi-
antly freed them, and the beer blast boiled onward.

Forty-nine arrests were made, for the most part on charges of
public intoxication, disorderly conduct, indecent exposure, and assorted misdemeanors, to a point where a special session of night
court ran until dawn on Sunday to process the offenders. Roughly
fifty of the celebrants were treated at the local Hazel Hawkins Hospital, but aside from the aforementioned trio who damaged them-

selves in botched trick riding displays, there were no serious injuries. Considering the lurid tales generated by the incident, which implied death and destruction rivaling the St. Bartholomew's Day Massacre, the so-called Battle of Hollister was at best a skirmish and at the least a glorified drunken binge.

On Sunday, Hollister police sergeant Roy McPhail called the California Highway Patrol for help. Thirty CHP officers, armed with riot gear and tear gas and joined by several Monterey County deputies, finally restored order. By Monday morning, most of the rioting bikers had blearily wobbled out of town. The great confrontation, a puny squabble when compared to the vast antiwar campus conflicts that would erupt twenty years later, dribbled to an end amid the reek of stale beer and the crunch of broken glass. Yet the seismic shift it caused for the world of motorcycling was the cultural equivalent of the immense, ominous Calaveras earthquake fault that bisected the little city two blocks to the west of the riot scene.

Surely the event would have been long forgotten had it not been for a veteran *San Francisco Chronicle* photographer named Barney Peterson and reporter C. J. Doughty. They had been assigned on Friday evening to fly via a small chartered airplane the ninety miles to Hollister to snap some photos of the brawl. But by the time they landed, the action was apparently at a low enough level that Peterson needed some theatrical license to produce a properly dramatic picture.

Peterson's shot, picked up by the Associated Press and *Life* and then seen around the world, was probably taken the following morning, in front of Johnny's Bar and Grille on San Benito Street. Despite the seminal impact it had on motorcycling in general and on Harley-Davidson in particular, there is considerable doubt about its veracity. Surely Peterson took the picture at the riot, and there is no question that the Harley-Davidson in the photo is an authentic precursor of the "choppers" that became favored among future bikers. It was a battered big twin, probably a prewar 74 with its front fender removed (this was to become a favored styling trick as more and more effluvia was removed from the basic motorcycle in the years to come). But there is more to the story, as has been revealed by motorcycle historian and columnist Jerry Smith of Coos Bay, Oregon. Long fascinated with the Hollister incident and the sea change it effected in worldwide motorcycling, Smith has done extensive research into the circumstances surrounding Peterson's photograph. In searching the archives of the *San Francisco Chronicle*, Smith discovered that the now-dead Peterson shot several pictures with his 4 x 5 Speed Graphic while in Hollister. Smith found three versions, notably different, of the famous photograph. What fascinated him was the litter of beer bottles at the rider's feet. In one photo the bottles were standing upright, although in the exposure used by *Life* they are strewn helter-skelter around the front tire and under the engine of the motorcycle. It appears that the bottles were carefully arranged for maximum impact. In another of Peterson's unpublished shots, the rider has repositioned his booted feet on the front forks and pretentiously draped a jacket over his left shoulder. On the back of the jacket is an emblem of a winged skull surrounded by the words "Tulare Raiders." The letters "DAVE" are clearly visible.

Smith and local historian Daniel Corral located eighty-three-year-old Gus DeSerpa, who was present at the scene as a curious local and confirmed that the pictures were in fact posed, with the bottles planted on the pavement and the motorcycle positioned for maximum impact. The rider has also been identified by Smith as one Eddie Davenport, although his current whereabouts, or even if he owned the motorcycle upon which he was sprawled, remain a mystery. While associates of the late Barney Peterson deny that he would stoop to faking a news photo, there is no debating that several poses were assumed by Davenport during the shoot. Whether Davenport did this on his own or at Peterson's instigation is a moot point. More central to the issue is the fact that a person or persons staged the infamous Hollister *Life* photograph simply to generate public outrage.

In an interview with Smith, DeSerpa recalled the incident in a way that calls into question the validity of the infamous photograph:

> My former wife and I said, "Let's go uptown and see all the excitement." And then we ran into these people. They were on the sidewalk, and there was a photographer, I think he was from the *Tribune* [sic]; anyhow, they started to scrape up the bottles with their feet, you know, from one side to the other, and then they took the motorcycle and picked it up and set it right in the glass. I told my wife, "Hey, that's not right, they shouldn't be doing that." Yeah, he [the guy on the bike] was pretty well loaded. He was just in the vicinity right there. I think they just got him to sit down there. Because there was a bar right there, Johnny's Bar. I think he came wandering out of that bar. He comes staggering out, and "Hey, here's just the guy we want; hey, how about you sitting on there so we can take a picture?"

This was not the first time that the media made ad hoc "adjustments" to a scene for maximum drama (the Marine flag-raising on Iwo Jima's Mount Suribachi comes immediately to mind). What is amazing is the durability of the picture and its impact. *Life*'s caption writers also managed to amplify the drama, implying that "4,000 members of a motorcycle club" did the damage. In fact, it was a tiny cadre of perhaps 10 percent of that number, representing perhaps a dozen small California clubs. The distortion was unconscionable, but considering the novelty embodied in the notion of a helpless rural town being terrorized by a mob of Huns on motorcycles, who cared if the facts were stretched a bit? Surely the people who actually saw the picture in that issue of *Life* half a century ago represented but a minuscule percentage of the population (although the magazine reprinted it in its "25 Years Ago in *Life*" section in 1972). Yet its imagery is pervasive, as if it had been branded into the brains of every citizen as a paradigm of motorcycling — as the quintessential portrait of every man and woman who ever rode a Harley-Davidson. Hollister was perfect for the *Life* cultural spin. Like most of the elite media of today, the magazine was New York based, urban and sophisticated to a fault, and endlessly disdainful of the tall-grass population. Motorcycles were (until Malcolm Forbes end-ran the elitists in the 1970s) the worst sort of proletarian gadget — especially the hulking, noisy, oil-spitting Harleys from that provincial brewery town called Milwaukee. Riots among the great unwashed were to be expected. *Life* editors, perusing the national landscape from their Olympian perch high above Manhattan, felt more than qualified to pass judgment on a collection of grease-stained blue-collar hooligans. That these images of outlawry and lawlessness would be transferred to their own children at unlikely venues like Yale and Columbia in another twenty years was inconceivable. But in the summer of 1947, it was obligatory to sneer at the slobs bullying a hick town in nowhere and not worry about any broader implications the incident might have for society.

Today Hollister's downtown is part of a national historic dis-

trict. San Benito Street's rows of Gothic and Greek revival buildings have been neatly restored. In the middle of the small business
district still sits Johnny's Bar and Grille, the seedy metacenter of
the infamous riot and the backdrop for the Peterson photograph.
While Hollister celebrates its eighteenth-century Spanish mission
and the growth of its agricultural empire, the notorious Battle of
Hollister is unmarked by sign or symbol. Only in 1997 did bikers return in appreciable numbers for the fiftieth anniversary of the legendary event. The gathering was pure theater. As opposed to the
original rioters like the Booze Fighters and the Tulare Raiders, who
wore Levi's and T-shirts, the newcomers were decked out in expensive black leathers, looking infinitely more ominous than their predecessors. But this was faux menace. They were average citizens in
search of a communal identity embodied in the swashbuckling raff-
ishness of the Booze Fighters and their like. A noted Harley rider
from the upper echelons of government, Colorado senator Ben
Nighthorse Campbell, appeared briefly, properly costumed. He mingled with corporate executives, lawyers, doctors, and other profes-
sionals who came to Hollister to pose in front of Johnny's and to
transport themselves, in spirit at least, to that wild moment when a
cipher of a human in the grand scheme of things named Eddie Davenport drunkenly launched himself into immortality.

Hollister's original moment of fame appeared to pass quickly.
Several major dailies, including the *New York Times* and the *Los
Angeles Times*, gave the incident cursory coverage, but this being a
time when television network news was in its infancy, videotape
unknown, and satellite feeds unthinkable, coverage was limited to
Peterson's staged photograph and a brief dispatch from the news
wire services.

If there was any reaction to the Hollister riot among the Harley-

Davidson management in faraway Milwaukee, there is none on the public record. With the prospect of strengthening sales in a pent-up postwar market, the company, led by second-generation president William H. Davidson, was surely more concerned with increasing production and adding new models than reacting to a ruckus in a dusty California farm town. The company's major rival remained much-hated Indian, America's only other serious motorcycle manufacturer, while the steadily increasing influx of lightweight, high-performance motorcycles from British manufacturers like Norton, BSA, Triumph, Royal Enfield, and Ariel posed a new threat. Imperiously, the Harley-Davidson management passed the word to its dealers that any servicing of the English bikes, even including the sale of lubricants, was forbidden. Meanwhile, plans moved ahead for the acquisition of a large former military propeller–manufacturing factory on the outskirts of Milwaukee and the introduction of a new cylinder head design for the big V-twin sixty-one- and seventy-four-cubic-inch models that formed the core of its business. These major advances were to be announced at a lavish dealer meeting set for Milwaukee's Shroeder Hotel in late November of 1947, where optimism about the company's seemingly robust future was sure to blot out any memories of the brief flurry of bad publicity surrounding Hollister and the *Life* magazine photograph.

But the brand on the American psyche was deep and permanent. As the St. Valentine's Day Massacre in Chicago had defined gangsterism and the Kent State shootings became a symbol of the Vietnam antiwar movement, Hollister's impact far exceeded the damage wrought by the actual incident. The little town would forever be linked with motorcycle hoodlums in general and specifically with Harley-Davidson riders. A few cuts and bruises, some arrests, and broken beer bottles were seemingly unimportant at the time, but thanks to Peterson's photograph, Hollister was elevated into the folklore of American violence along with the seven dead thugs of the "Bugs" Moran gang and the four students who would fall at Kent State in the spring of 1970. Four years later, *Harper's* magazine, a much-respected monthly celebrating its hundredth birthday, published a short story by a writer named Frank Rooney titled "Cyclists Raid." It chronicled an assault on an unnamed town by a gang of motorcyclists that ended in the death of a central character, the daughter of a hotel owner named Joe Bleeker. Bleeker spotted the menace, in Rooney's words, as he stood "quietly looking, without appearing to stare, at a long, stern column of red motorcycles coming from the south, filling the single main street of the town with the noise of a multitude of piston [sic] and the crackling of exhaust pipes." Rooney's reference to a technically meaningless "multitude of piston" reveals a notable lack of knowledge about his subject, as do the accompanying drawings by a long-forgotten artist named David Berger. His motorcyclists are impeccably dressed like aviators, with leather flying helmets, khaki shirts and riding breeches, and high leather boots — as opposed to the scruffy denim of the drunks who rumbled in Hollister.

Rooney's raiders behave well enough at the beginning of the story, but soon go berserk, with "the motorcycles racing up and down the street, alternately whining and backfiring and one had jumped the curb and was cruising on the sidewalk." In the end the bikers ride off in quasi-military formation, leaving Bleeker's sweetheart daughter dead and others injured. There is little point to the story other than to imply that out there in the hinterlands roved bands of motorized maniacs ready to blast into towns like modern-day Quantrill's Raiders to rape and pillage and kill. *Harper's* was a widely read monthly, and Rooney's story prompted horrified comment in genteel suburban circles — circles removed by sociological light years from a small group of motorcyclists who had formed up in the sooty steel town of Fontana, California. There, at roughly the same time Rooney was composing his hyperbolic fantasy, the real thing — the motorcycle club that would rise into the realm of international legend — was coalescing in beat-up bars and rented shacks on the edge of town. The little band, organized in 1948, was composed of young men who traded the conventions of middle-class American life for a rigid cultism built around motorcycles, free-form sex, and endless boozing supported by small-time thievery, and bound together by a code of ethics based on fanatic collective loyalty. They would, for reasons lost to history, call themselves the Hells (sic) Angels.

Some believe this fearsome name was derived from a B-17 squadron — the 358th — of the 303rd USAF Bomber Group based in the English Midlands during World War II. The fact that Clark Gable, who was a known Harley-Davidson enthusiast, flew a few missions with the 358th may or may not relate to the story. Another theory sources the name from the 1930 Howard Hughes–produced extravaganza *Hell's Angels*, starring Jean Harlow and Ben Lyon. Either way, the Hells Angels would establish themselves as the ultimate motorcycle club, the baddest, hardest riding, most rigidly disciplined, and ruthless of them all, at least in the minds of the general public. By 1950, a handful of similar clubs had been loosely organized up and down the West Coast, for the most part in hard-knuckle industrial towns like Fontana, Long Beach, San Pedro, Oakland, San Jose, and San Bernardino. The motorcycle of choice was the Harley-Davidson, which, in a sense, won by default, it being the most prolific brand in the nation. Indians were accepted by the clubs' membership, as were the few Triumphs and BSAs reaching the market. But slowly, with the demise of Indian in 1953 and the rise of jingoism among the clubs during the Vietnam conflict, the Harley would reach an exclusive, iconic status. During the formative years of the outlaw gangs, any number of motorcycle makes were acceptable — provided they bore the distinctive brands of their owners. This involved cutting or "chopping" away effluvia like fenders, saddlebags, and chrome trim in order to reduce weight and thereby increase performance. But more important, chopping branded the motorcycle as beyond the fringe, openly contemptuous of mainstream riders and their mindless compliance with convention.

If the formation of the Angels and their ilk was a symptom of disillusionment with middle-class life, it was but a footnote to the widely chronicled beat movement blossoming during the early 1950s in the mildly addled brains of a twenty-one-year-old ex–merchant mariner and aspiring novelist named Jack Kerouac and his pal, twenty-four-year-old poet Allen Ginsberg. They, along with William S. Burroughs, the drug-fogged heir to the business-machine fortune, and twenty-year-old sometime poet Gregory Corso, were the pioneers of a post-transcendentalism that some critics claimed linked them, in a broad sense, with Thoreau and Whitman. It centered on a fascination with pacifism and a suspicion of the modern industrial age. But their open rebellion against middle-class mores, which involved flirtations with Zen, heavy drug use (Burroughs was a pioneer heroin addict), boozing, and wild sex (Ginsberg was openly homosexual), elevated them into a realm of outrageous behavior heretofore unknown to the good burghers of America. In 1950, even as the motorcycle gangs were forming on the cultural fringes, Kerouac was setting out on a disjointed, drug-and-alcohol-blurred journey aboard his beat-up Buick. His odyssey would lead to a marginally coherent semi-autobiographical novel featuring his alter ego Sal Paradise, and his pals Carlo Marx (Ginsberg) and Dean Moriarty — a pseudonym for longtime counterculture Olympian druggy Neal Cassady. *On the Road* was published seven years later. During this same time frame, Ginsberg produced his murky, controversial poem *Howl*, the subject of several showcase pornography trials, and Burroughs published a disjointed chronicle of a permanent state of heroin-crazed addiction called *Naked Lunch*. These three men, along with a few acolytes in Greenwich Village and San Francisco, were the founding fathers of the beat (shorthand for "beatitude") movement, which created the bedrock foundation of the counterculture that followed in the early 1960s. While Kerouac slowly drank himself to a hermit's death that would come in 1969, Ginsberg gained icon status among the hippies, leading demonstrations against the Vietnam war and becoming, with Bob Dylan, an informal poet laureate for the entire movement. While Burroughs and Corso drifted off center stage, Neal Cassady made an easy transition from beatnik to hippie and became a fixture in San Francisco's Haight-Ashbury scene before drugs and alcohol resulted in a lonely, drug-fogged demise before the decade had ended.

Operating on the perimeter of this vast, robust but ill-defined shift in the youth culture of the nation was a new breed of motorcyclists — also devoid of a defining political philosophy but surely better structured, more violent, and more scatological than the counterculturalists. The overall themes were similar: denial of the viability of normal middle-class life and the expression of that disdain with openly antisocial and shocking acts. But while the joint, acid, the hookah, love beads, and the guitar became the accoutrements of the beatniks and the hippies, the angrier, tougher men who formed the motorcycle clubs employed other, more culturally infuriating symbols, including German iron crosses, the hated Nazi swastika, and frightening club "colors" — the embroidered emblems worn on the back of leather or denim cutoff jackets. These quasi-military trappings often utilized SS-style death's heads, snakes, crossed bones, laughing skulls, etc., as symbols of supreme menace. The Hells Angels' colors were centered around the profile of a helmeted skull trailing a large feathered wing, displayed with fanatic reverence on an embroidered patch surrounded by the words "Hells Angels M.C. [motorcycle club]" with the name of the chapter ("Berdoo" for San Bernardino, Oakland, Vallejo, etc.). The exact origin of biker clubs' colors is unclear, although they probably date to pre–World War II and their use by more benign motorcycle organizations. By the late 1950s, colors were in universal use by the clubs (or "gangs," as they were known in the press and among the general public). Rivals to the Angels, like the Outlaws, which formed up at roughly the same time, also employed colors centered on a motorcycle theme. The Outlaws' colors, for example, presented a skull flanked by a pair of pistons — surely from a motorcycle. All the clubs, regardless of their location or size, formed their tightly knit organizations around a single talisman: a lusty, rackety brute of a motorcycle more often than not bearing the Harley-Davidson label.

It was sometime during this period that a particularly poetic motorcyclist (whether a gang member or not is lost to history) labeled his Harley a "hog." He was no doubt rhapsodizing about the machine's bulk and its sloppy, ill-mannered demeanor as compared to the smaller, more effete European bikes. The name stuck, much to the distress of the decent folk who rode Harleys, although in the future this colorful, if clearly pejorative, nickname would be heartily embraced by the most lily white of the marque's devotees.

The men in Milwaukee were aware of the rise of the new outlaw clubs but chose to ignore them. Their surrogates who ran the 50,000-member American Motorcycle Association denounced the Angels and their ilk as "one percenters," an outlandish minority of thugs and outsiders who bore no resemblance to the real world of motorcycling. This assault delighted the outlaws, who saw it as affirmation of their presence and began wearing patches denoting themselves as "One Percenters," the ultimate imprimatur of the hard-core biker.

The lifestyle of the clubs centered on unflagging group loyalty and mutual support, whether in bar fights or in paying debts. Revenues, used primarily to maintain low-rent clubhouses and for endless communal parties, came from petty thievery and trading in stolen motorcycle parts. Initiation rites — made frighteningly lurid by rumors that oozed through straight society — often involved group sex with the flinty women who rode with them but could not be members. Scruffy fashions featuring filthy, oil-soaked denims, long hair, tattoos, headbands, handcrafted jewelry, and beards were in many ways prototypical of the look adopted by the hippies a few years later, as were some of the more shocking, antisocial mores originated by the outlaws. But while conventional society reeled in stunned fury over the antics of the bikers, similar behavior was tolerated in the counterculturists in the sixties — mainly because Mr. and Mrs. America's sons and daughters were participating.

Assaults on the establishment by middle-class college students were generally viewed as acts of conscience by sympathetic media and academia, although they were often more violent and overtly antisocial. After all, the Hells Angels never spun off gruesomely homicidal mutations like the Weathermen, the Symbionese Liberation Army, or the Manson family. No Angel ever burned down an ROTC building or blew up a university laboratory or machine-gunned a bank guard in the name of a hazy people's revolution. Much like the Mafia, the motorcycle clubs were essentially isolated, tightly knit cults whose battles were turf wars and who only ventured into the public domain when the media chose to spotlight them.

The Harley-Davidson company, operating in splendid isolation in the hinterlands of Milwaukee, continued to view the motorcycle market within a narrow perspective as old-line, traditional customers heaving their overweight bodies aboard belit and bechromed Harley cruisers known in the business as "dressers" — as in military "full dress." The notion that a collection of punks would actually saw up a perfectly good motorcycle in the name of an outlandish, antisocial fad was as confusing to them as the news from trend-setting California that more and more riders were turning to midsized, high-performance British and German bikes made by such well-known manufacturers as BMW, BSA, Triumph, and Norton.

While historians have described the fifties as pallid and feckless in comparison to the wild sixties, there were stirrings of discontent, as evidenced by the beat movement, the exploding popularity of rock 'n' roll, the California hot-rodders, and the rising tide of motorcycle gangs. The nation had changed radically since the end of the war. Paranoia about the Russian menace remained intense, and the nasty, undeclared war in Korea would kill and maim nearly as many Americans as the subsequent disaster in Vietnam, but the country appeared, superficially at least, to be heading, in the words of Arthur Schlesinger Jr., into a "state of repose." The devastation of the Depression, followed by the manic effort during

World War II, had enervated the nation, and despite Korea and the Cold War, much of the citizenry seemed to yearn for a return to the good life of the twenties. Save, of course, for a segment of young men who found the Babbitt-like normalcy insufferably boring. And at this point, the nation was able to afford such rebellions. Now the most powerful economy in the history of the world, America offered unprecedented opportunity for diversion and recreation — including alternate lifestyles like those of the beats and the bikers. Thousands of dissidents were therefore provided the luxury of hating the establishment — based, ironically, on the largesse of that very entity.

They had, in theory, much to whine about. The liberal elite was in high dudgeon over the excesses of the McCarthy hearings and the endless assaults on civil liberties by the House Un-American Activities Committee. The blackballing of a group of Hollywood screenwriters with decided left-wing sympathies energized the film industry for the first time since the 1930s. In 1952, Stanley Kramer, a producer with openly liberal sensibilities, began producing a much-revised version of Frank Rooney's *Harper's* magazine story, starring a pair of hot young actors as motorcycle gang members. Marlon Brando and Lee Marvin were cast with gritty character actor Robert Keith in a picture titled *The Wild One*, which would once again reinforce the depredations of Hollister in the public psyche. As Johnny Stabler, the leader of a motorcycle gang called the Black Rebels, Brando rumbles into a little town called Wrightsville with his buddies and begins hanging out at Bleeker's Café. There the pouty, punk-faced Brando, decked out in a leather jacket and a jauntily angled military-style peaked cap (no doubt a studio costumer's interpretation of proper motorcycle gang garb), meets the female star, the long-forgotten Mary Murphy, and utters the only memorable line of the picture when, replying to her question, "What are you rebelling against?" he mumbles, "What have you got?" While Brando uses a 500 cc Triumph Speed Twin in the movie, the bad guy, Chino, a semicrazed former gang member played with his classic malevolence by Lee Marvin, enters the scene aboard a scruffy, flathead Harley-Davidson, thereby linking the brand to the rising legend of motorcycle hoodlumism.

Kramer's film was a middling commercial success and quickly forgotten by the public. Its longevity as a cult favorite is based purely on the fact that it was among the first to identify 1950s-style antiheroes in the Brando–James Dean mold (Dean's immortal but equally simpleminded *Rebel Without a Cause* would be released a year later), as well as to confirm that motorcycles were mechanical predators ridden by a new breed of outlaw. Dean employed an automobile — a hot-rodded Mercury — in his movie, but the role of the machine was the same: a device for angry youths rebelling against the smarmy Ike and Mamie Good Life. Both pictures, *The Wild One* and *Rebel Without a Cause*, were fumbling attempts by Hollywood to describe a restlessness and isolation among the nation's youth that was being played out with infinitely more passion and intensity by Kerouac and his buddies and among the fledgling motorcycle clubs in grubby saloons and flophouses across the land.

Like most of middle America, the people of Milwaukee — most specifically those stolid citizens who ran Harley-Davidson — remained largely oblivious to these tumultuous trends. It was business as usual, with the company now enjoying what seemed to be an open field in the heavyweight motorcycle business. To be sure, inroads in the overall market were being made by the British imports, whose high-performance, lightweight 500s were appealing to much the same young, upscale customers attracted to sports cars and skimpy economy sedans like the spartan Volkswagen. This was unsettling to some of the more progressive of the firm's executives, who were convinced that the traditional Harley-Davidson customer was becoming an anachronism and that younger, more aggressive sporting riders had to be attracted. In response to this trend, the XL Sportster was introduced in 1957. It was substantially lighter, at 460 pounds, and offered a swing-arm rear suspension and sprightly performance. The Sportster was aggressively styled, faintly suggestive of the lean and mean outlaw choppers, and thanks to its improved nimbleness and power, it became a favorite among loyalists seeking to compete with the faster British bikes. It was the first Harley-Davidson to hint at the tough-guy image that became so critical to the firm's long-term survival. However, the company was hardly abandoning its traditional customer base. In 1958, the upgraded Duo Glide was introduced with a legitimate rear suspension — a component that had been offered on most imported bikes for at least a decade. The Duo Glide was a quintessential heavyweight dresser — a hulking 700-pound lump of machinery suitable for long-range touring and easy afternoon rides in the country, but light years away in terms of form and function from the quick, feathery, high-revving singles and twins from Great Britain that were nibbling at the edges of the Harley-Davidson market.

The most enthusiastic response to the British lightweights came from a small contingent of California custom builders who were altering the shape of motorcycles in the same way hot rod builders were modifying automobiles, sawing and shaving away superfluous weight in the name of speed and rakish good looks. They created the pure chopper, which featured a tiny custom "peanut" fuel tank; outrageously long, angled front forks; a small banana-shaped seat; sensuously curved exhaust headers; and bizarre "ape-hanger" handlebars. The resulting motorcycles, hand built with parts purchased from a group of fledgling independent suppliers, were aesthetic expressions that elevated them beyond simple function into the realm of folk art. They also exuded an aura of rebelliousness that melded perfectly with the outlaw gangs, the members of which began feverishly customizing their Harleys, if for no other reason than to visually separate themselves from the traditional, humdrum old-line riders.

With the Harley-Davidson now enjoying exclusivity in the domestic market, it was the only American motorcycle to become widely involved in the new custom chopper craze. British bikes were for the most part stigmatized by being "foreign" among the fiercely jingoistic outlaws. Moreover, the mini-industry of custom manufacturers was building aftermarket pieces almost exclusively to fit Harley frames. If a chopper was to be created, it had to be based on God's own American-made Harley-Davidson.

The trend angered and confused the Milwaukee management. Rather than attempt to exploit the potential business that was swirling around their brand, they opposed the chopper customers, arguing that converted bikes would not be covered by warranties, and they refused to stock parts that suggested a chopper theme. Old-line dealers rejected owners seeking to service or overhaul their converted machines, which only accelerated the movement toward small custom shops and accessory manufacturers exploiting the fad. Establishment riders belonging to the American Motorcycle Association and readers of the Harley house organ *The Enthusiast* ignored the existence of the choppers as if the fiendishly creative new machines were on another planet, along with the outlaws and renegades who rode them.

The Hells Angels remained a fringe organization with probably fewer than two hundred hard-core members scattered throughout California until the late fifties. It was on April 1, 1957, that the Oakland chapter gained a member who was to change the entire course of the Hells Angels and almost singlehandedly elevate them to legendary status. He was a nineteen-year-old warehouse laborer named Ralph Hubert Barger Jr., known to his friends as Sonny. After briefly serving in the infantry, this skinny, intense, intelligent, rodent-tough native of seedy Modesto hooked up with the Angels and within a year was elected president of the Oakland chapter. It was Barger, thanks to his supreme self-confidence, his penchant for publicity, and his innate sense of drama, who transformed the Angels into a nationally recognized organization, artfully balancing its image of thuggish villainy with that of a gang of raffish but essentially harmless cutups.

While conventional society smugly dismissed the club members as brainless, bottom-feeding slugs, many were in fact dropouts whose outrageous lifestyle shrouded their intelligence. Barger was such a man, and it was he, through guile and raw force of will, who regimented the Angels into a serious social force. Barger had the club's colors trademarked to protect them from imitators and, in a broader sense, to create a potential revenue source. He became an unofficial press agent for the Angels, which led to other clubs' developing a kind of public persona as well. On occasion the various club members would drift into the mainstream as movie extras, security guards, or even shock-value guests at chichi social functions. Barger would forever remain a pariah and a heretic within the precincts of the Harley-Davidson company, but in a broad sense his contributions to the ultimate success of Harley-Davidson rank with those of any of the personalities within the organization proper. Such was the impact of the scrawny tough guy from Modesto on the world of motorcycling and, perhaps, on the nation's self-image.

The executives at Harley-Davidson during the late 1950s had little reason to perceive the tectonic changes that were about to rattle their empire. After all, their company enjoyed a market dominance in heavyweight motorcycle sales, which had exploded from a total of 200,000 bikes registered in the entire nation following the war to triple that as 1960 approached. Imported BSAs and Triumphs, etc., were accounting for a small percentage of sales, while the California chopper phenomenon was discounted as a product of the One Percenters — idiots on the fringe butchering perfectly good Harley-Davidsons in the name of outlandish fashion.

Discounted, too, was a full-page advertisement that appeared in the November 1959 issue of *Cycle* magazine announcing a midget-sized motorcycle from a Japanese maker named Honda. While the company had made something of a name for itself in international racing competition, it was an unknown brand in the United States. Surely their tiny, ladylike Super Cub, with its minuscule overhead-camshaft, 50 cc engine, would have no impact on the market, despite its interesting electric self-starting mechanism. The tag line on the advertisement claimed, "You meet the nicest people on a Honda." Surely this was an oblique reference to the chronic perception among the American public that the Hollister incident and the *Life* magazine hoodlum photograph were not forgotten. Was it possible, whether Harley-Davidson's bosses liked it or not, that their motorcycles were being marginalized as the favored machine of lowlifes and outlaws? It would not be long before they found out.

3 · THE IMAGE DESTROYED AND CREATED

In a broadly tragic sense, the presidency of John F. Ken-
nedy served as a paradigm for the entire decade of the sixties.
Young, charismatic, and brilliantly theatrical, Kennedy launched
the decade by replacing the stodgy Republicanism of Dwight Eisen-
hower with the youthful, Democratic New Frontier seemingly able
to deal vigorously with rising civil rights unrest, the Cold War, and
the festering Far Eastern boil called Vietnam. That his brief term in
office would end in bloodshed and shattered dreams was to be a
bellwether for the mad era, which began in an atmosphere of optimism and ended with the nation riven with discord unlike any in
the previous century.

Harley-Davidson's fortunes would parallel that of the country,
beginning as it did with positive prospects and ending in a state of
disarray and shattered traditions. In early 1960, the company pur-

chased a half-share of the small, troubled Italian motorcycle manufacturer Aermacchi. The intent was to produce a high-tech, 250 cc
lightweight under the Harley-Davidson banner called the Sprint.
This undersized machine would, in theory, give Harley-Davidson a
franchise in the rapidly growing market dominated by the British
middleweights. Smaller versions of the Sprint, including one called
the Hummer, were also built by Aermacchi, but none was well received by either the Harley loyalists or the Triumph, Norton, and
BSA aficionados. The company also produced a scooter called the
Topper, which was intended to compete with a brief late 1950s
craze in imported Italian motor scooters by Lambretta and Vespa. It
was also during this period that Harley-Davidson diversified into
the boat building and golf cart businesses with the purchase of the
Tomahawk boat company.

The scooters and Aermacchi lightweights would linger diffi-
dently in the Harley-Davidson lineup until the midseventies before
being quietly discontinued, underlining the reality that Harley-
Davidson was branded with an identity centered around outsized,
lumbering motorcycles. Yet its approximately eight hundred dealers served a serious subculture rapidly mutating into three distinct
groups. Still dominant were the traditional Harley riders: docile
blue-collar lugs devoted to their bespangled, overweight dressers.
They rode sedately, often with their wives perched regally behind
them. But growing more numerous each day, to the frustration of
the company, was a wild new breed of enthusiasts who — in a stylistic sense, at least — aped the outlaws, who maintained the purity
of the chopper theme on their older Panheads and Knuckleheads as
well as on the newer Sportsters. The new breeders embraced the
Sportster as well, often customizing them on limited chopper
themes and outfitting themselves in outlaw fashions with leather

jackets and Levi's. Headwear of any kind — including the leather aviator helmets of yore and the cornball peaked military caps preferred by the dresser crowd — was rejected. Their long hair swirling in the wind and their Sportsters yapping at full cry through open exhaust pipes, the new breeders were rising up to challenge the imported bikes and the more sophisticated crowd who rode them. They were for the most part politically conservative working stiffs who would ardently support the Vietnam war effort and openly reviled the smaller English bikes as well as the new, increasingly high-performance machines from Honda, Suzuki, and Yamaha. The 250 cc Honda Hawk, for example, was a masterfully engineered machine, beautifully balanced, elegantly styled, and so efficient that its small-displacement twin-cylinder engine would outperform the Harley Sprint and rival even the Sportster, with a power plant three times larger.

It was during this period that Japan was radically revamping its image as the junk maker to the world. It was becoming a fountainhead of high technology in the areas of automobiles, motorcycles, optics, and electronics. Nikon and Canon cameras were challenging the old-line German Leicas and Contax 35 mm's, not to mention the crude American-made Kodaks. Datsun and Toyota were about to launch superior small cars against the Volkswagen and other European products. The Japanese were exploiting a fascination with high tech centered among younger, better-educated American consumers. This trend completely escaped the ossified brain trust in Milwaukee, which continued to serve a less-affluent, less-sophisticated, traditional customer base.

The company's dreaded outlaw image made national headlines again in September 1964, when four Hells Angels named Terry the Tramp, Mother Miles, Marvin, and Crazy Cross were arrested in

Monterey, California, for allegedly raping a pair of underage girls. The incident, which the press amplified to imply that it had involved as many as four thousand frothing Angels in a mad gang rape, took place during the club's annual Labor Day ride to that picturesque beach town. The local press screamed with outrage that these thugs had victimized a pair of innocents, although the four outlaws were never formally charged. But the damage had been done. Once again the Angels were back in the headlines as degenerate predators, and images of Hollister once again raced through the public's brain.

The incident prompted California attorney general Thomas Lynch to compile a fifteen-page "report" on the activities of the Angels. He released it to the national media in March 1965. It seemed on the surface a stunning description of lust and depravity. The pages outlined what appeared to be levels of criminality and bestial behavior that made Bonnie and Clyde look like Jack and Jill. Lynch chronicled eighteen outrageous "Hoodlum Activities," which upon close examination involved little more than a series of bar fights and some admittedly weird sex acts among apparently consenting adults. Taken individually, the eighteen incidents were little more than lewd and disgusting. But viewed collectively, they appeared to indict the Angels as the most degenerate barbarians to hit the planet since the Mongol hordes. California senator George Murphy, the former song-and-dance man, denounced the Hells Angels as "the lowest form of animals," and the media rush was on. The *New York Times*, then as now a compass rose of national opinion, treated the Lynch report with prim outrage. In a two-column story titled "California Takes Steps to Curb Terrorism of Ruffian Cyclists," the paper accepted the Lynch report at face value, outlining the depredations at Monterey and elsewhere with icy, terrifying prose. The implication was clear: Somewhere out there in the tall grass lurked legions of weirdos on motorcycles ready to invade decent neighborhoods to rape proper citizens' wives and daughters.

The two major newsweeklies, *Time* and *Newsweek*, both leaped on the story, titling their treatments with versions of Kramer's decade-old *Wild One* film. *Newsweek* made much of a 1963 bikers' rumble in the California town of Porterville that was, in essence, a drunken brawl and a hollow imitation of the Hollister rumble. But once the writers, based three thousand miles away in a Madison Avenue office tower, completed their imagery, Porterville sounded like Little Big Horn. In all of the reports, Harley-Davidson was specifically mentioned as the exclusive mode of transport for the lowlifes. This totally obscured any positive publicity the company might have garnered for introducing its Duo Glide and Electra Glide cruisers with new electric starters (denounced as "button pushers" by the Harley traditionalists). The big bikes would become favorites of the California Highway Patrol and other police agencies, but the reality was flooded under by the media's fascination with the raging wild men on their choppers.

Hollywood too continued to play its role in shaping the public's perception of motorcycles, often obliquely. The hit 1963 WWII adventure film *The Great Escape* featured Steve McQueen on an epic motorcycle ride (although on a Triumph rather than a Harley). McQueen himself was a serious and skilled rider and at his untimely death in 1980 had accumulated a collection of classic Harleys. *The Great Escape* had no direct impact on the public image of Harley-Davidson but did enhance the reputation of the motorcycle as a fearsome and rebellious machine capable of prodigious acts against the establishment — in this case the Nazis and their "escape-proof" POW camp.

It was during this same period that Hunter S. Thompson began work on a pivotal examination of the bikers, publishing in 1967 his wonderfully quirky firsthand look at the phenomenon, *Hell's Angels: A Strange and Terrible Saga.* Thompson, who with Tom Wolfe was the most daring and creative of the so-called new journalists, spent nearly a year hanging out with the Angels and wrote what remains a fascinating, clear-eyed, and candid account of the club and its members.

There was in Thompson's mind no doubt that the major media were responsible for the notorious reputation of the Hells Angels and their associates. "If the Hells Angels proved anything," wrote Thompson, "it was the awesome power of the New York press establishment. The Hells Angels as they exist today were virtually created by *Time* and *Newsweek* and the *New York Times.*" There is little debating this assessment, because Thompson's own account depicts a different and more mundane lifestyle among the Angels than that described by the media. Rather than a collection of hard-riding rapists and murderers, Thompson's Angels appeared more a subculture of disaffected petty thieves and layabouts, who occupied their time drinking, doping, messing with their Harleys, trading their women for bouts of group sex, and brawling over turf with rival gangs. Their encounters with the general public were rare and generally involved boozy weekend outings designed to spread fear and outrage but little else among the populace. Operating under a strict set of club bylaws and fiercely loyal to each other, the Angels were, outside the media attention (which amused them and which they sometimes courted for shock value), little more than societal outriders content to operate within their own private code of ethics. As a threat to the general public, they seemed to rank somewhere below white-collar embezzlers and chronic speeders.

But the biker gangs and their infuriating behavior seemed yet another assault on the establishment coming from a variety of sources. On a more noble but no less alarming scale were the increasingly violent civil rights demonstrations in the South, where activists were being rousted and beaten and killed by redneck segregationists. On the nation's elite campuses, the prime-fed youth of America were busying themselves with rioting against local police forces and concocting explosives and drugs in chemistry labs. The escalating Vietnam war had everyone on edge, including the so-called baby boomers, who were entering early adulthood as the most pampered, indulged, and overflattered generation in history. It seemed inevitable — based on their intrinsic if misguided sense of moral superiority — that they would rebel against the nation that fed them. Kerouac and Ginsberg's beats had created an initial fascination with drugs, but it was tame stuff: a few marijuana joints, amphetamines, and peyote consumed in private for fear of draconian jail sentences. But it was LSD, the breakout drug of the sixties — a chemical tripper — that addled an entire generation and defined the psychedelic, brain-fried counterculture. LSD was the centerpiece of Dr. Timothy Leary's crackpot reveries and the defining chemical for novelist Ken Kesey's Merry Pranksters, who in many ways set the behavioral standards for those who became known as hippies around the world.

Kesey was a brilliant former all-American boy whose first novel, *One Flew Over the Cuckoo's Nest*, published in 1962, had employed a nuthouse as an allegory for a dehumanized American society. He inherited the Kerouac, Ginsberg, and Neal Cassady legacy — the latter of whom became an integral member of Kesey's little claque, based at his La Honda, California, log cabin, planted on six acres in the redwoods south of San Francisco. Kesey's cross-country trip in a Day-Glo 1939 International Harvester bus in late 1964 to promote his second novel, *Sometimes a Great Notion*, was masterfully chronicled in Tom Wolfe's *The Electric Kool-Aid Acid Test*, as was the unique gathering of the Pranksters and the Hells Angels on August 7, 1965. This beer-soaked, acid-dropping blast at La Honda was also covered in detail by Thompson in his book on the Angels, thereby giving it near immortality at the hands of two of the most influential writers of the late twentieth century. It attracted not only scores of counterculture regulars and wanna-bes from the Bay area, but earnest intellectuals including the aging beat guru himself, Allen Ginsberg, and Leary sidekick Richard Alpert.

It was a confluence of two strangely diverse groups, linked only by a common antiestablishment history and a self-image of operating with unfettered freedom of action on the outer boundaries of society. The gathering was organized by Kesey, who had been introduced to the Oakland Angels by Thompson. While they disdained the Berkeley intellectuals and druggies who composed the hippie culture of the day, the Angels were more comfortable with Kesey, who had been to the ramparts, in a sense, by being busted on a marijuana charge. Run-ins with the law were a badge of honor with the Angels, and his arrest automatically elevated Kesey into a realm beyond the effete artists, dropouts, and college kids who appeared to make up a majority of the counterculture. Thompson attended with his wife and small son, implying he did not expect trouble.

Wolfe described the arrival of the Angels at Kesey's place "like a locomotive about ten miles away. It was the Hells Angels running in formation, coming over the mountain on Harley-Davidson 74s." The big guns were there: Sonny Barger himself, Terry the Tramp, Freewheeling Frank, and the other badass Bay area Angels. In Wolfe's account, they gang-banged Kesey's bevy of women, dropped acid with his sidekicks like Cassady, and grumped about Ginsberg, who trilled a medley of Hindu chants. The bearded poet, a Jewish, homosexual intellectual, was the antithesis of the white, Anglo-Saxon, wildly heterosexual Angels. The Pranksters were initially titillated by the bikers, embodying as they did outlandish, almost suicidal physical courage and a fuck-you attitude that made their bongo playing and dope smoking seem positively feeble by comparison. The party waxed and waned for two days, an acid-soaked free-for-all (LSD was legal at the time), while a squadron of cops stood guard outside the compound waiting for a blowup that never came, deafened by the rock 'n' roll that rattled the redwoods and blinded by the searing light show that lit up the night.

In the middle of the madness were the motorcycles, the dreaded, rattle-throated Harley choppers, which had become the one true totem of the bikers from coast to coast. Each time one of them roared, the police were reminded of the savagery of Hollister, *The Wild One*, and the most recent assault on humanity — a riot at the annual July bike races in Laconia, New Hampshire. Again, the fracas had made national headlines. Again, the incident was blown out of proportion by respected newspapers reporting that up to twenty-five thousand beer- and drug-crazed bikers — led by savage, chain-wielding Hells Angels — tore the town apart. But this time the media smugly reported that hundreds of cops and National Guardsmen in riot gear had descended on the place and restored order. There were scores of injuries, for the most part inflicted by law-enforcement billy clubs, tear gas, and shotguns. The media breathlessly reported that "hundreds" had been arrested. The actual number was thirty-two, all of whom were locals, and included not a single Hells Angel. Still, the bad-biker image was reinforced, and when Kesey and company blearily entertained Barger and his pals a month later and three thousand miles to the west, there seemed to be reason to believe that perhaps a common hatred of the "pigs" with badges and a proclivity for weird drugs and sex might provide sufficient glue to bond the two groups together. That was not to be, based on their radically different socioeconomic backgrounds and political outlooks.

The Hells Angels and the other outlaw clubs maintained a curious ambivalence toward the straight world. Though they hated the police, they seldom resisted arrest. For all their death's-head, German military–based accoutrements, they were originally apolitical, according to Thompson and other reliable observers. But as the Vietnam war escalated, their ranks swelled with angry, burned-out veterans. They, like most of their fellow Angels, tended to view the hippies as draft-dodging wimps, geeky cowards who spit and cursed at cops from behind the protection of college dormitories while real men fought and died, no matter how hazy the cause. While the counterculture became more openly strident and violent, the Hells Angels continued to make headlines as the ultimate street warriors, although their numbers were pitifully small — perhaps fewer than five hundred — and their antiestablishment acts generally involved little more serious than punch-ups, public intoxication, and small-time drug dealing. But the cultural divide between the grubby, blue-collar Angels and the educated, middle-class hippies placed the Angels at an instant disadvantage. They had no poets like Ginsberg, no bards like Bob Dylan, no philosophers like Herbert Marcuse, to rationalize their cause and were therefore marginalized as nihilistic slobs bent on destruction.

The Angels supported the war, confirming in a broad sense the findings of Ben Wattenberg and Richard Scammon in their penetrating 1970 book *The Real Majority* and other researchers and pollsters who found that most American males endorsed the war effort. During the 1968 election, when antiwar fever was at a peak and the alleged counterculture appeared to pervade the youth of America, Richard Nixon and third-party candidate George Wallace — hardly advocates of "flower power"— drew 57 percent of the eighteen- to twenty-one-year-old vote. While a few hundred young men gained national publicity by burning their draft cards, no fewer than 8.7 million served in the armed forces during the Vietnam campaign. That the Hells Angels and their subliminally violent Harleys were to become separated from the liberal, supposedly peace-loving hippies was inevitable from the start. Had he lived in the twentieth century, Henry David Thoreau, the paterfamilias of the counterculture, would never have ridden a Harley-Davidson to Walden Pond.

There were, however, several cultural and stylistic overlaps. The hippie word *bummer*, employed for bad drug trips and as a catchall description for misfortunes, was first used by the bikers to describe a nasty motorcycle spill. *Bitchin'*, as in *great* or *wonderful*, was a biker term. The bandanna headband was first employed by bikers to keep their hair out of their eyes, as were leather jackets for protection in cold weather and from high-speed crashes. Denim, cheap and durable, was probably first employed by bikers. Khaki pants, a favorite among the more educated classes of the day, were a well-known fashion item of Kerouac's. Levi's did not become favored hippie garb until long after the bikers had adopted them and cutoff denim jackets as standard issue. Long hair and beards date to the 1950s, but whether the bikers or the beats chose them first is open to question. Tattoos were never popular within the hippie culture, while no Angel would be caught dead in sandals or bell-bottoms.

The two groups' brief love-in ended little more than two months after Kesey's party, when an antiwar demonstration march from Berkeley to the Oakland Army Terminal led by Ginsberg was broken up, first by the police, then by a few Angels, who waded into the Berkeleyites and beat several severely. The Angels slapped the protesters around, calling them "Commies" and "traitors," which clearly defined their political orientation, at least as far as the war was concerned. Shocked at the turnabout and stunned at the behavior of a bunch they had deluded themselves to be brothers in the cause, Ginsberg had the protesters retreat at the Berkeley-Oakland city line, their fifteen thousand yapping schoolkids and academics buffaloed by a dozen snarling thugs.

Several peace parleys at Barger's scruffy little house in Oakland were held between the Angel leadership and Ginsberg, Kesey, and Cassady. The meetings descended into semicoherent, drug-laced political rhetoric. But somehow Barger grew to like Ginsberg, who plied him with Hindu and Buddhist chants and woozy claims of personal love that baffled and amused the iron-tough Angel boss. Being wooed by a semicrazed, queer Jewish poet with radical left-wing sentiments made no sense, but it was sufficiently quirky and perverted to defuse Barger's plans for another assault on the protesters' planned return to the base the following month. For the first time, the Hells Angels went public. In an artfully worded press release composed by Barger, the Angels called off the hippie war while retaining their strangely patriotic values:

Although we have stated our intention to counter-demonstrate at this despicable, un-American activity, we believe that in the interest of public safety and the protection of the good name of Oakland, we should not justify the Vietnam Day Committee by our presence . . . because our patriotic concern for what these people are doing to our great nation may provoke us to violent acts. Any physical encounter would only produce sympathy for this mob of traitors.

The statement was part of the baroque political and cultural theater being played out in the Bay area during the 1960s. The Hells Angels came down on the side of Jefferson and Lincoln — or perhaps in a more realistic sense on the side of most middle Americans and the actively prowar Johnson administration. At the same press conference announcing the new policy, Barger went over the top by reading an open letter to President Lyndon Johnson volunteering the entire Oakland Angels chapter for covert duty in Vietnam: "On behalf of myself and my associates, I volunteer a group of loyal Americans for behind the lines duty in Vietnam. We feel that a crack group of gorillas [sic] would demoralize the Viet Cong and advance the cause of freedom. We are available for training and duty immediately."

The president's reply, if there was one, is lost in history, as is the Angels' V.C. body count. This brash burst of publicity was probably the apogee of the Angels' political clout, but not their power and reputation. In 1966, the club incorporated and issued five hundred shares of stock. Shortly thereafter, Barger applied for a patent on its death's-head emblem. It was finally granted in 1972. But the short-lived alliance between the hippies and the bikers had ended. The gulf was too broad. The Angels could deal with the counterculture notion of radical individualism but parted company with their ideas on radical egalitarianism, which defied the powerful tribal links required for club membership. As Hunter Thompson, the only outsider ever to make salient observations about the Angels, noted, "The only difference between the student radicals and the Hells Angels is that the students are rebelling against the past while the Angels are fighting the future. Their only common ground is their disdain for the present, the status quo." As if to place an exclamation point on the breakup, a small band of Angels beat up Thompson on Labor Day, 1966, pounding him fiercely until another member interceded and stopped the mayhem. No explanation was ever given for the rousting, although Thompson observed in his book's postscript that it is likely the attackers felt he was taking advantage of them (which he did, in a sense, by employing their confidences to produce a bestseller). Thompson's book was the first serious peek inside the world of bikers, although pop musicians had already rhapsodized about their lurid lifestyle. In 1965 the Shangri-Las had hit the charts with "Leader of the Pack," which featured the rumble of a Harley V-twin. This marked the first time that many Americans had been exposed to the mysterious, rhythmic rumble of the old engine — a sound that was to become as much a representative of the great revolution of the sixties as the hard-driving drumbeats of rock 'n' roll.

As Americans sweated in fear and clutched their daughters over the Angels' menace, Hollywood was about to boost the legend of the biker gangs into hyperbolic outer space. Roger Corman, supreme schlockmeister of B pictures, had already produced and directed such epics as *She-Gods of Shark Reef* (1956), *Teenage Caveman* (1958), and *X: The Man with the X-Ray Eyes* (1963). The Hells Angels seemed a natural subject for the forty-year-old engineer-turned-moviemaker who had become a rich man generating ragged, low-budget sci-fi thrillers, bloody horror pics, and underworld shoot-'em-ups.

Madison Avenue and Hollywood had only recently discovered the "youth culture" — later to be known as the baby boomers —

and recognized this postwar population bulge as a potentially giant market. Ford's ad agency was among the first into the fray with its shameless "Lively Ones" campaign with pop idol Vic Damone. Post-pubescent cuties like Frankie Avalon and Annette Funicello were starring in such fluffy romances as *Beach Blanket Bingo*. But as the counterculture rose up screeching its new mantra, "Don't trust anyone over thirty," filmmakers like Corman realized that the demonstrations boiling out of Berkeley, Columbia, and elsewhere evidenced a hard edge to the flower children that could be exploited on film. With the confrontation between the Angels and Kesey's hippies still in the headlines, Corman and his screenwriter, Charles Griffith, came up with a brilliant notion: combine the two cultures. Hippies on bikes! Corman set to work on the first of dozens of biker films portraying the Angels and their ilk not as unemployed blue-collar grubs, but as disaffected kids rebelling against a stiff, uptight, conformist society. The 1966 film was called *The Wild Angels* and was in retrospect the best of a dismal genre of exploitation and corrupted imagery.

The story centered, as always, on bikers terrorizing the straights, portraying them as lost souls seeking their own visions of freedom in a hostile world. The cast included Peter Fonda, the twenty-seven-year-old son of superstar Henry Fonda and younger brother of brilliant actress Jane, who was at the time gaining speed in her notorious anti–Vietnam war crusade. Peter, like most film business trendies of the day, was caught up in the counterculture, offering such profundities as "Civilization has always been a bust," perhaps as a rationale for signing on for Corman's production. He was originally assigned to play the role of the Loser — a psycho on wheels whose death formed the plot's centerpiece. But when it was discovered that the intended star, George Chakiris,

couldn't ride a motorcycle, Fonda was assigned the role of gang
leader Heavenly Blues (a drug-related reference that Fonda insisted on). In a brilliant move, all-star motion-picture psycho Bruce
Dern was assigned to play the Loser. This was the first among
Dern's early pictures to give him a chance to play a crazed degenerate — an onscreen persona he was to raise to high art in the years
to come. Playing the female roles were no less a thespian than
Nancy Sinatra and Dern's wife, Diane Ladd. The film's loopy plot
follows the gang through the Loser's crash, his subsequent death,
and the biker funeral in his backwater hometown. This permitted
Corman and his assistant director, twenty-six-year-old Peter Bog-
danovich, to reel off the standard Hollister–*Wild One* finale wherein
the gang goes insane on acid and grass and engages in rape and
gruesome anti-Christ rituals in a small church. As the bikers roar
away from the scene of their depredation, pillage, and paganism
laced with swastikas and other outrageous trappings, Fonda, the
ultimate martyred lost soul, gallantly chooses to stay behind with
his fallen comrade and await his fate at the hands of evil "pigs."
"There's nowhere to go," he whines as the picture ends. The San
Bernardino chapter of the Hells Angels supplied background stories and advice to Griffith and Corman, thereby beginning a lucrative career for club members as extras in the picture business. The
"Blue's Theme" for *The Wild Angels* was written and performed by
Davie Allan and the Arrows, a minor-league rock band that would
compose and play a veritable symphony of forgettable songs for
dozens of biker and hippie rebellion flicks during the late 1960s.
Wild Angels was reportedly produced for about $360,000, but over
its long run in drive-ins and backwater movie theaters, not to mention a successful European distribution, the picture grossed close
to $10 million in box office revenues. Clearly biker flicks had "legs"

Rise of biker movies

in the picture business, and Corman's pioneering effort opened the floodgates for dozens of imitations.

Harley-Davidson choppers played a major role in *The Wild Angels* and scores of pictures like it, but the company was faced with other problems besides its unwanted reputation as the centerpiece of a renegade culture. Midsize British motorcycles like the Triumph Bonneville, the Norton Commando, and the BSA Gold Star were seizing big chunks of the market, while exquisitely crafted Japanese machines from Honda, Suzuki, Kawasaki, and Yamaha were beginning to attract thousands of buyers. The residue of the "legitimate" motorcycle market — aging, overweight cruiser traditionalists — was all that remained as Harley loyalists. The company and its surrogate satrap organization, the American Motorcycle Association, fought back with lopsided rules to prevent the European and Japanese bikes from winning big races, but in the trench warfare for cultural domination, they were clearly losing.

The outlaws remained an arm's-length ally of Harley-Davidson, much to the company's displeasure. Because of the bikers' perverse sense of patriotism, foreign motorcycles — the "Trumps" (Triumphs), "Beezers" (BSAs), "Beemers" (BMWs), and all Japanese machines ("Jap scrap," "rice burners") — were verboten. The Harley being the only American-made motorcycle, it was the outlaws' marque of choice — although graybeard traditionalists occasionally rode antique Indians, which were an acceptable alternative. Within the hard-core biker culture, in reality and as represented on drive-in screens across the nation, the chopped-down thundermakers from Milwaukee were king of the road, but it would be years before the men who made these strange and wonderful machines would have the chutzpah and creativity to take advantage of such a pervasive image.

The success of *The Wild Angels* sent Corman and others into a frenzy of filmmaking. Dozens of small-budget drive-in detritus were produced, carrying titles like *Born Losers, The Glory Stompers, The Savage Seven, Devil's Angels, Cycle Savages, Angels from Hell, Hell's Angels on Wheels, Run, Angel, Run!, Angel Unchained, Hell's Chosen Few, Rebel Rousers, Naked Angels,* and *Angels Die Hard.* The female bikers were not to be ignored, which brought to the screen such classics as *Angels' Wild Women, She-Devils on Wheels, Sisters in Leather,* and *The Mini-Skirt Mob.* The genre probably hit bottom with *Pink Angels,* in which the bikers were a bizarre collection of transvestites. It was released in 1971, when the drive-ins were dying and even the most cretinous of customers had been sated. After all, almost every perversion and aberration had been explored, with bikers being involved with lesbianism, homosexuality, devil worship, sadomasochism, necrophilia, monsters, space aliens, Nazis, the Mafia, and every aspect of the occult. The great biker flick explosion was over, leaving Americans even more convinced that anyone who rolled down the highway on a Harley was at best a gang member and at worst a neo-Nazi-hippie drug-crazed sexual predator with the social conscience of Attila the Hun. The spate of biker flicks actually involved some major talents, including John Cassavetes, who starred in *Devil's Angels* and other B pictures to finance his more serious efforts as a filmmaker. Also to be found in such films are Harry Dean Stanton, Scott Glenn, John Carradine, Broderick Crawford, and Gary Busey, as well as such serious actresses as Tyne Daly, Susan Strasberg, and Ann-Margret — whose *C.C. and Company* (with Joe Namath) gained her pinup status in every outlaw clubhouse from coast to coast. Tom Laughlin introduced his Billy Jack character in the 1967 biker picture *The Born Losers,* and the great cinematographer Laszlo Kovacs (*Five*

Easy Pieces, New York, New York, Ghostbusters, etc.) also shot a number of such films during his early career. Sonny Barger and the real Angels, including Terry the Tramp, worked as extras in a number of biker pictures and had significant roles in the 1969 production *Hell's* [sic] *Angels '69*, starring Jeremy Slate.

In 1983, the club produced its own documentary, complete with Dolby sound, titled *Hells Angels Forever.* It was a good-natured frolic, portraying the boys as fun-loving rogues and featuring the music of such luminaries as Willie Nelson, Johnny Paycheck, Bo Diddley, and Jerry Garcia and the Grateful Dead. Don Imus, then in a drug-fogged miasma of self-admitted addiction to cocaine and alcohol, served as the curbside master of ceremonies at the Manhattan premiere on October 3, 1983. The Angels, looking scrubbed and amazingly presentable, were led by Manhattan chapter president Sandy Frazier Alexander, who had conceived of the project over ten years earlier. The evening was capped by a party at Studio 54, the flashy midtown celebrity den. Like the Mafia before them, the Hells Angels were a major celebrity attraction, drawing the weaker and more febrile among New York status slaves into their orbit, there to bask in the glow of their reputation for nihilistic power and fearlessness.

The Angels movie, which enjoyed modest success, brought the club into the company of such Hollywood production houses as AIP (American International Productions), Avco Embassy, and New World, who were generating millions from low-budget biker exploitation flicks. Perhaps the most shameless of the lot was Mike Curb, the ardent right-wing California lieutenant governor in the Jerry Brown administration, who, as well as Los Angeles radio personality Casey Kasem, produced a number of such pictures. Kasem also acted in several biker films, including *Wild Wheels* (1969) and *The Girls from Thunder Strip* (1966).

But all of these dramatic efforts (which have been excised from the résumés of several of the more serious actors mentioned above) paled in comparison to the mightiest motorcycle-based film of them all, the 1969 hit *Easy Rider*. The ragged cooperative effort of Peter Fonda, Dennis Hopper, and novelist-screenwriter Terry Southern was the tragicomic saga, oft-told, of innocent outsiders who fall victim to a narrow-minded and cruel establishment. Both Fonda and Hopper were veterans of biker flicks — the latter having made his mark in the American International Pictures release *The Glory Stompers*, in which he played the typically demented leader of a gang called the Black Souls. Joining Hopper and Fonda in the project was thirty-two-year-old Jack Nicholson, himself a veteran of Corman's and others' biker dramas, including *Hell's Angels on Wheels* and *Psyche-Out* (with Dern, Strasberg, and former child star Dean Stockwell). *Easy Rider*

In a broad sense, *Easy Rider* stands as a paradigm for the entire self-pitying, paranoid, drug-crazed, self-destructive era of the 1960s. The original concept was surely Fonda's; he claims to have gotten the inspiration during a visit to Toronto in 1967. He then shared the idea with his sometime friend Dennis Hopper, who at the time was the raging rebel of the Hollywood scene. Married to Brooke Hayward, the Brahmin daughter of producer Leland Hayward and actress Margaret Sullivan, Hopper fancied himself as the heir to hard-drinking, frantic-living actors of yore like John Barrymore and W. C. Fields, although acid, heroin, and grass had replaced the scotch and bourbon of the old order. It was planned that Fonda would produce the picture — originally called "The Loners" — while Hopper would blearily direct. Terry Southern, whose major triumph was the antiwar screed *Dr. Strangelove*, was assigned to write the script. But his association with the pair quickly degenerated into acrimony and confusion. There is little question that Southern wrote the screenplay — at least that which was not made up, ad hoc, on the set — and suggested the title *Easy Rider*. But in the end, after endless disputes, the screenwriting credit was shared by Fonda, Hopper, and Southern.

Easy Rider is remembered as a mawkish ode to drugs and the counterculture, again involving a melding of the bikers with the hippies, thereby creating freaked-out, aging flower children (Fonda and Hopper) drifting around the country on custom choppers of the kind ridden by hard-core outlaws. Fonda's bike, a bechromed custom Panhead chopper built by the studio, featured ape-hanger handlebars, a towering sissy bar, and a peanut gas tank painted like an American flag with, symbolically, thirteen stars. The story, as unformed and essentially simpleminded as the loopy automobile-based imitation *Two Lane Blacktop*, starring rockers James Taylor and Dennis Wilson, that was released two years later, involved Wyatt or "Captain America" (Fonda) and Billy (Hopper) on a drugged meander toward the Mardi Gras in New Orleans. On the way, they encounter a hopeless collection of dweebs and squares from the straight world, including George Hanson (Nicholson), who is exposed to the liberating glories of pot smoking and acid before being killed. He departs to the big commune in the sky before poor Wyatt and Billy meet their ends at the hands of who else but yahoo rednecks out to crush and dismember placid, peace-loving souls like the hapless pair. Cocaine was the drug of choice in the picture (baking powder was actually employed during the shooting), which is believed by many to have popularized the then rare and expressive drug (which at the time was believed to be nonaddictive).

Fonda had purchased four Harley-Davidson patrol bikes from the Los Angeles Police Department for $500 each and, with several friends who were expert customizers, converted them for the picture. Two were altered for Hopper, while the other pair became Fonda's famed Captain America machine. One was burned during the final scene in the movie; the other three were stolen from a Simi Valley shop during the shooting and never seen again. They were probably scavenged for parts and sold, although if one were to reappear, it would be celebrated as perhaps the most valuable motorcycle artifact in history. The four Harleys created for *Easy Rider* were the very antithesis of the kind of motorcycle their manufacturer was stubbornly trying to sell, yet stylistically they were perfectly attuned to the expressionism of the outlaw customizers operating out of small, obscure shops around the nation.

Easy Rider was a continuation of the trend popularized by the 1967 Warren Beatty production *Bonnie and Clyde.* This "new wave" of filmmaking combined violence and comedy in weird juxtaposition and suspended moral judgments while breaking ground in cinema verité filming techniques. *Bonnie and Clyde* shredded the old Hollywood rules of plotting structure and became a hit after its 1968 rerelease. It would spawn a group of antiestablishment films, including *Easy Rider.*

Crazed on drugs, Hopper insisted that the original cut of the film be four and a half hours long, including endless footage shot at the 1968 Mardi Gras in New Orleans without script. The picture was finally cut to ninety-four minutes and produced for a cost of $501,000. It would ultimately gross over $19 million after its New York release on July 14, 1969. As *Easy Rider* was glorifying antiauthoritarianism and its subliminal message against parental figures in theaters, the Manson gang committed its heinous murders in Los Angeles. Surely the movie's message of "peace and love" unraveled almost as quickly as Fonda's Captain America Harley-Davidson blew up in the final scene — an explosion that was intended to symbolize the destruction of the entire decadent American middle-class establishment. The result was quite the opposite.

Nicholson reached stardom through the picture, having been nominated for a supporting actor's Oscar, while Hopper and Fonda gained immortal status as heroes of the counterculture. Laszlo Kovacs shot *Easy Rider* in vivid, often psychedelic colors, which only enhanced its appeal to young audiences who, in acid-laced states of self-pity and self-importance, celebrated the picture as a profound statement and a paradigm for their sacrifices on behalf of the antiwar movement. It being a period of agonizing tumult in the nation, with the increasingly pointless and bloody war in South Vietnam dragging on and the civil rights movement in brutalized chaos following the assassinations of Dr. Martin Luther King and Robert Kennedy, *Easy Rider* widened the rift between the embattled establishment and a small but vocal minority of kids now so alienated that they had long since forgotten what made them angry in the first place.

Easy Rider remains a blearily portentous relic from those angry and confused days before most of the hippies shed their denims and their tie-dyeds, butted out their last joints, and headed for graduate school. For all *Easy Rider*'s celebration as a seminal comment on the times and its social impact, the biggest box office hit of the year was a mindless Disney production about a Volkswagen called *The Love Bug*. Today, the madness of the late sixties is remembered as a time of enlightenment and universal love by sentimentalists, whereas others think it a turning point when scatological cynicism, the culture of victimization, and an all-pervasive lassitude about drugs gripped the nation.

Surely *Easy Rider* helped glorify dope and cocaine, the long-term benefits of which remain murky at best. So too did it drive motorcycles into the mainstream psyche once again, to join musty images of the Hollister drunk and Brando's punkish *Wild One*. Although both Fonda and Hopper would forever be associated with the freewheeling biker lifestyle, only Fonda had a real enthusiasm for motorcycles. Over the years he not only became a serious and highly respected actor, but rode Harleys both privately and publicly. Most recently he and a friend made an extended cross-country cruise to attend the celebration of the company's ninety-fifth birthday, descending with an estimated two hundred thousand other keepers of the flame on Milwaukee in midsummer 1998. Hopper's career steadied up, and he too came to be regarded as a serious and talented actor. But he made no effort to continue riding. He has privately admitted that he has hated and feared motorcycles ever since he dumped one on Sunset Boulevard in the midsixties and spent ten days in a hospital as a result. "I can't stand the goddam things," he told author Peter Biskind. "When I made the movie, every time a shot was done, that bike went right back on the truck."

Attempts by Harley-Davidson to brush aside unpleasant images radiated by *Easy Rider* and earlier biker flicks were increasingly futile. Their motorcycle, like it or not, oozed rebellion and antiestablishment gropings for independence and self-styled freedom. For all the sound and fury generated by the counterculture during the final years of the sixties and the early part of the seventies, much of it has been overblown and sentimentalized with the passage of time. Little cultural residue exists today beyond FM oldies stations and a chronic problem with illegal drugs that remains its most enduring legacy. Harley-Davidson, the stodgy Milwaukee company that unwittingly interfaced with the hippies through the brief Ken Kesey–Hells Angels love-in, far outlived the Great Revolution. While fantasies of flower power persist on a few college campuses and in throwback neighborhoods in San Francisco and on Manhattan's West Side, the Harley-Davidson mystique rides on, enhanced and expanded by that brief encounter. Based on the publicity generated by Hopper, Fonda, and others, by mid-1970, progressives inside the company suggested that perhaps it was time to shuck its traditional customers and seek out the younger, wilder ones and the crazy machines they embraced. Surely the shock troops of the sixties shook the old firm to its foundations, generating a call for a new beginning. Now was not the time for more business as usual. Outside forces, beyond the purview much less the control of the company, had radically altered its image. The hippie-motorcycle connection portrayed in *Easy Rider* was a contextual reach at best, and it obscured the reality that it was the Vietnam veterans, not the flower children, who formed the nucleus of the new Harley culture. They too were embittered and isolated from the mainstream, in no small part because of the hostility generated by the antiwar movement. It was men like Dave Barr, not movie stars or hippies, who formed the core of the hard-bitten rebels who rode Harley-Davidsons. A double amputee following an encounter with an Angolan land mine, Barr accomplished an incredible journey on his Harley — a four-year circumnavigation of the globe. It was Barr and his kind who established the patterns for courageous, no-nonsense, independent motorcycling that were to energize Harley-Davidson's corporate image in the years to come.

Since its formation in 1903, little had changed in the firm's overall corporate philosophy: to build strong, reliable motorcycles for decent folk who embodied the same bedrock Midwestern American values as the four founders. It had worked for nearly seventy years, leaving Harley-Davidson the sole survivor in a war for supremacy in the American market that had seen hundreds of domestic rivals fall by the wayside. The simple goals of the founders, based on straightforward technology and hard-knuckled work ethics, had produced great success through two world wars and a crushing depression. Those elemental themes had made eminent sense in a time long past, when America was young and places like Milwaukee, Wisconsin, roiled with audacious men seeking to exploit the booming opportunities embodied in the miracle of the internal combustion engine.

PART TWO · ORIGINS OF THE LEGEND

4 · AN HONEST MACHINE

When William Harley and the brothers Arthur and Walter Davidson rolled their first prototype motorcycle into the harsh Milwaukee sunlight early in the spring of 1903, they were but three of thousands of young men in America and Europe consumed by dreams of conquering space with all manner of contraptions powered by the internal combustion engine.

The craze had begun in Europe in 1885, when two Germans, Gottlieb Daimler and Karl Benz, working independently within sixty miles of each other, developed the first roadworthy vehicles employing a four-cycle gasoline engine developed ten years earlier by Cologne engineer Nikolaus Otto. Daimler's Einspur ("single-track") two-wheeler is considered the first motorcycle; Benz's little three-wheeler is credited with being a primitive automobile. This trio — Otto, Benz, and Daimler, in company with Wilhelm Maybach (who, with Daimler, developed the basis of modern carburetion) — launched civilization into the era of powered automobiles, boats, and aircraft.

By 1903, the world was on a technological binge. Within the past quarter century, the invention of the lightbulb and the telephone, and rapid refinement of the internal combustion gasoline engine, had altered the perception of mankind's horizons, prompting soaring optimism and rosy predictions for the new century. Americans were particularly brash in their visions of the future. After all, they had recently shamed Spain in a lopsided 112-day war involving overt flexing of imperialist muscle. The Spanish-American War thrust the nation onto the world stage as a power to be reckoned with. In another classic example of gunboat diplomacy, in November 1903, the United States seized tiny Panama from Colombia, thereby setting the stage for completion of the great interocean canal that had stymied the French. Brimming with jingoistic bombast, America stood on the brink of a charge into international geopolitics that would make her the most powerful nation in history by the half-century.

The youths Harley and Davidson and their spindly little motorcycle would rise with their nation's tide, but in the broad scheme of things, their accomplishments would pale in comparison to those of three other men who were, at the same time in the great heartland, poised to rock the earth with their machinery. In Dayton, Ohio, a pair of bicycle mechanics named Wilbur and Orville Wright were completing fabrication of a crude machine they called Flyer I, powered by a twelve-horsepower engine that would leave the ground for 120 feet at Kitty Hawk, North Carolina, later that year. In Detroit, a few hundred miles east of Milwaukee across Lake Michigan, Henry Ford, following a series of false starts, incorporated the

Ford Motor Company and began production of a small eight-horsepower Model A two-seater that would be sold to 658 customers within the first twelve months. The age of the gasoline engine was about to accelerate to maximum speed.

The Safety bicycle developed by the English Rover company in Coventry in 1885 had offered enormous impetus to modern transportation. Chain driven, with equal-sized wheels fore and aft, and employing the all-metal construction and wire-spoked wheels first seen on the Ariel bicycle fifteen years earlier, the Safety bicycle was a major hit. By the early 1890s, four million Americans, men and women alike, were astride bicycles, and the industry, led by Massachusetts industrialist Albert Pope, was generating revenues of $60 million a year.

Thanks to the invention of the modern pneumatic tire by Scottish veterinarian John Boyd Dunlop in 1888 and the development of mass rubber-tire production by the Michelin brothers, André and Edouard, in 1895, the bicycle became a useful, relatively cheap means of transportation until it was replaced by the automobile and the motorcycle in the early years of the twentieth century. With the development of the gasoline engine and the pneumatic tire came major advances in electrical technology, welding processes, roller bearings, and metal casting techniques, along with stronger, lighter steel and the newly developed aluminum alloy, all of which energized the mad rush to build and sell motorized two-, three-, and four-wheeled vehicles by thousands of backyard mechanics, bicycle makers, blacksmiths, machinists, and woozy dreamers in every corner of the civilized world. Nearly 10,000 companies would be formed between 1890 and 1920 in Europe and North America to build such machines. Today, a century later, only a handful of those remain in business.

Among the multitudes hoping to cash in on the brave new world of gasoline-powered transportation were William Harley and the brothers Davidson. They were of stolid immigrant artisan English and Scottish stock and boyhood pals with a penchant for things mechanical. Harley and Arthur Davidson had been working at Barth Manufacturing, a small Milwaukee machine shop, when, in the late 1890s, a German draftsman named Emil Kruger showed them drawings of a French single-cylinder De Dion-Bouton engine based on the Otto principle. The pair then began creating their own patterns for a small engine, not for a motorcycle but to power a small boat. Arthur Davidson had made some patterns for neighbor Ole Evinrude, who is credited with creating the first outboard motor, and the connection is logical, although within a year the young pair had transferred their energies to building an engine to serve as auxiliary power for a bicycle.

Being practical young men, they logically concluded, like many contemporaries, that motorized bicycles, or "motorcycles," could serve as reliable transportation for the masses. The automobile, now being built in tiny quantities, was slow, heavy, and expensive. Worse yet, automobiles were unsatisfactory for use on the rutted cow paths that formed the majority of roads in America. A motorcycle, conversely, might be built for a reasonable cost using the basic technology inherent in a lightweight, tubular-framed steel bicycle. Others had already begun to probe the market, including aviation pioneer Glenn Curtiss; the Thomas Company of Buffalo, New York; the aforementioned Albert Pope; and most important of all, a pair of Springfield, Massachusetts, businessmen named George Hendee and Oscar Hedstrom, who in 1901 teamed up to build Indian motorcycles — and were destined to become archrivals of the Milwaukee trio. At the same time, dozens of English manufacturers were entering the motorcycle business, including such brands as Excelsior (1896), Matchless (1899), Ariel and Norton (1902), and J.A.P. (1903), all of whom would endure to struggle with Harley-Davidson for market share in the decades to come.

In the beginning there was no reason to believe that William Harley and the Davidson brothers enjoyed any unique opportunity to succeed. They possessed no particular design or mechanical ingenuity. They were uneducated technically, had little or no financial resources and no reputation in the business world. Beyond being intelligent young men with a bent for mechanics, they were virtually interchangeable with literally thousands of workaday Americans dreaming of glory in the burgeoning business of motorized transport.

Mechanical drawings for various engine designs by William Harley and Arthur Davidson date to 1901, but it was not until a year later that the operation began to gain momentum. Bill Harley, twenty-one, was an apprentice draftsman and Arthur Davidson, a year younger, worked as a metal pattern maker. Both were hampered by a lack of hands-on mechanical skills — like those of Arthur's brother Walter, who was an apprentice machinist working on the railroad in Kansas. Lured home by a letter from Arthur offering him a ride on the new motorcycle, he arrived in Milwaukee to discover no more than a set of blueprints and a legion of high hopes. But convinced of the merit of the project, Walter Davidson joined the part-time operation in the basement of the Davidson family home at Thirty-eighth Street and Highland Avenue. His connections with the railroad would remain valuable in that the team would utilize its machine tools and foundry to create their early prototypes. Like his two cohorts, Walter realized that most of the new motorcycles on the market were little more than gussied-up bicycles with weak frames and underpowered engines. Their Achilles heels were their front forks and steering heads, which often broke while absorbing a majority of the road shock. If there was any singular goal that set the early Harley-Davidson efforts apart from those of their rivals, it was to build simple, rugged machines with extra strength designed into the traditionally weak points. Davidson's steering head was to achieve new standards for durability in the nascent industry. Utility and practicality were to form the philosophical core of the tiny organization. If a machine is the manifestation of the personalities of the people who create it, the pioneer Harley-Davidsons were perfect images of the founding trio. Straightforward, tough-minded, and intensely loyal both to their friends and family and to their engineering and business ethic, they would form an alliance that would last until their deaths and be passed on to future generations. Such was the gritty intensity of the creators of the Harley-Davidson.

The first prototype that the three young builders bounced over the rutted Milwaukee roads was, like most of its rivals, little more than a converted bicycle. Legend, still unproven by company historians, maintains that the engine's crude carburetor was fabricated out of a tomato can. Bill Harley would later recall that "the first spark plugs were as big as doorknobs and cost three dollars each" (a prodigious sum in those days). Its small but sturdy engine would generate about twenty-five miles per hour in short bursts. Harley immediately set to designing a somewhat larger engine, for which Arthur Davidson again created the casting patterns. The second edition was radically stronger — a pure, purpose-built motorcycle, with the rear wheel powered by a flat leather belt, which they deemed to be tougher and more reliable than the linked steel chains being employed by others. The machine — the first legiti-

mate Harley-Davidson — worked well, exhibiting good performance
and reliability, to a point where several locals professed interest in
purchasing duplicates if they could be built. Encouraged by such
positive reviews, the three men, still employed in regular jobs, decided to gamble more of their futures in the new world of motorcycles. William Harley, realizing that he needed more technical
training if he was to continue design work, enrolled in the fall of
1903 in the engineering school of the University of Wisconsin at
Madison, while Arthur and Walter Davidson remained home to
thrust the fledgling business forward. William C. Davidson, the boys'
father, who had emigrated from Aberdeen, Scotland, in the late
1870s, used his skills as a professional carpenter to erect a small
ten-by-fifteen-foot wooden shed behind the family residence. There
a secondhand lathe and drill press were installed and above the
door was painted "Harley-Davidson Motor Company" (Harley's
name being given primary billing by mutual agreement because of
his contributions to the original design of the engine and running
gear).

During the harsh Wisconsin winter of 1903–04, Arthur Davidson assembled two more motorcycles for customers, using his elemental tools and a local foundry to create the castings and forgings
from his patterns. By spring, potential business seemed sufficient
to prompt brother Walter to quit his railroad job and aid in both fabrication and building an addition to the shop that doubled its size. A
small group of part-time help was also enlisted. While the exact
number of motorcycles built during this period is unclear, most historians believe that three more machines were completed during
1904, with another five being sold the following year. In comparison
to the booming business being enjoyed by Indian or such English
makers as Norton and Excelsior, Harley-Davidson remained a non-

entity, apparently but one of hundreds of upstart organizations manned by novices and doomed to failure.

Still, the solid if unspectacular performance of the handful of machines that rolled out of the little shop was gaining an enthusiastic following. But it was not until mid-1905 that the fledgling operation began its breakthrough as a serious motorcycle manufacturer. Until then the early bikes had been only modest improvements over the competition, still haunted by weak, flexible frames prone to breakage and promoting erratic handling. Historians celebrate the 1905½ model Harley-Davidson as the first truly competitive machine produced, and the model that would help the company rise above the ruck of competition. Potential for expansion was sufficient for a prosperous Davidson uncle named James McKay to open his generally tight Scottish purse and lend his nephews funds to purchase a vacant lot on the corner of Twenty-seventh and Chestnut Streets (soon to be changed to Juneau Avenue). It was a fine site for a factory, being located on a spur of the Chicago, Milwaukee, and St. Paul Railroad. There, during the winter of 1904–05, a two-story frame building was erected and a modest inventory of machine tools installed to begin serious production. With increased capacity and an expanded workforce, nearly fifty Harley-Davidsons were sold in 1906.

Slowly, steadily, the nation was awakening to the potential of motorized transportation. The tiresome jape "Get a horse" was losing impact, and the railroad cartels, which had actively inhibited highway improvements, were losing political clout, both in the new trust-busting atmosphere of Washington and at the local level, where bicyclists and motorists of all kinds were demanding better surfaces upon which to travel. Despite Ford's dream of a cheap automobile for the masses, four-wheeled vehicles, still propelled by a variety of primitive steam, electric, and gasoline power plants,

were essentially rich men's toys with little relationship, either fi-
nancially or functionally, to the average citizen. Conversely, the motorcycle, with good power and speed, plus the maneuverability to
negotiate clogged urban streets and lumpy, dusty country roads,
seemed a viable alternative to the venerable horse and buggy.
Therefore, the earliest Harley-Davidsons were intended purely as
mundane transportation devices, with no idea that they would ultimately become wildly sybaritic machines intended for pure sport
and pleasure.

The Harley-Davidson Motor Company was formally incorporated on September 22, 1907. The president was Walter Davidson,
doubtless selected as the most senior of the founding three. Arthur
served as secretary and general sales manager, and Bill Harley, still
laboring toward his engineering degree, was named, in absentia, as
treasurer, chief engineer, and designer. It was at this point that the
fourth member of the team and the third Davidson brother was
added. William A. Davidson was, at age thirty-seven, the eldest and,
like his father, a native of Scotland. A beefy, square-jawed man with
a direct, deliberate manner, Bill Davidson left his job as a toolroom
foreman in the repair shops of the Chicago, Milwaukee, and St.
Paul Railroad and came aboard as vice president and works manager. An experienced machinist and hands-on mechanic and fabri-
cator, he was to become a brilliant manufacturing expert, although
historians note that during his long tenure with the company, he
seldom if ever rode a motorcycle. It's noteworthy that despite the
overwhelming advantage enjoyed by the three Davidson brothers
over Harley in terms of management and financial weight in the
company hierarchy, there is no evidence that anything but total
unity existed between the four men until their deaths.

While temptation tugged at them to modify and update their
single model in response to a madcap variety of machines entering

the market from all quarters, the decision was made to maintain the course, although in late 1905, new paint was adopted to replace the all-black scheme offered on the earliest models. A muted, quasi-military gray hue was chosen, which, combined with the improved muffler system that reduced the normal blat of the thumping, slow-revving engine to a civilized rattle, gave rise to the most successful of the early Harley-Davidson production models, known as the Silent Gray Fellow.

Another technical advance was critical: the development of a sophisticated front-wheel suspension employing a pair of coil springs that dampened the tooth-jarring ride — a nod to rider comfort that would be enhanced in 1912 by the addition of a patented "Ful-Floteing" (sic) seat featuring a large coil spring concealed in its mounting. No rear suspension of any sort would be offered by Harley-Davidson until 1960.

Arthur Davidson was a compact man with the piercing, deep-set eyes shared by his brothers. More than the rest, he was an adept salesman, with a searing curiosity to find out how to best create a network of dealerships, which the Indian organization had developed out of the existing network of bicycle shops around the nation. His first goal as general sales manager was to organize a consortium of dealers to sell the motorcycles being manufactured by the new company. He packed his bags and hit the road from coast to coast to establish dealerships, primarily within the small network of bicycle shops converting to the new motorcycles, while pitching all manner of municipal agencies — police forces, rural mail carriers, surveyors — in hopes of convincing them that the motorcycle was a viable alternative to the horse and the automobile. His pitch was to sell Harley-Davidsons as utility machines: strong, simple, reliable units capable of probing into locations unreachable by the primitive automobile. Major sales resistance came from the harsh reality that the motorcycle required considerable skill, both in terms of physical dexterity and mechanical aptitude, to ride effectively. Worse yet, the motorcycle left the rider as vulnerable to the elements as if he had remained mounted on a horse.

Despite the disadvantages, sales notched steadily upward, reaching 456 machines in 1908. But any dreams that Harley-Davidson — or any other motorcycle manufacturer, for that matter — was on the verge of becoming a major factor in America's workaday transportation mix were about to be dashed. By 1913, Henry Ford would hit his stride. Employing mass-production assembly-line techniques adapted from the meat packing industry, Ford and his team of manufacturing and design experts, led by Charles Avery, began mass-marketing their famed Model T, the world-shattering "Tin Lizzy" or "flivver" that would rival the lightbulb, the telephone, and the airplane as the most influential invention to be introduced since the steam engine over a century earlier. Ford initially priced the Model T at $850, but volume production, ruthless marketing, and overwhelming public response soon drove the cost to below $500 and within a few hundred dollars of a motorcycle, which cost between two and three hundred dollars. As adaptable and tough as a cockroach and nearly as mobile, the Model T "put America on wheels," as the saying went, and doomed the motorcycle to a secondary position as a device for specialized utility duties or a pure sporting machine.

The conservative Harley-Davidson management evidenced little interest in reaching the so-called sports market, even after the Federation of American Motorcycles (FAM) began organizing all manner of races and endurance events. However, with Indian, Excelsior, Iver Johnson, Merkel, Pope, et al., competing and gaining publicity, it was decided that the factory had no choice but to enter competition on a limited basis. Walter Davidson, who was the most accomplished rider of the founders, was selected to enter a well-prepared Silent Gray Fellow in a major endurance run in June 1908. It would start in Catskill, New York, and circumnavigate Long Island in a series of carefully timed competition legs. Eighty-four riders, astride nearly two dozen different makes, entered the event marked by miles of pocked and rutted roads traversing steep grades. Nearly half the motorcycles broke down on the first day, but Walter soldiered on, relying on the Harley's durability rather than its outright speed. He won the two-day marathon with a perfect score, then backed it up with a victory the following week in an economy run that saw his same machine record a stunning 188 miles to the gallon. Both triumphs were widely celebrated in the trade press, bringing a bump in sales and orders. But beyond a few endurance demonstrations, the company's policy against racing remained in place.

William Harley, now holding an engineering degree — awarded with honors — returned to the company full-time with plans for a great leap forward. The trend in the industry was toward twin-cylinder engines, a design that would offer double the displacement (and power) with a modest penalty in weight and size. Multiplicity of cylinders was energizing all forms of gasoline power plants, with six-, eight-, and even twelve- and sixteen-cylinder engines being created for cars, airplanes, and boats. But weight and space considerations limited motorcycle designers in terms of increasing motorcycle engine capacity. Like his archrivals at Indian, Harley chose a V-twin design, i.e., two cylinders mounted on a common crankcase in a V shape, with the cylinder barrels angled at forty-five degrees. This produced an excellent package when fixed in the roughly triangular shape of the motorcycle frame and offered both compactness and good balance to the machine. Harley employed an old technology wherein each cylinder's connecting rods were mounted on a common crankshaft journal (called a "knife and fork" configuration by aficionados). Coupled with the narrow forty-five-degree angle between the cylinders, the layout limited rpm's and power output. Offsetting this was lusty, low-end torque, which was valuable in digging through the ruts and mud encountered on most of the nation's still-awful rural roads, and the distinct, tub-thumping, cadenced exhaust note that was to become a priceless Harley-Davidson asset.

The company offered its first V-twin in 1909, but hard starting and other problems delayed serious introduction of an improved model until 1911, when the 6.5-horsepower Model 7D joined the Silent Gray Fellow in the lineup. This model would establish the technological bedrock of Harley-Davidson, its forty-five-degree, air-cooled V-twin engine embodying the same overall design themes still in use today. Also entering the lineup in 1915 was an optional sidecar that converted the Harley-Davidson into a three-wheeler capable of carrying an extra passenger or additional cargo. This would enhance the utility of the machine and offer limited help in staving off the onslaught of the Model T.

By 1913, Europe was on the brink of the nightmare of trench warfare, with Hiram Maxim's machine gun doomed to become the most influential machine on earth. Far away and impervious to Continental political upheavals, the American motorcycle industry continued to thrive. Nearly 75,000 machines were manufactured — with nearly half of those being produced by industry leader Indian, trailed by Harley-Davidson with 11,000 singles and twins. But with Henry Ford now operating at full steam and annually selling more than 300,000 Model Ts, and with the Dodge brothers coming into the market with their own low-priced, all-steel-bodied sedan, the motorcycle was on the verge of becoming marginalized as a mass-market vehicle. Its destiny was already cast in stone: to serve as alternate transportation to the automobile, as sport and light-duty utility, nothing more, nothing less.

While most of the nation's population remained clustered east of the Mississippi, balmy Southern California offered a perfect all-year, all-weather market for motorcycles, although it was unsuited to vehicle manufacture due to the absence of resources like iron, coal, limestone, and timber. The railhead city of Los Angeles had grown from a dusty backwater town of forty thousand in 1880 to a booming metropolis of five hundred thousand by the early part of the twentieth century. The vast, open spaces surrounding it, coupled with excellent weather, made L.A. nirvana for motorcyclists. Arthur Davidson worked hard to develop a solid network of dealerships within this fertile sales territory. The Southwest would become the primary market area for Harley-Davidson over the years, creating not only enormous profits but powerful social trends that would concurrently alter, enhance, and curse the machine's identity.

Ford's spidery flivver created a rift between automobile drivers and motorcycle riders that would never be breached. Cars, soon to be equipped with self-starters and rigid steel tops — with such conveniences in the offing as automatic transmissions and later air conditioning and power-assisted everything — were on the verge of becoming appliance-like devices capable of being operated by the most ham-fisted citizen. Conversely, the motorcycle would always remain a challenge in terms of the balance, dexterity, endurance, and courage demanded of the rider. After nearly a century, the modern motorcyclist remains, for all intents and purposes, as vulnerable to weather and the laws of physics as when Walter Davidson and Bill Harley first threw their legs over their prototype in 1903. Motorcycle riding was — and is — sufficiently difficult that despite the dreams of many early manufacturers, its acceptance among a vast percentage of the population was automatically narrowed, especially in substantial portions of the nation where rain, snow, ice, hail, mud, high winds, and freezing temperatures limited its use to all but the most skilled and intrepid riders.

The company, which had openly disdained involvement in competition since the Long Island marathon victory, was in 1913 forced onto the tracks and board speedways that were rising up across the nation. With rival brands winning big races, the absence of Harley-Davidson, which still openly bragged that it was building no "special racing machines," became a source of adverse publicity within the industry. After all, challenged critics and rival manufacturers, if Harley-Davidson motorcycles were so strong and powerful, why were they not able to win races? As the lack of a motor sports program became an increasingly effective sales tool against them, the founders made the decision to develop purpose-built motorcycles strictly for high-speed-track competition. Because Bill Harley was a competent but hardly inspired engineer, outside help was sought to create a truly high-performance motorcycle. William Ottoway, the brilliant competition manager of Thor motorcycles in Aurora, Illinois, was hired away to inject real power and speed into the reliable but rather slow and heavy Harley-Davidson twin.

Ottoway's first act was to work with Harley in designing a reliable three-speed transmission, also needed to aid in hauling around a sidecar, which was becoming a popular option. His great leap forward would come a year later with the introduction of the light-

The founders: bright, tough, hard-edged, and ready to take on the world. L to R: Arthur Davidson, Walter Davidson, William S. Harley, and William A. Davidson. (Harley-Davidson Motor Co.)

Harley-Davidson "Number One" is on display in the Juneau Avenue office lobby. Its single-cylinder engine is stamped "Number One," dating it to 1903 or early 1904, and the frame has been dated to 1905. No earlier, complete Harley-Davidson is known to exist. (Harley-Davidson Motor Co.)

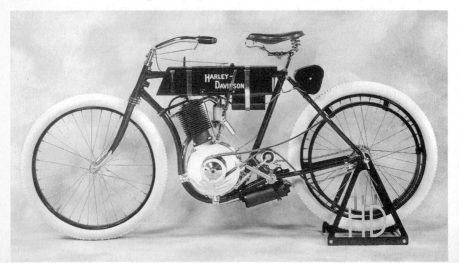

Walter C. Davidson poses with the stock Silent Gray Fellow he rode to a stunning victory in a June 1908, 180-mile endurance run around Long Island. It would mark the motor company's first entry into formal competition. (Harley-Davidson Motor Co.)

The 1936 overhead valve 61E Knucklehead is considered by many to be the finest motorcycle produced by Harley-Davidson and among the best in history. The 61E forms the technological bedrock of the Harleys being produced today. (Harley-Davidson Motor Co.)

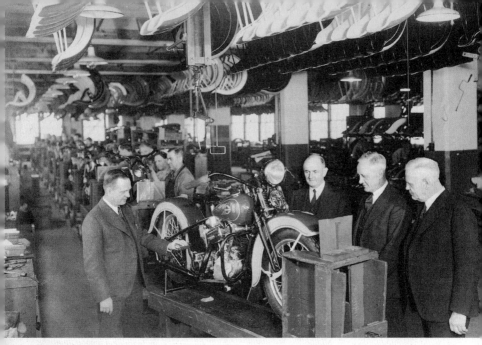

The four founders examine a completed 61EL as it rolls off the Juneau Avenue assembly line in 1936. L to R: Arthur Davidson, Walter Davidson, William A. Davidson, and William S. Harley. (Harley-Davidson Motor Co.)

While these U.S. Army soldiers appear ready for combat aboard their forty-five-cubic-inch, military version Harley Davidson WLAs, motorcycles were in fact used primarily for dispatch service and behind-the-lines patrol duty in World War II. (Harley-Davidson Motor Co.)

The shot that changed everything. Eddie Davenport poses for San Francisco photographer Barney Peterson during a lull in the July 1947 Hollister bike riot. The photo's appearance in a subsequent issue of *Life* magazine permanently transformed all motorcyclists into "bikers" and "outlaws." (*San Francisco Chronicle*)

A second shot, never published, indicates that someone, either the photographer or perhaps the rider, believed to be Tulare, California, resident Eddie Davenport, repositioned the empty beer bottles and the jacket, thereby creating the suspicion that the entire scene was posed. (*San Francisco Chronicle*)

Johnny's Bar and Grill is considerably more peaceful today than when it was the epicenter of the great Hollister, California, riot of July 4, 1947. (Brock Yates)

This happy couple, suited up in their quasi–highway patrol getups, exemplifed the image the motor company was trying to project on the same July 4, 1947, weekend the Hollister riot altered Harley-Davidson's image forever. (Harley-Davidson Motor Co.)

The menace on the move. Hells Angels funerals were (and are) mass events, often attracting hundreds of bikers, who ride in grim-faced formation to the cemetery — often accompanied by fleets of police cars and the press. (San Francisco Chronicle)

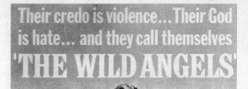

The 1966 Roger Corman–Charles Griffith feature *The Wild Angels* was the first of dozens of low-cost drive-in pictures that linked the hippies with the biker gangs in a contrived juxtaposition of the two cultures. The picture was produced for $360,000 and reportedly made American International Pictures nearly $10 million during its run in the United States and Europe. (MGM Clip & Still)

Peter Fonda hauls Jack Nicholson aboard his *Easy Rider* Harley-Davidson chopper on their ill-fated odyssey toward New Orleans. Dennis Hopper rides shotgun on a second Harley that was doomed to obscurity compared to the Fonda machine, which was to become the single most famous motorcycle in history. (Archive Photos)

Willie G. Davidson, the Olympian figure who serves as the life source of the Harley-Davidson mystique. (Harley-Davidson Motor Co.)

Sonny Barger (center), the greatest Hells Angel of them all, checks out his Harley with the help of a girlfriend while other club members pay rapt attention. (San Francisco Chronicle)

weight (300 pounds) Model II-K racing twin, which, with the bravest and most accomplished riders aboard, could reach a stunning ninety miles per hour. This motorcycle would form the basis of Harley-Davidson's long and much-honored competition career and raise Ottoway to a level of influence in the design department that would finally transcend Harley's revered position.

As the company stolidly held course by producing both the increasingly quick and potent V-twin and the aging single-cylinder model, Arthur Davidson began looking overseas to exploit additional sales. Indian and Excelsior had already encountered success in the United Kingdom, and now Harley-Davidson set up an export department to tap a growing enthusiasm in Europe for American V-twin motorcycles, which were larger and faster than their home-built counterparts. Edwardian England still resisted the widespread intrusion of motor vehicles of all kinds, and taxation policies, plus the high cost of gasoline, restricted manufacturers like Triumph and Norton to single-cylinder models with engine sizes under 500 cc (approximately thirty cubic inches). Conversely, there were no strictures on engine displacement in the United States, thanks in part to the fact that the nation was awash in petroleum. Enormous oil fields were being developed in west Texas and California, providing citizens with copious amounts of cheap gasoline. This, coupled with the vast expanses over which Americans were forced to travel, encouraged the manufacture of large, powerful, and essentially inefficient automobiles and motorcycles until the OPEC fuel crisis of the early 1970s. If companies like Harley-Davidson, Ford, and General Motors are to be pilloried today for building oversized "gas guzzlers," they ought to be excused in part because they operate in a marketplace that since the beginning has offered no advantage to the makers of small, economical vehicles, regardless of their engineering excellence or efficiency. While European governments discouraged the selling of oversized machines like the Harley because of a near-total dependence on Middle Eastern oil, there were from the beginning wealthy sportsmen willing to pay the egregious taxes in order to gain the extra speed and acceleration available from a Harley-Davidson and its American ilk.

The Harley-Davidson export plan briefly ran aground when the candidate to operate the export department — one Eric von Gumpert — was rejected because of dark suspicions that he was Jewish. This made him verboten to the Davidson brothers, and von Gumpert was hired only after he convinced them he was a gentile with proper German ancestry. This would not be the last time that this nasty prejudice would blur the Davidsons' business judgments. Von Gumpert, once vetted, worked with a Scotsman, Duncan Watson, to set up a handful of dealerships in England and on the Continent before World War I broke out, thereby setting the stage for Harley-Davidson's active and successful export business, which thrives to this day.

Bill Ottoway's influence truly manifested itself in late 1914 with the introduction of the great Model J — an improved sixty-one-cubic-inch V-twin featuring chain drive and a neat three-speed transmission snugly mounted behind the engine. Ottoway's improvements in the valve mechanism, lubrication system, and cylinder head design offered a substantial boost in performance that, with the company's reputation for building high-quality, anvil-tough frames, made the Model J an instant success. Sales soared to 8,000 units during its first twelve months and hopes remained high for 1915 until the bloody war in Europe, which had broken out in July 1914, began affecting not only export sales but the American economy as well. The nation did not enter the conflict until 1916, however, and the new J-11 twin, now featuring full electric lighting and a kick starter, sold at the rate of 15,000 units per year until the fighting began. Ottoway and the brilliant English engine designer Harry Ricardo developed a prototype eight-overhead-valve engine for the competition Model 17 that produced a stunning fifty-five horsepower on the test bed — a number approaching the magical but rarely attained one horsepower per cubic inch. Had it not been for Ottoway's incessant drive for more engine efficiency and performance — sometimes in direct opposition to the conservative, pinchpenny policies of Harley and the Davidsons — it is possible that the company would have foundered on its reputation for building slow, boring, and outdated machines that were about to be completely outclassed by the competition. Such was the dynamic influence of William Ottoway.

So too for "Old Bill" Davidson, the burly boss of production, whose energetic, hands-on ramrodding of the fuming Juneau Avenue factory resulted in a steady train of well-fabricated motorcycles flowing off the assembly line. A tough, hard-nosed but fair man, Davidson presided over a generally loyal and devoted workforce. It was in no small part due to his stewardship that over its long history Harley-Davidson has enjoyed labor relations well above American industry standards. If there are men among the early cast of characters whose influence in the company soared above that of the others, the list would have to include Ottoway, Bill Davidson, and his brother Arthur, the peripatetic demon of sales.

Ottoway having created legitimately high-performance motorcycles, the management entered competition with a vengeance. A group of the finest racing riders available was hired, including the brilliant Red Parkhurst. Harley-Davidson became a winner on all manner of tracks, including the giant, abundantly dangerous, bowl-shaped board speedways being constructed around the nation. This enhanced competition reputation, plus the overall excellence of the Model J series, positioned the company among the top three competitors in the domestic market. Indian remained the sales leader, and Excelsior, now in the hands of powerful bicycle maker Ignatz Schwinn (who had also acquired the floundering Henderson firm), was still able to manufacture excellent big twin motorcycles. But thanks to Harley-Davidson's conservative fiscal management, enhanced product lineup, and efficient manufacturing policies, the upstart company from Milwaukee was about to parlay circumstance and missteps by the competition into a major sales breakthrough. Meanwhile, other smaller makers steadily dropped out of business, unable to compete in terms of cost, quality control, and dealer outlets. In 1917–18 both Pope and Merkel ceased production; Glenn Curtiss had ended his motorcycle business three years earlier. Some bit players still hung on, but the trend was clear; within a decade the battlefield would contain but two combatants, named Indian and Harley-Davidson.

In a brilliant act of marketing, Arthur Davidson began publishing a small magazine titled *The Enthusiast* in the summer of 1916. It was sent to all Harley-Davidson dealers and owners, serving as a conduit for information regarding company policy and product development. This publication, which remains in print to this day, served as a link — both spiritually and in terms of hard news — between the company and its thousands of customers in the hinterlands. *The Enthusiast* was the opening gambit in a well-conceived strategy to create a special bond between the company and its customers, one that would ultimately create a unique sense of loyalty and clannishness among Harley-Davidson owners everywhere. The magazine also served as a valuable promotional tool for selling a widening line of motorcycle clothing first offered in 1912 — leather jackets, boots, jodhpurs, riding breeches, sweaters, helmets, goggles, etc. — that would remain an integral part of the company's marketing efforts.

As the war in Europe accelerated in savagery and the bloody standoff inherent in trench warfare became apparent, America's entry on the side of the Allies was inevitable. There appeared to be a wartime role for the motorcycle as a vehicle suited to scouting and courier duties following the role it had played in General Pershing's frustrating pursuit of Mexican villain and sometime revolutionary Pancho Villa across the great southwestern desert in 1910. Small numbers of Harleys, Indians, and Excelsiors had been employed by Pershing in the campaign and had acquitted themselves nicely in the rugged terrain.

As the war effort accelerated, the Indian company management made a critical error. They decided to dominate the new military business and cut prices to absurd levels to gain contracts. Arthur Davidson instantly recognized an opportunity, understanding that if Indian obtained volume orders from the army, it would be unable to service its civilian customers. Davidson immediately hit the road, offering lucrative incentives to Indian dealers to switch sides, assuring them that their parent would be unable to provide product to both civilian and military markets. He was right. Indian was to sell 41,000 of their big sixty-one-cubic-inch side-valve twins (with a rudimentary leaf-spring rear suspension) to the military. Harley-Davidson sold but 15,000 army models, while craftily reserving half its production for the civilian market. This strategic move radically improved Harley-Davidson's sales position when the war ended — at the expense of Indian, which had ignored both its dealers and its traditional customers in search of short-term military profits.

Moreover, the fates smiled on the Milwaukee firm. Legend would build up around the blunders of U.S. Army corporal Roy Holtz, who, after becoming lost in a rainstorm along the Belgian front, wandered into German hands on November 9, 1918 — two days before Armistice. Released on the eleventh, Holtz chugged into a German border city aboard his muddy, side-car-equipped Model J, there to be photographed by the army and touted as "the first Yank to enter Germany." Harley-Davidson wisely trumpeted the dubious Holtz exploit as an example of their machine's indomitable wartime contribution, embellishing the incident to imply that Harleys had led the charge in defeating the hated Hun. In fact, motorcycles played only minor roles as courier vehicles behind the lines in both World War I and World War II.

Peace appeared to offer tremendous opportunities for Harley-Davidson, and the founders were quick to exploit it. Shortly after the troops began returning home, ground was broken for a major expansion of the Juneau Avenue factory. Five stories of floor space would total 600,000 square feet to accommodate 2,500 workers and a shiny new inventory of advanced machine tools. Once completed, the facility would be the largest motorcycle factory in the world, capable of cranking out 35,000 machines annually. Less than fifteen years after Bill Harley and the Davidson brothers had wobbled around their Milwaukee neighborhood on their rickety and anonymous prototype, their company possessed the potential for becoming the most powerful motorcycle manufacturer on the face of the earth.

5 · BURDENS OF LEADERSHIP

America was a vastly changed place in 1920 from when the Davidson brothers and Bill Harley had first toyed with the notion of building and selling motorcycles. A series of massive legislative reforms had altered the economic and social structure, redistributing wealth and naively attempting to govern morality. The Sixteenth Amendment to the Constitution (1912–13) had introduced the income tax in an effort to rectify the reality that 2 percent of the population controlled 20 percent of the wealth. The income tax, coupled with the toughened Clayton Anti-Trust Act in 1914, dealt a death blow to the nation's grotesquely rich aristocracy. The Eighteenth Amendment, ratified in 1920, was a disastrous attempt to legislate the citizenry's behavior. Prohibition outlawed the consumption of liquor while introducing an atmosphere of lawlessness and cynicism that would mark the decade as "the Roaring Twenties."

Hard on the heels of the hated and universally ignored Volstead Act came a series of blows to the national confidence. The 1920 Black Sox scandal, wherein it was discovered that Chicago's Black Sox American League team had thrown the World Series to the Cincinnati Reds, blighted the beloved national game of baseball. Hundreds of millions were lost and numerous banks failed as scores of citizens went broke, victims of the notorious Ponzi pyramid scheme. Meanwhile, the administration of sleazy, smooth-talking Warren G. Harding was being exposed as responsible for the Teapot Dome scandal — an outrage that surely would have led to his impeachment had he not done the nation the courtesy of dying on a vacation trip in 1923.

Worse yet, the transition from wartime business to peacetime expansion had proven difficult. Unemployment soared and businesses failed during the adjustment phase. Companies like Harley-Davidson and Indian found themselves haunted by enormous overcapacity. Both firms were capable of building 35,000 machines annually, only to discover that sales were roughly one-third that in a population mesmerized by cheap automobiles. The Model T, now joined by multitudes from Dodge, Star, and Chevrolet, dominated the market, which had soared to a total of eight million cars and trucks. Road building was in a frenzied state, with nearly four hundred thousand miles now paved with concrete and macadam — from fewer than ten thousand miles at the turn of the century.

The mix of the population had changed radically. Twenty years earlier, a majority of the nation — Protestant and Anglo-Saxon — had lived on farms. Now the 1920 census revealed that fewer than a third of the 105 million Americans were rural dwellers. The nation was urbanized, and increasingly Catholic, Central European, Jew-

ish, and black. America was motorized and about to be intercon-
nected by the twin miracles of the long-distance telephone and radio in a mass intimacy unimagined a few decades earlier.

The Harley-Davidson hierarchy could gain little solace from
these altered social states. Sales in 1920 slumped to about 11,000
motorcycles, which gave them sales leadership over Indian — a
hollow victory that offered little relief on the ledger sheets. It was
apparent that too much emphasis was being placed on the big
Model J twin and the performance image it embodied. The motorcycle, like its sixty-one-cubic-inch Indian counterpart, was heavy
(nearly 400 pounds) and tricky to handle, requiring an expert young
man to ride it effectively. Aside from applications as police units
employed in traffic duty, the big twins were exclusively the province of sportsmen who rode for pure recreation. The old dreams of
the motorcycle rivaling the car as a device for utilitarian transport
was long dead.

The new breed of motorcyclist, young, lusty veterans recently
home from the war, were fiendishly hard riders, hammering across
the back roads of the nation at insane speeds, scattering pedestri-
ans and chickens while easily outrunning all but the fastest and
most exotic automobiles. These lads, blue-collar types and raccoon-
coated collegians alike, embodied the rebellious spirit of the age
and put the lie to any lingering notion the Davidsons harbored that
their machine would serve the workaday needs of the population.
Bad-ass boys straddling blowsy, sideways-by-the-silo motorcycles
were altering the face of Harley-Davidson whether anybody liked it
or not. The influence of their progeny, the restless, ferociously adventurous veterans of thirty years hence, would solidify this image,
casting in stone the Harley as a machine of romance and not a little
menace.

It was time for ruthless action, and the Davidsons were more than ready. Their racing team, now called the "Wrecking Crew," was indomitable, winning major races all over the country. Expert riders on powerful, specially built lightweight Harleys marshaled by Bill Ottoway were lapping the big board speedways at well over 100 mph, and their fame — in a sports-crazed nation — was growing by the day. That is, until Walter Davidson quickly and without warning decided that racing was a promotional expense that had to be eliminated. As the crew readied themselves for a big race on the one-mile horse track at the Arizona State Fairgrounds in Phoenix, they received a terse telegram informing them of their immediate termination. No polite thank-yous were included, much less any severance pay. Telephone calls to Milwaukee were not accepted. Communications were cut forever, leaving men who had risked their lives in the name of Harley-Davidson to pawn their watches and other valuables in order to generate train fare home. The simple, down-home methods of the founders were giving way to hard-nosed business tactics that often pushed their ethical boundaries to the limit.

In order to expand the market beyond the high-performance big twins, Harley-Davidson introduced a smaller Sport Twin, a neatly packaged middleweight machine using a thirty-seven-cubic-inch, horizontally opposed, air-cooled engine similar to the one BMW would employ as its traditional power plant two years later. The Sport Twin was a modest success; if it had dominated the market on a grand scale, it is possible that Harley-Davidson might have abandoned its lumpy, rough-running V-twin in favor of the silky opposed layout — thereby unwittingly eliminating the uniquely dominant element of its personality. Indian came to market at the same time with its similarly sized Scout, but despite these efforts, both companies were to discover that the core of their market lay with adventurous, athletic young men who demanded the lusty levels of acceleration and speed available only from motorcycles packing powerful large-displacement engines. Both firms would make other attempts to build lighter, cheaper, more user-friendly motorcycles in the years to come, but their indelible trademark would be the loud, evil-sounding heavyweights.

During the height of the war years, the Juneau Avenue factory had employed nearly 2,500 workers. In response to the 1920s slump, brutal downsizing cut the staff to about 1,000, while Arthur Davidson embarked on a campaign to upgrade and improve the firm's 1,200-member dealership body. Some of his more successful franchises had given up the motorcycle business altogether in order to take on a line of cheap automobiles. Many others were planted in remote rural environs now abandoned by a population that had fled to the city. Still more had let their premises decline into grease-stained warrens attractive only to a tiny coterie of regulars and repellent to new customers. Art Davidson tried to correct this by canceling his weakest and most disheveled dealerships while seeking new opportunities in cities. This would be partially successful, but the trend toward Harley-Davidson dealerships being run in shabby sections of town by even more shabby proprietors would take decades to correct. Try as it might, the Harley-Davidson management would be helpless in preventing the motorcycle from becoming marginalized as a crude, often violent proletarian machine with a tarnished public image. A classic example was the notorious "Motorcycle Row" in downtown Los Angeles, where rowdy dealers and repair shops engaged in an active trade of stolen bikes and parts. Recognizing the critical nature of that market, Davidson rooted out his established dealer there and replaced him with a reputable individual in freshly enovated premises miles from the dingy thieves' market.

While well-crafted corporate hagiography, working through a generally docile press, has created the legend of the four founders as prim Midwestern gentlemen, they were in fact classic representatives of the bumpkin entrepreneurs who rose out of the late industrial revolution — blunt-edged artisans who, thanks to a combination of guile, hard work, luck, and bare-knuckle business tactics, managed to best a multitude of similar rivals. The automobile, aircraft, and motorcycle industries were especially attractive to such men, relying as they did on such basic skills as welding, pattern making, lathe operation, and other manual crafts. The greatest example of the breed was Henry Ford, an uneducated Michigan farm boy who, through fateful circumstance, managed to overpower thousands of brighter, better-educated combatants in the early car wars. Like the Davidsons, Ford was suspicious of the immigrants pouring into the nation from Italy and the Balkans and was, in his late, semimad years, to become anti-Semitic, with open sympathies for Adolf Hitler. This level of swinish behavior did not exist, so far as it is known, among the Davidsons and Harley, but they were far from sophisticated egalitarians, remaining private men operating in a tight circle of Protestant, Anglo-Saxon peers their entire lives. Hard-drinking within the confines of their clubs and homes, publicly they were pillars of the Milwaukee community: starched, grim-faced, board-stiff businessmen singularly devoted to building and maintaining the most powerful motorcycle company on earth.

Because of the weakness of the home market in the twenties, Arthur Davidson continued to seek sales overseas, where the broad-shouldered V-twins were attractive to affluent enthusiasts seeking more performance than that available from domestic brands. He and von Gumpert hired a young Englishman named Alfred Rich Child, who was to exert a major influence on Harley-Davidson's overseas international sales, especially in Japan. After he had convinced a suspicious Davidson that he was not Jewish, Child was taken aboard and immediately left for Africa, beginning a life of travel that would carry him — and the Harley-Davidson message — to the world's major population centers.

While Child hunted new markets, the company abruptly and mysteriously canceled its Sport Twin after a mere 6,000 units had been sold and reverted to the manufacture of even larger motorcycles. A seventy-four-cubic-inch version of the traditional Model J sixty-one-cubic-inch mainstay was introduced, while at the same time the company ruthlessly moved to solidify its market position. Harry V. Sucher, the author of a detailed, often critical history of the company (*Harley-Davidson: The Milwaukee Marvel*, Haynes Publishing, Great Britain), reveals that in the autumn of 1922, Arthur Davidson — who was, among the four founders, the most aggressive — arranged a secret meeting with Indian motorcycle boss Frank Weschler at New York's elegant Astor Hotel. The purpose of the gathering was simple and hopelessly illegal: to fix prices between the two manufacturers, thereby assuring their joint survival in a rapidly narrowing marketplace. This was an extraordinary act, not only because it openly violated antitrust laws, but because it was a contradiction of the Davidsons' open hatred of the competition. Their pinched clannishness theoretically countenanced no quarter for the enemy. But Sucher reports that the Astor meeting marked the beginning of annual sessions between the two rivals that would settle such issues as dealer exclusivity, model lineups, and ongoing price adjustments. Faced with such choreographed opposition, other manufacturers soon faded from the market, leaving the two colluding giants to fight to the death. Ignatz Schwinn's Excelsior, which was building the popular Henderson in-line four-cylinder, would remain a marginal third player until 1931. But for all intents and purposes, by the mid-1920s the American motorcycle business had become a two-company game.

Indian, long since having lost the energies of its two founders, staggered along in chaotic financial condition, now playing second banana to the better organized, better focused Milwaukee firm. Indian continued to participate in racing, but with the demise of the huge board tracks through the vagaries of weather and fire, the sport had been reduced to the county fair level, where horse-track venues and carnival midway "death defying" barrel riding entertained a poor and generally unsophisticated public. Harley-Davidson continued its nonracing policy, although numerous privateers competed independently on Harley-Davidsons. The founders still maintained that the company's sales tactics centered on a split strategy of utility and sport — with their big machines being aimed at applications like law enforcement, border patrol, military use, light delivery (with sidecars), and the legions of young men who rode for pure recreation. Unfortunately for Harley-Davidson, the automobile industry boomed, and as Ford was able to chop the price of a new Model T, the used-car market was flooded with aging Ts that were cheaper than a new Harley 61 or 74. Dreams of motorcycles becoming mainstream transportation had disappeared, except in Japan. There, thanks to the amazing Alfred Rich Child, Harley-Davidson became a major presence in the 1920s. In many ways the company was to serve as the parent of the Japanese industry that would nearly drive it out of business a half-century later.

Through a series of clever business maneuvers, Child organized an import operation in Japan that began selling more than 2,000 machines annually by the mid-1920s, for the most part with sidecars for utility work. The Japanese domestic motorcycle industry was essentially nonexistent, and Harley-Davidsons (as well as some Indians) were valued as small, light trucks in Japan's crowded cities, where their maneuverability and relative fuel economy made them adaptable for hauling all manner of freight. Child set up his Harley-Davidson Sales Company of Japan and prospered mightily — and quietly. He established more than 400 dealerships across the main islands before contracting with the giant Sankyo Trading Company to manufacture complete machines under license. Not only would large V-twin bikes be built by Sankyo, but also a three-wheel shaft-drive utility vehicle for pure business applications.

Because of the increasingly tense relations between Japan and the United States involving trade and tariff barriers, strict immigration policies, and political differences over Japan's expansionist military plans — plus racially and culturally based bad blood — the Milwaukee firm entered into this arrangement in strict secrecy, fearing its public image as an all-American company might be compromised. This strange alliance would lead to Sankyo's building a Japanese Harley-Davidson clone in the mid-1930s called Rikuo, or "King of the Road." Child and Harley-Davidson left Japan in 1937 as the clouds of World War II gathered, but the Rikuo became a mainstay of not only the Japanese motorcycle industry but the Imperial Army as well. It was to serve as the basic military motorcycle of America's archenemy during the most savage conflict in history. More than 18,000 Type 97 Japanese Army–version Harley-Davidson imitations were built for the Imperial Army. Production continued until the middle of the 1950s, when the booming domestic industry, led by Honda, seized control of the market.

The irony of this story is staggering. Here is Harley-Davidson, viewed by millions of loyalists as the supreme example of star-spangled American purity, serving as the parent of the Japanese motorcycle industry during a period when such trading arrangements bordered on consorting with the enemy. Moreover, it would be the Japanese who would rise up, under the banners of Honda, Suzuki, Kawasaki, and Yamaha, to drive Harley-Davidson to the mat in the 1970s while the Milwaukee firm wrapped itself in Old Glory for survival.

While this strange and highly profitable Japanese interlude was taking place in the late 1920s, the Harley-Davidson management was engaged in an intense campaign to overpower all the competition but Indian, which it was careful to keep on the ropes but not knock out, lest the attention of the Justice Department antitrust lawyers be attracted. The company offered steady improvements to its mainstream Model J, even going so far in 1922 as to alter the basic color from muted olive tones to a livelier green with gold striping. Three years later, the seventy-four-cubic-inch JD was introduced with the first "teardrop" fuel tank, a styling fillip that was to be adopted, in one form or another, by virtually every other motorcycle manufacturer in the years to follow. The new tank shape marked the beginning of an emphasis on styling and aesthetics that would become a powerful marketing tool for Harley-Davidson, although technical improvements were also made on all models during the 1920s, centering on efficient electrics and front-wheel brakes, which had been common in European motorcycles for a decade. Many American riders were disdainful of the front-wheel brakes, convinced that a lockup would send them pitching over the handlebars. This led many owners to disconnect them, an example of the hardheaded traditionalism that was already becoming a component of Harley-Davidson ownership.

The company further solidified its industry domination in 1928 by seizing control of the American Motorcycle Association. The firm's on-again-off-again racing policy had given way to a privately held conviction that victories on the speedway could be translated into sales. The Indian management believed the same thing, which generated tremendous on-track rivalries between the two marques and their most avid supporters. After installing its own puppet president and board of directors at the AMA, Harley-Davidson — while publicly feigning continued disinterest in racing — established an iron grip on competition policy, skewing rules in order to blunt Indian's efforts and exclude faster imported machines.

New motorcycles were slowly brought into the lineup, including the larger, heavier, 550-pound VL twin that finally replaced the aged J series with a side-valve seventy-four-cubic-inch engine of the type long employed by Indian. The VL design was intended to offer more power as well as easier maintenance. It was the first V-twin from Harley-Davidson that did not have a direct thematic connection to the nineteenth-century De Dion-Bouton configuration, displaying once again the company's crablike approach to engineering adventurism. Aside from a few forays into other engine layouts, including the short-lived but well-conceived Sport Twin and flirtations with four-cylinders and singles, Harley-Davidson would remain technologically ice-bound, with the same forty-five-degree V-twin, for essentially its entire history. Critics derided this as a Neanderthal idiocy until the latter part of the century, when it came to be celebrated as an act of perverse genius.

The new VL was flawed by a poor flywheel design that caused insane vibrations above fifty miles per hour that even veteran Harley riders could not tolerate. In an act of high-handedness that came to typify its early relationship with dealers, the company manufactured a modified unit and ordered dealers to dismantle the VLs in their inventory and make the repair — at their own expense. The choice was simple: follow orders or surrender the franchise. Facing the prospect of losing the only viable motorcycle brand in the nation, the dealers angrily complied.

As Harley-Davidson grew stronger and Indian and Excelsior continued to decline, Arthur Davidson, surely the most gregarious and energetic of the founders, continued to upgrade the dealership body, which remained shabby and inelegant and served a customer group that was becoming increasingly poor and uneducated. Davidson added a vast inventory of accessories, including windshields, crash bars, saddlebags, and better seats, and an extensive wardrobe of clothing designed for riding. Early motorcyclists wore outfits inspired by aviators, who in turn had adapted the riding breeches and high leather boots employed by cavalry officers and other horsemen. Leather jackets were preferred not only for protection from the elements but as a natural barrier against scrapes and abrasions (called "road rash" in later years). Leather aviator helmets (linen in warm weather) and goggles completed the ensemble. Some riders traded the leather helmets for peaked military caps of the type worn by police officers and gas-station attendants of the day, giving them a faux-official stylishness. Competition riders favored padded leather helmets for crash protection, but decades would pass before they would be worn by highway riders — and then only after endless legal wrangling and public protests over government incursions into personal freedom.

As second-generation family members began to enter the business — led by hulking Walter Davidson Jr. and cousins Gordon, Allan, and William H. Jr. (as well as youthful apprentice William J. Harley Jr., who was planning to begin his engineering studies at the University of Wisconsin) — the company's hierarchy appeared to be in place for the long term.

Although the nation continued to booze and Charleston its way through the flapper-era twenties, disaster lay on the horizon. The stock market, offering absurd margins, was hopelessly inflated. Congressmen, feeling their oats as representatives of a new and major economic power, unwisely passed strict tariffs on a variety of agricultural and manufactured foreign products. This brought instant retaliation against numerous American export items, including motorcycles. The ensuing trade war helped trigger the Great Depression, which began on Black Tuesday, October 24, 1929, and forced Harley-Davidson and Indian to the brink of extinction. It did in fact deal a fatal blow to Excelsior, which produced its last — and technically superior — Henderson Super X two years later.

If paranoia had pervaded the executive suite at Juneau Avenue before, it was nothing compared to the level reached in 1930, when news arrived that one E. Paul Du Pont — a principal in the mega-rich Du Pont chemical and manufacturing empire — had scooped up the ruins of the Indian Motorcycle Company and was entering the business with massive infusions of cash and financial expertise. Walter Davidson, reports Sucher, raged endlessly about the upstart rich kid — "the New Jersey Jew," in his special brand of alliteration (although Du Pont's family was of course French Roman Catholic and its traditional residence Wilmington, Delaware). Such was the backwater isolation of the men who formed the Harley-Davidson hierarchy — an isolation that was the basis of a rigid business phi-

losophy that viewed all rivals as hated enemies. An object of special enmity was Du Pont, whom they despised as a member of the
effete, privileged Eastern aristocracy and utterly unqualified for entry into the hard-knuckle world of motorcycling.

In a daring response to Du Pont, and to take advantage of the
demise of Henderson, a brand that had been favored among many
police forces, Walter Davidson offered a stripped VL model to
law enforcement agencies at the cut-rate price of $195 — direct
from the factory. The dealers were to be circumvented in an open
violation of their franchise agreement. The deal specified that a
trade-in motorcycle of any brand had to be included in the purchase. This used machine would be scrapped, thereby ridding the
marketplace of older motorcycles that might be reconditioned for
continued use. The plan caused a bitter outcry from the dealers,
who, as in the case of the VL repair debacle, were left with little
choice but to complain or get out of the business. Most, in a state of
cold fury, stayed. Indian dealers, who saw Harley-Davidson playing
a brutal game of product dumping, seethed in anger, creating a rift
in small towns and cities everywhere that would never be repaired.
The uproar was so great that after six months, Davidson was
forced to recant the policy. But the damage, created in a time when
the motorcycle business, not to mention the entire economy, was in
a state of chaos, weakened the industry for decades.

While the company's paranoia about competing brands, especially Indian and its "Jewish" gentleman owner, simmered, meetings to set prices continued with the hated opposition. Oddly, in
this atmosphere of plunging sales, a certain frivolity evidenced itself in the products. In keeping with Henry Ford's Model T policy of
"You can have any color you want, as long as it's black," Harley-
Davidson had painted most all of its models olive green since the

demise of the Silent Gray Fellow. But avant-garde paint schemes were appearing on all kinds of machinery now, thanks in no small part to the development of Du Pont enamels that were brightly hued and easy to apply. The art deco movement came to Milwaukee, and suddenly the flathead side-valve 74s and 80s hit the marketplace dressed up in hot oranges and flashy lime greens. The paintwork, done ad hoc by in-house artists, was masterful folk art and transformed the Harleys of the 1930s into splendid rolling sculpture that would become an enduring corporate trademark. Sometime during 1933, a painter applied an eagle to a tank logo, thereby introducing a powerful Harley-Davidson symbol. Small eagles had been employed intermittently in earlier years, but from the 1930s onward, the great birds would be an integral component of the company's identity, thanks in part to the artistic brilliance of a long-forgotten, lunch pail–lugging employee.

Both Harley-Davidson and Indian tried to exploit the sour economy by offering "Servi-Cars": three-wheeled models with hefty cargo boxes mounted between the twin rear wheels. It was hoped that these machines would offer cheap alternatives to light trucks for local delivery and various municipal duties, and indeed they became a fixture on big city streets in the hands of small businessmen, postmen, and police departments until the 1950s.

Due to its lugubrious engineering policies, the company was falling behind its European competitors. A steady flow of new motorcycles from BMW, Triumph, Norton, and others offered new design elements such as four-speed, foot-operated transmissions; dry-sump lubrication systems; hydraulically damped telescopic front forks; exotic rear suspension layouts; high-efficiency overhead camshaft cylinder heads; and stiff, lightweight frame designs. Its eyes glued exclusively on Indian in Springfield, Massachusetts, and having successfully closed out the faster European machines from competition through rule-jiggering with the AMA, the Harley-Davidson management, much like their counterparts in Detroit, became isolated in a technological sense. Ultimately, though, this ossification in the engineering department formed the basis for the company's legend and its ultimate survival.

By 1933, when the Depression truly hit bottom, Harley sales dribbled to a mere 5,689 units, and total motorcycle registration fell below 100,000 for the first time in thirty years. In the midst of this slump, a new star was rising in the fusty, inbred Harley-Davidson organization. He was a San Francisco kid, the son of Italian immigrants, named Joe Petrali. A daring and skilled rider, Petrali was an instinctive, hands-on engineer with great creative energy. He had joined the company upon the demise of Excelsior, where he had raced with great success. For several years in the mid-1930s Petrali served as a lone gun, Harley-Davidson's only factory-sponsored competition rider, while at the same time he developed new and radically improved machines for the mass market.

The remnants of the great early-century motorcycle boom had been reduced to tiny pockets of enthusiasts huddled in crumbling garages and clubhouses in seedy sections of town. The clannishness inherent in minority brotherhoods was forming up among them. Motorcycle riding took devotion, mechanical skill, and not a little bravery. Breakdowns were frequent, and the diligence and creativity of the rider, fiddling with baling wire and bits of scrap metal, generally made the difference between mobility and long walks for help. This distillation process produced a perverse elitism among those who chose to endure the challenge of motorcycle riding, as opposed to the increasingly mindless operation of automobiles, with their self-starters and roll-up windows. With it came the creation of riding clubs and small enthusiast groups. They met to ride together and to organize hill climbs, tours, rallies, and flat-track races on local fairgrounds, as well as grueling European-style endurance events that shook the riders' bones and skulls on ragged cross-country routes. Try as the marketers of motorcycling might to halt this progression, the customer was becoming hard-core, defensive, and mildly fanatic about his machine as the rift between the car and the motorcycle widened.

Thanks to the input of Petrali, William Ottoway, and racing engineer Henry Syvertson, an impressive new machine was on the drawing board in 1935. It would be the first truly modern Harley-Davidson and one that would serve as a mother lode for the machines that make up the legend to this day. It was called the 61E, and it would rise from a sheet of paper to leave the VL drifting into antiquity. The 61E retained the classic Harley-Davidson V-twin architecture and traditional one-liter or sixty-one-cubic-inch displacement. Its overhead valve design doubled horsepower to thirty-six. Many contemporary design elements were introduced, including dry-sump lubrication, a system derived from automobile and motorcycle racing whereby engine oil was stored in an independently located tank, or sump. This enhanced oil flow and reduced the chance of starving the engine during hard cornering. A rugged new four-speed transmission was also included, although the shift mechanism remained hand-operated on the left side of the fuel tank, as opposed to the more ergonomically friendly foot-operated shifters that were beginning to appear on some advanced European makes. The 61E was designed with a low-slung frame and a shapely teardrop fuel tank with bright graphics and chrome fittings. The new machine was a stunner, and as it moved into the marketplace, customers quickly nicknamed it the "Knucklehead," based on four lumpy bolt housings protruding from the polished aluminum valve covers on the engine's right side. This initiated the long-standing tradition of enthusiasts and customers naming models on the basis of visual cylinder-head profiles ("Panhead," "Shovelhead," etc.).

Although the 61E was well conceived, early test rides by young Bill Harley Jr., fresh out of college with his engineering degree, revealed a nasty propensity to leak oil from the valve train. Petrali and others recommended further development before the model was released to the public, but Walter Davidson stubbornly ordered the flawed machines to head for the hapless dealerships. As they were with much of the rest of American industry of the day, warranty and service were minor considerations for the company. The dealer and the customer were expected to make do with flawed products and jury-rigged repairs. While time has blurred memories of the early Knuckleheads' teething problems, there is little question that had not Petrali, Ottoway, and company worked overtime in 1936–37 to make running fixes in the leaky valve gear and to provide dealers with repair kits, the fabled 61E — the motorcycle that set Harley-Davidson on the road to long-term success — might have ended up on the scrap heap, a failed and rejected venture.

As the improved 61E was gaining a reputation as the finest big V-twin in the world, the first of the founders was dying. "Old Bill" Davidson, the eldest of the brothers and the tough-talking boss of production, gave in to years of consumption of local Milwaukee brew and starchy German food. He passed away on April 21, 1937. This tough old Scotsman had been key to the development of the company's efficient factory layout and its generally loyal and well-paid workforce. Had not Old Bill been able to ramrod the large and unwieldy Juneau Avenue factory into a downsized Depression-era posture, it is likely that Harley-Davidson would be but a historical footnote, one of hundreds of manufacturing concerns that collapsed and died in the mid-1930s. Of the four founders, William and his intrepid sales genius brother, Arthur, seem to have been treated most kindly by history.

William Ottoway replaced the burly old founder as production chief and was forced in late 1937 to capitulate to the labor union movement that was rampaging through American industry. An agreement with Walter Reuther's rough-and-tumble United Auto Workers was signed, and Harley-Davidson thereby made a relatively peaceful transition — as opposed to Ford and General Motors, to name but two firms that battled the movement — into the new world of collective bargaining.

The steadily improving 61E (to be enlarged to seventy-four cubic inches in 1941) and relatively stable working conditions plus a modestly improving economy and minimal competition helped business increase slightly in 1937–38. It was during this period that many aficionados believe the finest Harley-Davidsons in history were manufactured. By 1939, the sixty-one-cubic-inch, overhead-valve Knucklehead EL, with its improved valve train assembly and modified oiling system, was fast (about 100 mph), nimble, beautifully balanced, and vividly styled. The EL Knuckleheads of this period are among the most cherished by classic motorcycle collectors around the world, and perfect originals sell for upwards of $30,000.

But despite the commercial and artistic success of the EL, Harley-Davidson was heading into a long-term transportation limbo. The motorcycle was totally marginalized, an oddball machine with limited utility employed primarily by a tiny band of intense enthusiasts who yearned for the special challenge inherent in balancing a high-powered machine between one's legs and propelling it down deserted highways at unseemly speeds. Motorcycle competition for the most part was long played out, taking place on obscure country dirt tracks and attractive only to small but intensely devoted audiences. Harry Sucher, an overt Indian supporter, charges that Harley-Davidson's domination of the American Motorcycle Association's officialdom sometimes led to scandalous favoritism at competitions. He claims that the Indian Sport Scout was the fastest flat-track racer of the day and generally waxed the Harleys in any given race. But the winning Indian was often relegated to second place or disqualified over some niggling rules infraction. This race-fixing, says Sucher, created enormous antagonism between the two loyalist camps and often led to brawls in the pits and grandstands, "further tarnishing motorcycling's image as a roughneck sport."

Business improved short-term, thanks to the 61EL and its larger brother, the seventy-four-cubic-inch FL introduced in 1941. These designations introduced a complex and confusing alphabet soup of model names that continues to this day and that only the most loyal of aficionados cares to decipher. A total of 11,000 61ELs were built, better than half of which were sent to overseas customers. Even in those dark years, Harley-Davidson was a strong and established brand in Europe and South America. Also in Hollywood, where major stars like Clark Gable, Randolph Scott, Tyrone Power, and Robert Taylor were seen rumbling around the great Los Angeles basin on various Harleys and Indians. Some were drafted to ride by studio publicity departments to boost their macho image, but several of the actors and directors — Gable and gritty character actor Keenan Wynn among them — were legitimate enthusiasts. Gable loved fast cars and motorcycles. During the 1930s he owned and seriously rode Harley-Davidsons and attended a number of California Harley gatherings. Victor McLaglen, the gravelly-voiced veteran of both silent films and talkies, organized a motorcycle drill team wherein thirty-six experts, all aboard Harleys, executed intricate low-speed maneuvers during parades and other civic functions. Such teams became popular across the nation, for the most part favoring Harleys because their excellent gearboxes and clutches would endure the endless stops, starts, and low-speed lugging employed in such exercises. The involvement of luminaries like Gable and McLaglen helped somewhat to polish the image of motorcycling, as did the creation of the Motor Maids of America, a group of female enthusiasts who, decked out in snappy uniforms, appeared at public functions wheeling their hulking, 600-pound Harleys with élan.

Both Harley-Davidson and Indian went to considerable lengths to stress in their house organs — Harley's ardently agitprop *Enthusiast* and *The Indian News* — the chummy sociability of motorcycle riding (while totally excising the rival brand from their pages — to the point where an *Enthusiast* reader would be led to believe that no such make as Indian even existed). The AMA and progressive dealers organized clubs into quasi-military groups, with members sporting riding boots and breeches and nearly starched shirts. Many clubs concentrated on civic functions, laboring as volunteer police auxiliaries while working hard to upgrade the image of their sport. Regardless of their efforts, the motorcycle community was fragmenting into two distinct elements — the well-organized, good-little-soldier club members and the hard-riding, grease-stained independent rabble who would, in subtly perverse ways, ultimately define the image of America's greatest motorcycle.

The nation was rooted in the seemingly endless Depression and at war with itself. The Dust Bowl and its pitiful, dreamlike westward migrations created a vast chasm between the common folk and the so-called Café Society. With it arose energized fascinations with socialism, communism, and the labor union movement, not to mention the phenomenon of populist gangsters like John Dillinger and Bonnie and Clyde, who gained a certain macabre celebrity. Great left-leaning writers of the day like John Steinbeck, John Dos Passos, and Erskine Caldwell, and painters like Edward Hopper, Grant Wood, and Thomas Hart Benton turned away from the rich elite of the Jazz Age, who had been treated a decade earlier by novelists like Fitzgerald and Maugham, and began dealing with the proletariat with sentimental intensity. For the first time in America's turbulent 150-year history of helter-skelter growth and furious expansion, the little guy, the working stiff, the grizzled laborer, and the callus-handed farmer were looked upon as dignified human beings. They became worthy of both the broad-reaching ministrations of Roosevelt's New Deal and the attention of the formerly elitist community of the arts.

From this raw underside of life the motorcycle emerged as a "real man's" machine, a machine bereft of the complex trappings of the new industrial age that had shattered the lives of so many Americans. Slowly, subconsciously, it was rising out of the ruck, identified by icons like Clark Gable as an honest, useful, and valuable egalitarian device for all but sissies and the hopelessly effete. This manliness factor would take a decade to become evident, but the embracing of the Harley-Davidson as a machine for real men was surely anchored in the great social upheavals of the 1930s.

Isolationism was rife, not only in the political realm, where a cabal of Midwestern senators was loudly denouncing any American involvement in the European cauldron being stirred by Adolf Hitler, but in technology as well. Save for a vital aircraft industry, which was in the vanguard, domestic automotive and motorcycle technology was in the dark ages compared to that welling up in Germany, France, Italy, and Great Britain. Automobiles from Detroit, while being manufactured with state-of-the-art mass-production techniques, were archaic designs employing ancient flathead engines, three-speed transmissions, and crude suspensions. So too were American motorcycles, which relied on large displacements for brute power but offered little sophistication. Gearshifts remained on the fuel tanks, and clutches were foot operated, as they had been for decades. By contrast, the best European machines from firms like Norton, Triumph, BMW, and Zundapp had already reversed the system, permitting the foot to operate the gearshift and the hand to work the clutch — a far better ergonomic arrangement that would not be adopted by Harley-Davidson until the early 1950s. This technological gap was exposed — accidentally — in the spring of 1937 at Daytona Beach, Florida, when a cheeky Canadian kid named Billy Matthews rode a 500 cc twin-overhead-camshaft Norton single-cylinder (a precursor of the famed postwar Manx) to an easy victory over a vast field of Indians and Harley-Davidsons. The Norton had been admitted into the race by accident, thanks to a provincial collection of AMA officials who were ignorant of British motorcycles and gave the little machine no chance against the big American iron. Had they known its potency, it would have been banned. Walter Davidson was apoplectic. After excoriating the AMA for its lapse, he made sure that Matthews and his Norton were censored from the captive motorcycle press, making the Canadian's victory in this major race one of the most obscure in history.

Surely the state of the motorcycle art in America suffered when Joe Petrali tired of Davidson's tightfisted policies and left the company amid considerable acrimony. He would go on to work with Howard Hughes as a key flight engineer (riding with the enigmatic billionaire on the single flight of his notorious *Spruce Goose*) before becoming a widely respected international motor sports official prior to his death in 1974. Petrali was truly a giant of the motorcycle industry and sport, and one can only speculate the course of the company had he remained with Harley-Davidson. Perhaps, because of his technical adventurism, he might have developed more advanced engine designs and abandoned the archaic V-twin. In retrospect, this might have been a well-intentioned but fatal error. Either way, the departure of Petrali from Milwaukee marked, in a symbolic sense at least, the company's embarkment on a half-century decade of technological stagnation that would serve in turn as its death knell and then as its singular blessing of survival.

With the country's December 1941 entry into World War II came a military contract for Harley-Davidson to build the army-specification forty-five-cubic-inch model WLA. The machine was slow but anvil tough, intended for courier duty and occasional scouting missions. Hundreds of riders were trained on the olive drab machines, and the army delighted in releasing publicity photos of young men astride the WLAs, armed to the teeth with Thompson submachine guns and .30-caliber carbines. But in reality, the Harleys and their counterpart Indians saw limited use in the war after it was discovered that the American Bantam–designed, Willys-Overland-produced jeep was far more versatile in combat than any motorcycle. Despite energetic attempts by the company to embellish the WLA's contribution to the fighting, its use was primarily limited to training-camp exercises, military police patrols, and behind-the-lines courier service.

Before the tap was turned off within the army's manic procurement process, about 88,000 WLAs would be built, not only for the U.S. military, but for the British, the Russians, and the Commonwealth allies. Thousands were never even uncrated and, following the end of the war, were sold as surplus to enthusiasts. These rugged but sluggish machines served the company well, not only as a profit center during the war, but to reignite loyalty to the brand during the 1945–46 conversion to peacetime production.

It was during this wartime period that the army discovered the advantages of the opposed twin-cylinder layout employed on German BMW and Zundapp motorcycle engines. Known as the pancake layout, it was smoother running than the forty-five-degree Harley-Davidson V-twin and produced a lower center of gravity for improved handling. BMWs captured from the Wehrmacht during the African campaign confirmed these advantages, and in late 1942, the army ordered both Harley-Davidson and Indian to develop flat-twin bikes with BMW-style drive shafts instead of the conventional chain drive used by the American bikes. Ottoway designed the so-called Harley-Davidson XA, which was, many believe, to be a superior machine to the WLA and a potential prototype for a postwar civilian version. Had the XA been perfected, it is possible that Ottoway, like Petrali a progressive, would have advocated its succeeding the aged V-twin, thereby creating a BMW clone as the company's mainstream product. But the army canceled the XA contract in 1944, after about a thousand motorcycles had been built, permitting the company to lapse back to its traditional practices and remain loyal to its proven and beloved V-twin layout.

The company's staff, hourly workers, and vast network of dealers were stunned by the news on February 7, 1942, that longtime company president Walter Davidson had died of a liver ailment.

This tough, often ruthless leader passed away accompanied by limited mourning among the many who had been victims of his predatory policies. While he was far from the saintly old paterfamilias portrayed in company hagiography, Walter Davidson devoted most of his sixty-six years to his family and the motorcycle they created. He could be faulted for unethical and marginally illegal policies, but never for his unfailing devotion to the cause of making Harley-Davidson motorcycles the dominant brand in the world. His three sons were hardly qualified to succeed him. Walter Jr. and Gordon worked within the company but eschewed greater responsibility. The third boy, Robert, worked outside the industry. Sixty-three-year-old Arthur was the brilliant salesman of the family and next in line, but years on the road socializing had revealed a tragic penchant for alcoholism. Although he was able to operate normally for months at a time, Arthur would lapse into periodic binges, plunging into a boozy stupor for weeks on end. He clearly was not able to handle the intense responsibilities embodied in the presidency. The new leader would be William Herbert Davidson, the son of the late production chief, Old Bill Davidson. Not only was he the largest single stockholder in the firm, but he held a bachelor's degree in business administration from the University of Wisconsin, which, in theory, offered extra qualification for the top job.

Less than a year after the death of Walter Davidson, a third founder met his maker while sitting on a bar stool in the Wisconsin Athletic Club. William Harley, the titular chief engineer, had long since ceased to be an influence in daily company operations and had turned most of his work over to his talented assistant, William Ottoway. A quiet and somewhat introverted man, Harley had seemingly lost interest in the company and was devoting most of his time to fishing on Wisconsin lakes when he died. Ottoway assumed his post with little or no interruption in the corporate cadence.

In late 1944, Alfred Rich Child, the intrepid salesman who had singlehandedly created Harley-Davidson's Far Eastern market, left his job at Lockheed Aircraft and signed on as the United States importer of the widely respected British make BSA. Child would therefore fire the first round at his old company in a revived war that would pit Harley-Davidson against an onslaught of cheaper, faster, better-designed imported motorcycles. It was a fight that would rage on for the remainder of the century.

In 1948, an improved version of the EL Knucklehead was introduced. Immediately dubbed the "Panhead" because of its skillet-shaped aluminum valve covers, the new model's aluminum alloy cylinder heads and hydraulic valve lifters were dogged by oil leaks and other reliability problems that were not totally solved until 1953. Offered in sixty-one- and seventy-four-cubic-inch engine sizes, the EL and FL Panheads were on balance more powerful, more user-friendly motorcycles than their predecessors. A year later, in 1949, the so-called Hydra Glide hydraulic front suspension was introduced to provide a smoother ride, and a smaller, entry-level 125S — based on a war-appropriated design from Germany's ravaged DKW firm — was debuted to attract younger, first-time motorcycle riders.

These were heady times for the company as demand from returning veterans gave the market a lusty boost. The acquisition of a former military propellor factory from A. O. Smith on Capitol Drive on the edge of Milwaukee nearly doubled available factory space, and by 1948 total production had jumped to 29,612 motorcycles, a new peacetime record for the firm. Included in that number were nearly 13,000 of the new FL Panheads, which poured into the hands of eager buyers despite the lingering reliability problems. Following its traditional policies, the company imperiously involved its 800-odd dealers as coperpetrators of the ailments and forced them to fend off complaints from customers with jury-rigged repairs and other delaying tactics. Over the near half century that Harley-Davidson had been in business, it had engaged in periodic warfare with its dealers, often unloading poorly engineered motorcycles onto the market and forcing the franchises to pick up the pieces. This bullheaded attitude was possible during the postwar years, when the domestic market was dominated by two manufacturers — Harley-Davidson and Indian — both of which enjoyed a cadre of fiercely loyal customers.

The company now enjoyed a strong market position in large-displacement cruiser-style motorcycles as Indian began to falter, while the $325, three-horsepower, DKW-based 125S single-cylinder opened the door to young customers at the bottom of the market. But a major gap in the lineup remained. As powerful, lightweight, midsized British and German motorcycles steadily captured a larger chunk of the market, Harley-Davidson dealers began demanding a 500 cc middleweight model to counter the invasion. The company ignored them. But as the foreign onslaught accelerated, the company sought redress before Congress. Its complaint was simple: While American tariffs on imported bikes stood at 8 percent, most European nations were charging up to 40 percent on Harleys, placing the company in peril in both the home and overseas markets. A Senate hearing was called with high expectations but immediately backfired. Alfred Rich Child, the man who had created Harley-Davidson's Japanese market, was now importing BSAs, and he appeared as a stunningly eloquent adversary. He recounted the Milwaukee firm's long tradition of predatory franchising, dealer abuses, price-fixing, and other antitrust illegalities with a clear intent to establish a monopoly within the heavy motorcycle class in America. The Harley-Davidson executives were sent packing with no corrective legislation pending and perhaps feeling fortunate that Child's indictments had not led to a great public outcry.

Another blow befell the firm in August 1950, when the last of the four founders, sales genius Arthur Davidson, died in an automobile crash close to his Milwaukee home. The final link to the creation was broken, and the company rule passed into the hands of offspring neither as talented nor as committed as the originators. Yet the firm's grip on the heavyweight motorcycle market tightened as its only rival, Indian, plunged deeper into debt and mismanagement, finally to close its doors for good in 1953. The last American motorcycle competitor from among hundreds but a half century earlier was gone. Theoretically the way was clear for Harley-Davidson to dominate the domestic market, assuming a certain constancy of taste and social stability among the American public. That was decidedly not the case.

The end of the war brought not peace but increased turmoil for the embattled company. The Hollister riot, which first revealed the existence of the nascent outlaw motorcycle gangs, Frank Rooney's *Harper's* magazine short story, and Stanley Kramer's *The Wild One* veered Harley-Davidson onto a wild and woolly course that it was helpless to alter, try as it might to maintain its traditional position in the marketplace. Those external forces were only further enhanced by the appearance in the 1960s of the outlandish Hells Angels and the glut of biker movies they inspired. Enormous, unexpected, and unwanted attention was brought to bear on the venerable, hidebound firm, which peaked — with laserlike intensity — with the release of Fonda and Hopper's *Easy Rider* in 1969.

For two confusing decades, Harley-Davidson played the unwitting tool in a tumultuous cultural revolution — a revolution that embraced their lovable old motorcycles with neither the compliance nor the understanding of the management. The entire image of their machines was transformed as they stood by in helpless witness. As the seventies dawned, it was up to new men within the company to somehow harness the outlandish energies that now controlled the corporate destiny.

6 · DESCENT INTO THE SEVENTIES

The 1970s saw the nation reach a nadir equaled only by the Civil War and the Great Depression. Within those dismal, sometimes absurd ten years, one president narrowly missed impeachment by fleeing the White House, and another, a well-intentioned but overmatched former governor, seemed cursed to have major accomplishments like brokering an Israeli-Egyptian peace accord counterbalanced by such farces as an attack by an insane rabbit. As the nightmarish Vietnam war disintegrated in a cloud of defeat and bloated body counts, the once-proud United States Army participated in a depraved massacre at My Lai and destroyed other Vietnamese villages "in order to save them," in a convulsion of Orwellian logic. Twice a cabal of militarily weak but oil-rich Middle Eastern sheikdoms brought the country to its knees by shutting off the petroleum tap, thereby disarming the most powerful nation on earth through its gluttony for black gold. In response, the government imposed a fifty-five-mile-per-hour speed limit that was to become the most ignored law since Prohibition, further enhancing the public disconnect from respected institutions. The consumption of illegal drugs soared, as did draconian efforts to control them, led in part by a legendary FBI boss who apparently preferred cocktail dresses and high heels to business suits during his leisure moments. The odd behavior of J. Edgar Hoover was but one strange symptom of the powerful sexual revolution that rose out of the 1960s and consumed America in the seventies. Sexual indulgence was an elemental component of what author Tom Wolfe described as the "Me Generation," wherein the entire nation seemed obsessed with endless self-analysis and probing pop-psychological examination. Somehow, in an oblique way, the motorcycle, with its fiercely noisy and overt phallic connotations, became part of this national self-absorption, in part stimulated by a perception that people were losing control, that the time-honored national ethos of independence and personal freedom celebrated during the 1976 bicentennial was being shredded into tiny bits.

The motorcycle, be it God's own American-made Harley-Davidson or one of the multitudes of new Japanese bikes pouring onto the roads, seemed to represent certain fundamental verities as opposed to the ennui and nannyism spewing forth from what appeared to be a helpless and corrupted government. It wasn't perfect, but a high-speed blast on an overpowered, noisy, and hopelessly antisocial machine like a motorcycle was one small gesture on behalf of personal independence in the decidedly unbrave new world.

The postwar years and the tumultuous sixties had passed with the Harley-Davidson management operating as witless tools of the times, mere bystanders for twenty-five years while tumultuous social forces rapidly altered their market. First came the outlaws, then the counterculture, and finally the Japanese importers to stunt and blur their business to a point where it bordered on irrelevance. While the company stubbornly ignored shifts in demographic trends and social attitudes, and the growth of entire new buying segments accompanied by increasing assaults from overseas, its business shriveled down to a tiny collection of cultists who would have ridden the chrome-laden, unreliable arks from Milwaukee even if the markedly superior upstarts from Japan had been offered free.

The hoggish 783-pound Electra Glide, essentially unchanged since its introduction in 1965, was a road-cruising leviathan compared to the Japanese middleweights. Even the smaller Harleys — the Sportsters — were slower and heavier than the imports. Worse yet, the Japanese were effectively driving the English out of the marketplace, leaving a hapless and vulnerable Harley-Davidson as their only competitor.

Harley-Davidson had made a feckless attempt to fight back in 1966 with yet another rehash of its basic 1936 EL engine, attaching a third-generation cylinder head that came to be known as the "Shovelhead." As a concurrent penalty in the search for more performance to compensate for the ever-increasing girth and bulk of the big cruisers, the modified engine produced more vibration, more oil leaks, more chain failures, and continued overheating. The only consolation to loyalists for this lackluster design were the equally unreliable British motorcycles being manufactured in factories easily as primitive as the ancient Harley-Davidson facility on Juneau Avenue. Facing them were energized Japanese companies like Honda and Suzuki, who were on the verge of introducing vividly advanced, high-performance machines like the 125-mph, four-cylinder Honda CB 750 and the unbelievable 247 cc, six-speed Suzuki X6 Hustler, which would easily surpass ninety miles per hour despite its tiny engine. These machines were but opening volleys in a technological and marketing onslaught that would virtually erase the British motorcycle industry and force Harley-Davidson to the brink of extinction in the next decade.

By the late 1960s, America's only remaining motorcycle company had seen its dealer body slump to about 650 disgruntled souls. Half its motorcycle production of M50 mopeds and small Sprints was sourced from the Italian subsidiary Aermacchi. Another 18 percent of the output involved golf carts and three-wheel industrial trucks. The big Electra Glides, Duo Glides, etc., that formed the traditional bedrock of the company were being sold at the modest rate of fewer than 10,000 a year. Gross sales for the tightly held company were roughly $43 million annually, with net profits dipping to about $1 million. Harley-Davidson remained barely in the black and faced bankruptcy unless new infusions of cash were found to update its creaking production facilities and its entire corporate philosophy. Two bidders appeared, both classic examples of the faddish conglomerates that had become fashionable in the 1960s. Bangor Punta Corporation owned divisions that produced everything from small engines and pleasure boats to designer clothing and jewelry. Its rival, American Machine Foundry, had expanded from its core business of building railroad cars into a hodgepodge of firms ranging from Brunswick (bowling equipment and pool tables) to bicycles, skis, tennis rackets, and golf clubs to industrial bakery machines. Its president, ex–West Pointer Rodney Gott, a Harley-Davidson riding enthusiast since the 1930s, successfully led a takeover bid for the Milwaukee firm in early 1969 for a $21.6 million stock trade.

During this transition, the static hometown management was producing a future star, who would come from behind a drawing board. William G. Davidson, the eldest son of president W. H. Davidson and grandson of founding production boss Old Bill Davidson, was a bright, bespectacled, gray flannel–clad graduate of the respected Los Angeles Art Center College of Design. He was a skilled rider who had initially appeared to be just another modestly talented third-generation member of the Milwaukee clan. But it was he who would come to be known to Harley-Davidson aficionados around the world as "Willie G." and who initially recognized the social and cultural shifts that were dooming his company.

Willie G. Davidson was nearly alone among the company leaders in understanding the rising popularity of so-called custom motorcycles (a sanitized term for the "chopper") favored by the One Percenters. Davidson was aware of the trend being celebrated in small-circulation fringe magazines, where choppers/customs were being elevated to the status of high folk art. Arlen Ness, a former carpenter in San Leandro, California, who began building customs during his off-hours, was a brilliant craftsman with an extraordinary eye for outré style. His motorcycles, along with those of such masters of homegrown fashion as Donnie Smith of Minneapolis, Wisconsin's Al Reichenback, Ness's son Cory, Massachusetts's Dave Perewitz, California hot-rodders Bob Bauder and Pete Chapouris, and the brilliant Iowa minimalist Don Hotop, transcended simple transportation devices and were elevated into the realm of rolling sculpture, late-twentieth-century kinetic art that gained approval from aesthetes around the world. The geographic range of the great customizers made it apparent to Davidson and others that the appeal of radically modified Harleys reached well beyond Southern California. The imagery of these outré machines

had not only energized a booming do-it-yourself customizing industry but amplified the notion that Harley-Davidsons were a source of
creativity and uniqueness unavailable in other brands.

The success of *Easy Rider* on the big screen and a pallid television knockoff titled *Then Came Bronson* had driven the reputation
of vagabond motorcycles drifting around the nation into America's
living rooms. Unlike Fonda and Hopper, the druggie bikers in the
movie, *Bronson*'s hero was an unemployed journalist played by
Michael Parks — first in a made-for-television movie with Bonnie
Bedelia and then in a weekly series styled as a shameless knockoff
of the popular series *Route 66*. Parks merely traded the *Route 66*
Corvette for a mildly customized Harley Sportster (without a logo
on its peanut tank). Operating with the theme song, "Ridin' down
that long, lonesome highway, gonna live life my way," Jim Bronson
cruised the California coast, once again amplifying the nomadic
biker's life, although from the unthreatening aspect of a G-rated
television hero far removed from the thugs and low-lifes who in-
fested the midsixties' biker flicks.

Bronson and *Easy Rider* were powerful engines of influence in
creating mass awareness of motorcycles, as were other pop stars
of the new decade. Surely the most spectacular was a brash
Montana-born daredevil name Robert "Evel" Knievel, who became
the most famous motorcycle rider of all time after a series of high-
flying, bone-cracking jumps aboard a modified 750 cc Harley-
Davidson XR racing bike. Knievel, whose physical courage and
pain threshold were equaled only by his penchant for publicity,
gained initial fame in 1968 with a spectacular televised leap over a
row of cars in the Caesar's Palace parking lot in Las Vegas. He
crash-landed — a not-uncommon ending to his stunts — and ended
up an international celebrity. After being foiled by the government

and the local Indian tribes from leaping the Grand Canyon, Knievel tried a jump of the Snake River Canyon in 1974 aboard a rocket-powered quasi motorcycle. The attempt fizzled, with Evel escaping death via a deployed parachute, and his career began a dive toward oblivion. He was later convicted of beating a former business associate with a baseball bat, and his long and effective sponsorship by Harley-Davidson was canceled. Today his son, Robbie, continues motorcycle jumping, while Evel — the most unique and press-worthy personality to ever ride a motorcycle — pursues a career painting western scenes and making occasional public appearances. He was recently diagnosed with hepatitis C and announced, at age fifty-nine, that he needed a liver transplant. After hundreds of body-wrecking tumbles, the irony that the old stuntman faced such a mundane demise could not be ignored.

George Hamilton played the daredevil in a 1971 bio-pic titled *Evel Knievel.* Six years later a second bio-pic, *Viva Knievel!,* was released, this time featuring the man himself and a cast that included such unlikely biker types as Lauren Hutton, Gene Kelly, Leslie Nielsen, Red Buttons, and the former evangelist Marjoe Gortner. Harley-Davidson also made the big screen in the 1973 story of a diminutive Arizona Highway Patrol officer played by Robert Blake. The picture, *Electra Glide in Blue,* predated by two years Bruce Springsteen's huge biker-based single, "Born to Run." Steppenwolf had already gained fame with the biker anthem "Born to Be Wild." The song had been employed in the sound track of *Easy Rider* after Crosby, Stills and Nash dropped out of the project following a dispute with Dennis Hopper.

Perhaps the best example of the image of the outlaw biker being absorbed into and co-opted by the mainstream media is the Henry Winkler character the Fonz in the television sitcom *Happy*

Days. This tough-talking, leather-jacketed but benign character rode a Harley. Yet he was properly housebroken for prime-time television, only hinting at the bad-guy reputation that dogged the company.

By 1970, Willie G. Davidson and other serious thinkers within Harley-Davidson had realized that the gargantuan dressers were unrelated to the rising new consciousness about motorcycles. But the latent public fear of the outlaw biker still appeared to create an unbridgeable marketing chasm. It would be madness to marginalize the company by pandering to a tiny but highly visible collection of One Percenters. Like the merchandisers of mass fashion exploiting the avant-garde dress of the hippies, or the Detroiters flirting with the glamour of the street-racing "muscle car" devotees, Davidson searched for a way to jerk his company toward more contemporary products without breaking the bank. A stagnant business with limited funds for developing all-new motorcycles led him to patch together existing bits and pieces into a breakthrough motorcycle he called the Super Glide.

It would mark Harley-Davidson's first tentative step into the biker culture. The challenge was twofold: to capitalize on the raffish image created for Harley-Davidson by Hollister, the Hells Angels, Roger Corman, and *Easy Rider* while still challenging the Japanese and their squeaky-clean, high-powered "café racers," which oozed the personality not of roving thugs, but of European grand prix heroes. Davidson's solution was to cobble together pieces from the monstrous dressers and the lighter Sportsters in a daring combination. The big twin's engine, frame, and rear suspension were mated to the smaller bike's fuel tank, its slightly extended front forks, and zoomy fiberglass seat and tail. Davidson then took a radical leap backward by eliminating the electric start to reduce weight. This was an open acknowledgment of the chopper riders who had long favored the older, more basic Harleys and their ancient kick starters. Davidson's final gesture was to paint the motorcycle in garish red, white, and blue, a clear paean to the confused patriotic themes swirling through the nation at the time. As Vietnam reached critical mass, both sides of the war issue were employing the American flag as a symbol. While the counterculturists burned them, the national colors were a safe bet to appeal to young Harley riders, who, for the most part, were noncollegiate, blue-collar types supporting the government's policies.

The FX Super Glide was hardly a major hit when it was introduced in 1971, but it marked a sea change in the way Harley-Davidson built and marketed motorcycles. The company was breaking free of its traditional customer base, reaching out to a younger, wilder, less conventional audience. As the Super Glide matured (an electric starter was added in 1974 and outsold the hard-core kicker), it would stand as a breakthrough machine that would elevate Willie G. to icon status within the worldwide Harley-Davidson cult. Although he was a member of the inner sanctum of old-line family leaders, Davidson had worked beyond the pinched precincts of the company, first with Ford Motor Company, then with the progressive Brooks Steven Design Studio in Milwaukee, before returning to his roots in 1963.

Despite the turnabout his Super Glide triggered, it barely jiggled the needle when compared to the terrible clashes of culture initiated by the AMF acquisition. When Rodney Gott took over the company, his goal for Harley-Davidson was a single word: expansion. He correctly identified the booming motorcycle market and pledged to make Harley-Davidson share in the bounty being mined by the Japanese. With the exception of newcomer Kawasaki, the

Milwaukee firm was the sole seller of so-called heavyweight motorcycles, and Gott reasoned that increased production would solve
the company's soft-profit problems. Major steps were initiated, including the conversion of an idle AMF military plant in York, Pennsylvania, to build frames and make final bike assemblies. The older
Milwaukee facilities, 700 miles to the west, were assigned to manufacture engines and transmissions, thereby creating a logistic nightmare exacerbated by transportation problems and the inability to
dovetail the modern York facility with the ancient Milwaukee factories. Worse yet, major policy decisions were made from AMF's
headquarters in faraway White Plains, New York. In a fumbling attempt to exploit demand, production was bumped nearly threefold,
to 60,000 units. This increase generated not only complaints among
the heretofore loyal workforce, but a nightmarish plunge in quality.
While Harleys had long been known for quirky oil leaks and unreliable electrics, their paintwork, fit and finish, etc., were world-
class — the result of careful assembly by old-fashioned hands-on
techniques. These were discarded in the mad rush for increased
volume, and soon dealerships were flooded with machines that literally shed pieces while sitting on the showroom floor. In many in-
stances dealers were forced to totally reassemble motorcycles
before they could be sold.

The blame was passed between the eager new owners, well
versed in mass-production techniques, and the old-line traditionalists within the company, who clung to the aged, low-volume policies of the past. The clash of cultures was all pervasive, infesting
the assembly line, the sales and engineering staffs, and the executive suites. The Harley-Davidson designers were for the most part
enthusiasts with vast empirical understanding of motorcycle dy-
namics but little or no formal training. This placed them at a

massive disadvantage when trying to interface with AMF engineers intent on updating both the design of the motorcycles and the volume in which they would be manufactured.

In 1971, William J. Harley, an amiable man who, like his father, had served as chief engineer of the company, died at age fifty-nine, thereby effectively ending the Harley family's influence within the top echelons of the firm. During the same year, Walter Davidson Jr., the son of the hard-driving founder, left the company under rather stormy circumstances. He was a staunch traditionalist and a rather bigoted defender of the old-time Harley-Davidson religion, and his tenure as sales manager had seen the company's dealership body decline from a prewar high of more than one thousand to about six hundred when he left office. Two years later, President William H. Davidson announced his retirement, thereby ending forty-five years of intense and productive involvement with the firm. A well-bred and courtly man, he had been marginalized during his final years by the new management team from AMF and was uncomfortable with the direction his beloved company was taking. His departure marked the end of the dynasty's centralized leadership, although other Harleys and Davidsons would remain in the organization. Only one, William H.'s son, design genius Willie G. Davidson, would exert significant influence as, sadly, the third generation saw a steady disintegration of the long link between the Harley and the Davidson families. Three years after William H. Davidson's retirement, John E. Harley, son of founder William S., died of cancer at age sixty-one. Though he was a stockholder, John Harley never held any senior positions in the company, and his son, John Jr., left the firm shortly after John Sr.'s death to seek other work. Insiders report that considerable bitterness persists on the part of Harley family heirs in that they do not share in the current prosperity, al-

though truth be known, major influence by any Harley — specifically William J. — ended in the early 1970s.

Although the 1960s are recalled as the desperate decade in
which the American social fabric was most seriously threatened,
historians may rate the seventies as having more serious long-term
effects. It was, after all, the decade in which America lost its first
war and first drove a president nearest to formal impeachment since
Andrew Johnson a century earlier. The nation's mighty military machine had been helpless against a furtive army of Vietnamese guer-
rillas armed with little more than bicycles and automatic rifles, and
a loose alliance of Middle Eastern potentates had embargoed the
world's oil market. The great drug enlightenment of the sixties
quickly unraveled when in late 1970, a spate of rock stars, including
Jimi Hendrix and Janis Joplin, cashed in from drug overdoses. The
Hells Angels were back in the headlines. In December 1969, the
club had been hired by the Rolling Stones to act as crowd control
during a concert at the Altamont Speedway near San Francisco.
With 300,000 screeching fans in attendance and the Maysles brothers, David and Albert, shooting their documentary *Gimme Shelter*,
Angel Alan David Passaro engaged in a brief but bloody fight with
eighteen-year-old Meredith "Murdock" Hunter. Although the circumstances surrounding the tussle remain unclear, it is known that
Hunter pulled a gun. Passaro then stabbed him with a large hunting
knife. Other Angels rushed into the melee swinging bats and
chains, and the youth thudded to earth. As Mick Jagger pleaded for
calm, Hunter died on the spot. Passaro was arrested for murder.
Following a protracted trial during which the entire seedy business
of monster outdoor rock concerts was called into question, Passaro was acquitted. But the club's troubles were not over. A year
later, Sonny Barger and three other Oakland Angels were tried and

acquitted in the murder of a Texas cocaine dealer. Barger testified that he and his fellow club members had been working with Oakland cops to prevent various underground leftist groups from obtaining weapons and explosives. In 1973, Barger was convicted of heroin trafficking and sentenced to ten years in Folsom Prison. He was paroled four years later after his lawyers convinced the courts that his sentence was related more to his sordid reputation as a Hells Angel than to the actual crime.

Slowly, owing to advancing age and a certain war weariness, Sonny Barger, the most vivid and interesting Angel, drifted into the shadows of the club. Surely as unique and purely American as any of the other great homegrown outlaws like Dillinger, Luciano, and Siegel, Barger managed to escape the violent death that befell so many of his counterparts and at last word was operating a small custom motorcycle shop in Oakland, the city where he almost singlehandedly created the worldwide image of the most powerful, most ominous, most intriguing motorcycle club of them all.

Thanks in no small part to the lurid imagery of the Hells Angels, which alternately fascinated and terrified the straight citizenry around the globe, the Harley-Davidson became branded with such diverse items as the AK-47, the Volkswagen microbus, and the Gibson guitar as a tool of the new underworld, a machine of menace and unfettered, Rabelaisian antiestablishment rebellion. Willie G.'s Super Glide was a tentative attempt to exploit the revolution, but that would take more bold action, based in part on the steadily disintegrating market position of Harley-Davidson.

By the middle of the decade, the company's fortunes had hit bottom. A three-month strike in 1974 cut production to a trickle. Honda was invading home turf, setting up shop in a vast, ultramodern factory in Marysville, Ohio, where state-of-the-art GoldWing cruisers were to be built. In faraway Nebraska, Kawasaki was building lusty KZ1000 cruisers that would soon replace Harleys in hundreds of police forces across the nation. In some heartland municipalities, a few of the old Electra Glides were kept in storage, to be hauled out for politically sensitive Memorial Day and Labor Day parades in which Japanese motorcycles might be booed off the street. By the middle 1970s, the last of the aged three-wheel Servi-Cars dribbled off the assembly line. Once valued by car dealers, small businesses, and parking meter attendants, the more powerful postwar models were employed mainly by police forces for routine traffic patrol, which included high-speed chases. But the Servi-Cars were handling nightmares anywhere beyond fifty miles per hour, and, following a number of fatal crashes, they were pulled from the market.

The nation's moral compass was spinning. The Watergate scandal was about to run Richard Nixon out of office, less than a year after his notably sleazy vice president, Spiro Agnew, stepped down to avoid indictment on charges of tax evasion. Meanwhile, Patti Hearst, the kidnapped daughter of publishing mogul Randolph Hearst, resurfaced during a bank robbery perpetrated by her abductors, yet another Bay area revolutionary closet gang calling itself the Symbionese Liberation Army. This bizarre episode was typical of the decade, which witnessed Richard Nixon protest that he was not a crook, then leave office only to be given full presidential pardon by his successor, Gerald Ford, and a free pass from any future indictments. Ford also pardoned all draft dodgers from the now-concluded Vietnam war. This helped to defang and dilute the antiwar movement. Once the fighting was concluded, the narcissism of the counterculture, veiled in lofty rhetoric about peace and love, lost steam, and by the end of the decade most of American youth had reverted to dreaming about sports cars, super-heated stereos, and maybe, just maybe, a zoomy Honda or Suzuki motorcycle. Under no circumstances was a Harley-Davidson part of their dreams.

Surely the low-tech image of the Harley-Davidson played little part in a rising intellectual interest in the motorcycle, exemplified by philosopher Robert Pirsig's 1974 chronicle of a ride across Montana with his young son. *Zen and the Art of Motorcycle Maintenance* employed Pirsig's bike (probably a BMW, although it was never identified) as a paradigm for man's search for meaning in a world he described as divided between the classical and the romantic. The motorcycle, said Pirsig, bridged the divide, combining the rigid, schematic rules of the classical with purely romantic ideals. Formal disciplines involving engineering technology apply to the motorcycle, as does the purely romantic act of riding — an act Pirsig describes as being "in the scene, not just watching it anymore, and the sense of the presence is overwhelming. That concrete whizzing by five inches below your foot is the real thing, the same stuff you walk on, it's right there, so blurred you can't focus on it, you can put your foot down and touch it anytime, and the whole thing, the whole experience, is never removed from immediate consciousness."

Complex and arcane (harsher critics suggest garbled, incoherent, and pretentious), Pirsig's book, after being rejected by dozens of publishers, became an international bestseller. While it meant nothing to the average biker, who seldom viewed lubricating his wheel bearings or tightening his drive chain as a Zenlike act, the book helped to temper the prejudices of academia regarding motorcycles and may have influenced such luminaries as megarich gadfly publisher Malcolm S. Forbes to embrace the machines. It was during this period that Forbes purchased a fleet of Harley-Davidsons and, with a small collection of friends and sympathetic journalists, embarked on several highly publicized rides into darkest China and the Soviet Union. More than any single person, Malcolm Forbes injected a much-needed note of credibility into motorcycling in general and Harley-Davidson in particular. His efforts did, however, veer into the theater of the absurd when he purchased a customized pink Sportster for his sometime companion Elizabeth Taylor — who, as far as is known, never rode the machine for more than brief jaunts in front of the show business press.

Pirsig's metaphysics and Forbes's public exhibitionism notwithstanding, it was evident by the middle of the decade that the AMF venture in Milwaukee was a disaster. The Japanese were gobbling up the market, and no amount of positive publicity resulting from the high-flying stunts of Evel Knievel improved Harley's business. Several mainstream motorcycle monthlies ceased testing the Milwaukee bikes, protesting that there was nothing new to report. In reaction, a collection of tatty, tough-talking magazines appeared that were exclusively devoted to the aged brand. Speaking directly to the biker crowd, monthlies like *Easyriders* and *Iron Horse* featured tattooed, bare-breasted bimbos sprawled on custom Harleys in open defiance of the pie-faced imagery being peddled by the manufacturer.

These publications were feverishly loyal to Harley-Davidson, exhibiting a biting jingoism that eulogized the old twin as not only the best motorcycle, but the *only* motorcycle worthy of ownership. The largest, most visible, and most successful of the biker magazines was *Easyriders*, which had been started by a singularly bright ex-Angel named Keith Ball. Ball's self-taught publishing skills would make him rich while altering the way Harley-Davidson marketed motorcycles — whether the company liked it or not.

Easyriders, Iron Horse, and their imitators surprised the publishing world by outselling many of the conventional motorcycle publications while dealing for the first time with a group of enthusiasts wilder and larger and more influential than anyone had realized. Now the bad-guy image of the Harley-Davidson transcended the outlaw clubs and entered the magazine racks of the nation's supermarkets.

Not only did the revolutionary biker magazines identify a large customer base of outlaw riders and wanna-bes, they championed causes that had been ignored by the establishment. As states began to impose helmet laws on riders in the late 1960s, it was the outlaws who rose up in protest, forming ABATE (American Bikers Aimed Toward Education) to battle the various state governments. Hordes of bikers heretofore unseen outside seedy bars and back roads suddenly appeared in front of state capitols to loudly protest what they considered yet another intrusion by the nanny state. ABATE was originally an acronym for "A Brotherhood Against Totalitarian Enactments," but it was modified and softened when serious legislative action began being introduced. *Easyriders* was a powerful force in the antihelmet movement, which again moved the once-reviled bikers closer to the mainstream and into the psyches of the Harley-Davidson leadership. Willie G. Davidson began actively courting this group, shucking his business suit and his cordovans for black leather and boots. His persona was transformed over a matter of years as he remade himself as a bearded, bandanna-wrapped, good-ol'-boy brother and a godhead of the Harley-Davidson cult. This Willie G. Davidson, once the bespectacled, gray-flanneled young executive, became the quintessential biker. Some critics viewed this transformation as a blatant public relations move, but those close to him insisted it was a genuine alteration in lifestyle based on his contact with the free-living bikers. As a trained artist and designer, Willie G. had been stimulated by the wildly creative, often brilliant folk art embodied in the bikers' custom motorcycles and their audacious leather and denim fashion statements.

Davidson's eye was aimed with laserlike intensity at the newly recognized cultists. *Easyriders*, ABATE, and the outlaw Modified Motorcycle Association were formed in part out of frustration with the national drift and a general malaise that had gripped the country. For the first time, the anger heretofore restricted to the outlaw gangs blossomed among the general riding public. *Easyriders'* 750,000 readers went far beyond the bikers it celebrated, all identifying a surliness and sexuality in motorcycles that had been sublimated for decades. Were the great thumping beasts menacing? Did they embody elemental sexuality? Of course they did, although before the appearance of *Easyriders* magazine no one had dared to admit it in print.

Willie G. Davidson, strapped as he was by a stringent budget and an AMF management team unwilling to countenance the outlaws, did his best to exploit the new reality. He and a canny AMF engineer named Vaughn Beals were among a tiny cadre of men within the Harley-Davidson management who understood that the biker image embodied a whole new market for motorcycles and accessories. The question was how to cozy up to a group the general public viewed as degenerate criminals while at the same time capturing customers attracted to the squeaky-clean Japanese brands. The AMF leadership, based in a starchy New York suburb, hadn't the vaguest idea about the nuances of the motorcycle market and cared less. Example: After Rodney Gott retired in 1978 as CEO, he was succeeded by Ray A. Tritten, who had run the firm's Ben Hogan golf club division. Tritten made his first appearance as CEO at the raucous Daytona Beach Bike Week celebration aboard a stretch limousine and, like a hopeless square, mingled with the true believers in a three-piece business suit. When a dealer group attempted to place a full-page ad in *Easyriders*, the magazine refused, running instead a blank page in a symbolic act of defiance, not against the motorcycle, but against the myopic AMF management. Such was the rift between a corporate conglomerate committed to modern mass-marketing techniques and a tight, mildly fanatic collection of loyalists carving out a lifestyle centered on an outdated, retro-fashion motorcycle.

Willie G. produced another tentative link between the two factions in 1977, when he offered up the FXS Low Rider, a parts-bin miracle of integrated styling that featured a rakish front fork, cast alloy wheels, and a deeply notched seat that dropped the rider's leather-clad butt to within twenty-seven inches of the road. The Low Rider's enthusiastic reception offered further proof that Harley-Davidson's future lay not in the frumpy cruiser market being lost to Honda's GoldWings, but rather in a rising group of traditionalists looking backward away from the seamless world of high tech and toward a simpler time when government intrusions, clogged highways, and foreign mercantile invasions were unknown.

The quest within the management was now under way at the Juneau Avenue headquarters to tap this new and energetic market for Harleys and to reach what appeared to be a mother lode of loyalists unlike any other in the nation. The "American freedom machine," as it began to be called in corporate promotions, subtly pandered to this rebellion, propagating as it did a sense of unity and uniqueness, real or imagined, among the customer base. The outlaw biker became a prototypical Harley rider, decked out in black leather and hooting patriotic themes, no matter how incoherent. The notion that these were authentic Americans, the nouveau cowboys, the unvarnished, oh-my-God, hellfire keepers of the faith, became dogma as the company found itself increasingly marginalized by the Japanese. Circle the wagons! The rice burners are coming! This was a ringing manifesto among the Vietnam vets who had returned home discredited and forgotten while their collegiate counterparts pranced and preened in victory. What better way to express rage than aboard a fuming V-twin motorcycle made in God's own Milwaukee by real guys like themselves? Included in this defiance were the nannies and the do-gooders, the pantywaists and the desk-riding bureaucrats who would take away a man's right to ride down a road full blast and, if he so chose, to bust his skull on the pavement with no questions asked. The hated helmets became a cause célèbre within the motorcycle community, led by the hard-asses on Harleys — who, if not a majority in sheer numbers, set a standard of in-your-face antiestablishmentarianism unseen since the 1960s. If this rabble wasn't a place to hang the corporate banner, what was?

Since forty-two-year-old Betty Friedan had published her pioneering feminist call to arms, titled *The Feminine Mystique*, in 1963, the American male had been under attack as a boorish, sex-obsessed slob. The creation of NOW (National Organization for Women) by Friedan and her cohorts two years later brought the issue of female stereotyping as mindless mommies and hausfraus into public focus. The war was soon joined by Germaine Greer and Gloria Steinem, who, after gaining national prominence by working undercover as a Playboy Bunny, began editing the advocacy magazine *Ms.* in 1972. The feminist movement, in all its sensible-shoed, bra-burning anger, was in full cry by the late 1970s, and males were in cultural retreat.

Reaction to this often militant movement was scattered and unstructured, if for no other reason than the feminists were articulating a reality that within the world of business, the professions, and in many homes, women *were* subordinated to second-class status. Often overstated and shrill to the point of absurdity, the feminists nevertheless opened a door that had been shut since the women's suffrage uprisings of the early 1900s. Males were threatened on all sides. The realities of the new age of computers and the nascent information revolution appeared to trivialize and reduce the status of their traditional roles in the so-called manly trades where physical strength, courage, and endurance played a part. It was apparent in the postmodern era that outside a few jobs like NFL linebacker and NBA center, women could handle about any assignment once restricted to men. Even at the hallowed Indianapolis Motor Speedway, the epicenter of chauvinism, where women were not even allowed in the garages or the pits until the late sixties, the barriers had collapsed. In 1976, a woman, Janet Guthrie, attempted to qualify for the 500-mile race, and two years later she managed to finish ninth. It was apparent that a modern woman was capable of driving a 200-mph racing car as well as a man, even in the most dangerous and grueling contest of them all.

One last bastion of maledom seemed to remain. The motorcycle, especially a hulking 600-pounder like a Harley-Davidson, required not only skill but a modicum of strength to ride effectively. It was a male precinct, although some plucky women had ridden for years, beginning in 1910, when an eighteen-year-old named Clara Wagner nearly won a 365-mile endurance race from Chicago to Indianapolis. Five years later, a mother and daughter, Effie and Avis Hotchkiss, rode a sidecar-equipped Harley-Davidson on a tortured 5,000-mile coast-to-coast trip — a trip that had seldom been duplicated by men up to the time. Still, the vast majority of motorcycles in the late 1970s were owned and ridden by men. Women were restricted to riding shotgun: "Seated by my man," to paraphrase the Tammy Wynette country-and-western hit.

As the world tilted on its axis and men faltered, full of self-doubt, the motorcycle, representing as it did maleness in full bloom, beckoned to many as a reassuring icon.

Simultaneous with this rise in the popularity of the motorcycle was the massive population shift to warmer — and more politically conservative — states, where traditional values acted to counterbalance the trendy liberalism of the Northeast. Beginning in the 1930s, great migrations began, first to California, then to Texas, Arizona, Nevada, and Florida, where a faint residue of the frontier mentality, coupled with warmer weather, opened the motorcycle market to unexpected dimensions. California alone experienced a population increase of more than 6 million immigrants from eastern states between 1940 and 1960. Another 7.5 million arrived between 1980 and 1993. Nevada — a wasteland of rocks and sand heretofore considered uninhabitable — saw its population jump nearly 100 percent from 1980 to the current day. Texas, led by giant megalopolises like Houston, Dallas, and San Antonio, became a boom state, as did swampy Florida, the former refuge of alligators, blue-hairs, and rednecks. This transfer of people and wealth to the new territories of perceived opportunity was in a sense a duplication of the enormous middle-and-southern European immigrant migrations to the United States in the late nineteenth century, giving rise to the same optimism and sense of pioneering. With it arose a population generally less tied to the conventions of the postmodern world and with a greater link to the more elemental traditions involving personal options and freedoms. A shift in political power would result, with four consecutive presidents (Carter, Reagan, Bush, and Clinton) rising out of the new southern and western power bases. So too would a conservative mood to displace the aged, elitist liberal nostrums of the eastern establishment — leading in some cases to strange, outcast antigovernment cranks who banded together as antitax protesters, militia groups, white supremacy thugs, proto-Nazis, and other bizarre manifestations of the American dream. While they played no central role, Harley-Davidson motorcycles served as statements of personal freedom and independence that, though not directly associated with any of the dissident organizations, represented a subliminal sympathy vote against government of all kinds.

Prior to the explosion of Harley-Davidson as an upscale status symbol and a favorite of the trend surfers in the late 1980s, it was firmly entrenched as a blue-collar machine. Repeated studies indicated that the average Harley owner generated a low income and was modestly educated and considerably older than the median buyer of Japanese motorcycles. He (with few female exceptions) was politically conservative and considered himself an independent thinker operating on the edge of the establishment. While only a small percentage belonged to outlaw clubs, average Harley riders were by the late 1970s suiting up in the leather and denim fashions originated by the hard-core bikers. They also expressed a certain surliness, perhaps for being marginalized as Neanderthals defending an ancient brand of motorcycle against the onslaught of better Japanese machines. From this arose a perverse sense of pride, like the citizens of Minneapolis bragging about their subzero winters or those of Phoenix defending their 130-degree, microwave-level "dry" heat.

The Harley-Davidson riders, discredited and disdained, congealed into a tightly packed mass. From these embattled enthusiasts, a small group of California devotees formed in 1977 what they called the Harley-Davidson Owners Association. Their goal was to create an alliance among Harley owners of all types and to establish a rapport with the company, which traditionally remained aloof from its customers. The little club's newsletter, *Gear Box*, was openly critical of the Harley's mechanical deficiencies, which angered the executive staff. But the germ of an idea was recognized: that of a formally organized collection of Harley-Davidson loyalists who could be brought closer to the corporation and its policies. This would ultimately lead in the early 1980s to the formation by the company of the Harley Owners Group, or HOG — a highly successful marketing venture that would link the brand's customers together under a single banner.

The financial community was aware of AMF's inability to dovetail its organization with that of Harley-Davidson, as the owners were of the need to make massive investments in new products to compete with the Japanese while needing funds for other segments of its business as well. AMF quietly shopped the company to possible buyers. There were no takers. Alone and struggling, Harley-Davidson entered into an agreement with Porsche Cars of Stuttgart, Germany, to develop fresh engine technology, based on the reasoning that Porsche engineers understood air-cooled engine design as well as anybody on earth. The link between Porsche and Harley-Davidson could be traced to the Indiana-based Cummins Diesel Company, where Vaughn Beals had worked as chief engineer. His associate there had been a German American named

Peter Schutz, who had recently been hired to head the fabled Stuttgart sports car builder. The friendship and mutual respect between the two men led to the alliance, although in a symbolic sense, a certain linkage already existed between the two firms. Both were steeped in tradition, until the 1970s controlled by a tightly knit family (paterfamilias Ferdinand Porsche had created the Volkswagen and was a favorite war machine designer of Adolf Hitler). Both companies were committed to a technical heritage that gave their products a patina lacking among their rivals; Harley-Davidson's V-twin was the equivalent of Porsche's rear-mounted, air-cooled, opposed four-cylinder engine and torsion bar suspension.

The joint Porsche-Harley NOVA project involved a proposed $10 million investment but was not pursued due to Harley-Davidson's serious shortages of cash. The government, now in the hands of activist bureaucrats appointed by the liberal Carter administration, was exerting pressure on the motorcycle industry to decrease exhaust emissions and engine noise.

Business got worse. Harley's once-dominant position in the big cruiser market had shrunk to 30 percent, the rest having been seized by the predatory Japanese. This prompted the company in 1978–79 to complain about dumping tactics to the International Trade Commission, much as it had done against the English following WWII. Again Harley-Davidson was rebuffed. The ITC countered that lax quality control, outdated designs, and poor marketing policies were more at fault for the company's problems than any actions by the Japanese.

It was at this point that Harley-Davidson could have taken a turn in the road that might have led it to oblivion. With enormous outside pressure being brought to bear to update and modernize its products, there was an obvious temptation to meet the Japanese toe-to-toe with brilliant, breakthrough designs and to shuck forever the wheezy, archaic, air-cooled, forty-five-degree V-twin engine that had been the heart and soul of the Harley-Davidson motorcycle for seventy years. Many outsiders opined that modern silky-smooth four-cylinder engines like those being offered by the Japanese were the key to the future. The V-twin ought to go the way of the buggy whip and the flintlock rifle, said the experts, choosing to ignore the cultlike support for the traditional Harley-Davidson rising out of unseemly quarters like those represented by the outlaw biker magazines.

To make such a change demanded a denial of the Harley-Davidson's heritage as a purely American machine, flawed but honest and forthright, bombastic and audacious like the nation that produced it — a machine whose value superseded any single mechanical component and nullified any simplistic technical deficiencies. To change or not to change, that was the question. Producing a modern power plant, which the Harley-Davidson design team and Porsche were perfectly capable of accomplishing, would place them in head-on competition with the seamless, high-tech Japanese bikes. But retaining the value inherent in the tatty old V-twin would be celebrated by a core ownership who evidenced a brand loyalty unequaled by anything in the entire world of powered vehicles. Much debate was carried on within the company in the late 1970s until the AMF management cleared the way for what was internally called the V-2, or Evolution, engine. This was the single most important decision in the survival of the company.

The V-2 would retain the traditional architecture of the ancient Harley-Davidson V-twin: two air-cooled cylinders mounted at forty-five degrees on the same traditional crankcase that dated, in essence, to the EL model created fifty years earlier. Much computer simulation was done before new cylinder heads, valve gears, ignition systems, pistons, etc., were decided upon for the final design. The new engine was to produce about 15 percent more power while offering better fuel economy, more reliability, and cooler operation than the old Shovelhead/Panhead/Knucklehead versions it replaced.

What is sometimes forgotten is that the much-reviled AMF administration sanctioned the development of the V-2, although it was not introduced until the conglomerate had been bought out and its memory had dimmed. While the marriage between AMF and the old Harley-Davidson operators was uncomfortable at best, loyalists choose to forget that without AMF's brief involvement, Harley-Davidson would (1) not have survived the 1970s, (2) not have obtained its modern York, Pennsylvania, facility and its tooling, and (3) never have been able to afford development of the V-2 engine. Much has been written about what a botched job AMF did with Harley-Davidson, but its contributions were substantial, not the least of which was to leave in place a group of talented executives who eventually leveraged a buyout and led Harley-Davidson on a course to its current prosperity. Without the involvement of AMF, as star-crossed as it was, it is likely that Harley-Davidson would today be lamented like Indian, Excelsior, Henderson, BSA, Norton, and many others as yet another victim of the Japanese in the international motorcycle wars.

The 1970s wound down in a fit of national ennui and despair. Iran, in an act of unprecedented international outlawry, took over the American embassy in Tehran and held its diplomats hostage. Chrysler Corporation was on the verge of joining venerable old brands like Hudson, Packard, Studebaker, and Nash on the automotive scrap heap. All the while, a weak and baffled but well-

intentioned Georgia peanut farmer occupied the White House. The
OPEC oil barons flexed their muscles once again and shut off the
petroleum. Interest rates soared to nearly 20 percent as the Carter
administration fussed helplessly. Within this scenario of frustration,
the woes of a small motorcycle manufacturer in Milwaukee were
unworthy of concern to either the government or Wall Street, which
set the stage for a comeback that would shock the business world
in general and the seemingly unstoppable Japanese industrial jug-
gernaut in particular.

7 · THE EAGLE FLIES ALONE

As Ronald Reagan swept into office in 1980 with his neon smile and feel-good nostrums about "morning in America," it appeared more like darkness at noon in Milwaukee. The Japanese were sweeping across the motorcycle business like the black plague, swallowing up competitors much as they seemed to be doing with hapless auto companies like Chrysler. Academics, economists, pundits, financial analysts, Wall Street brokers, and corporate executives were frozen with fear over the assault of a doomsday machine called Japan, Incorporated — a fiendish hegemony of monster banks, interlocking directorships, and ultra-efficient, predatory industries, all manned by hordes of worker bees mindlessly committed to worldwide economic domination. Industry after industry was crumbling under its headlong attack: electronics, cameras, machine tools, steel production, motorcycles, and automobiles.

In Detroit, Chrysler was saved — perhaps only temporarily — by $1.6 billion in government-guaranteed loans and the last-hour development of a new type of vehicle called the minivan. General Motors and Ford, operating with outdated management and production policies, seemed equally vulnerable, producing as they were oversized, inefficient, badly fabricated automobiles and trucks. But compared to hapless Harley-Davidson they appeared healthy. At least the Big Three composed such a powerful component of the American economy that not even throwback capitalists most committed to the laws of the economic jungle could afford to let them collapse. But Harley-Davidson, employing fewer than 3,000 workers in places like York, Pennsylvania, and Milwaukee, Wisconsin, was hardly critical to the domestic economy. Its demise would cause barely a ripple in the GDP, and aside from the few fevered loyalists who rode the rumble-gutted old monsters, nobody cared if Harley-Davidson lived or died.

By 1980, the company's share of the big-bike market — the cruisers and muscle-bound machines with engines displacing in the neighborhood of 1,000 cc's — had collapsed from roughly 80 percent a decade earlier to less than 30 percent. The Japanese, primarily Honda and Yamaha, had scooped up the rest. To make matters worse, Yamaha was taking a direct shot at Harley-Davidson. Word reached Milwaukee in 1980 that Yamaha was developing a Harley-Davidson clone to be called the Virago. It would be a V-twin — albeit with a seventy-five-degree engine layout for smoother running. The plan was to offer a Harley "custom" look with typical Japanese engineering excellence.

Although they had a substantial impact on the industry initially, the Virago and later V-twins from Honda and Suzuki aimed at the Harley heart would reveal a fatal flaw: they were *too perfect*. The Japanese industry, consumed by internecine warfare that had

turned into a technological game of can-you-top-this, refused to believe that the grand old Harley forty-five-degree V-twin, now near-
ing its fiftieth birthday since the introduction of the 1936 EL
Knucklehead, could not be improved upon. After all, it was lumpy,
noisy, and low powered; their engineers could make a better V-twin
with a few scrawls on the drawing board. But it would take a
decade of hard learning for the Japanese to discover that the elemental qualities of the Harley engine, including the ragged bark of
its exhaust, were precious commodities. In the meantime, Honda,
Yamaha, and Suzuki engaged in such engineering pyrotechnics as
V-twins with water cooling, four-overhead valves, and camshafts
connected to ultrasmooth drive shafts and silky transmissions —
all mounted on motorcycles costing nearly half as much as a big
Harley. This appeared an unbeatable combination: better, faster,
cheaper Harley-Davidsons! How could a bunch of bozos in Milwaukee, chained to a collection of three-piece suits in White Plains,
New York, compete against that?

Better than one might think, as it turned out. The first step was
a separation of Harley-Davidson and AMF. The marriage had simply
not worked, and a divorce was inevitable. Many at AMF believed
Harley-Davidson was doomed under any circumstances and simply
wanted to cut their losses. But some within the Harley-Davidson
management were convinced the company had a long shot at survival if it was permitted to reorganize outside the purview of the
parent conglomerate. A prime mover in this daring strategy was
Vaughn Beals. He had been hired by AMF president Ray Tritten to
head Harley-Davidson's engineering staff despite the fact that before 1976 he had never ridden a motorcycle. Tough and forthright,
Beals held both bachelor's and master's degrees in engineering
from the Massachusetts Institute of Technology and had a lengthy

résumé in the aerospace industry and with the aforementioned Cummins Diesel Company. He had come to believe that the beleaguered firm had a chance of surviving on its own based on its unique position in the market and the intense loyalty of its customer base. After all, as one financial type observed during initial buyout discussions, "I guess you won't find too many companies whose customers tattoo their logo on their bodies."

It was Beals and a small coterie of loyalists, including Jeffrey Bleustein, a former Yale engineering professor who had been with the company since 1971, and Richard F. Teerlink, who would ultimately become the chairman, president, and CEO of the reorganized company, plus Willie G. Davidson, who maintained the true faith: that with some creative thinking, a little luck, and about $80 million, they could turn the tide against the Japanese. Citicorp Industrial Credit, the lending division of the immense banking institution, agreed. Slowly a deal was put together — which was nearly aborted by a union walkout when the *Wall Street Journal* reported the rumor that AMF was planning to sell Harley-Davidson to Honda. Beginning in February 1981, a group of thirteen executives anted up roughly $1 million in personal equity for the buyout — and finally, after a decade of strife and ill will, AMF was freed of its albatross. Surely the Harley-Davidson management felt the same way.

There was reason to be cautiously optimistic. After all, what group of customers was writing novels like Bob Bitchin's *A Brotherhood of Outlaws* (1981) that glorified a product as an icon of personal freedom? Bitchin (real name Robert Lipkin) was an immense, tattooed outlaw biker and former bodyguard of Evel Knievel who held degrees from USC and UCLA in psychology and business administration. He was editor and founder of the hard-edged *Biker*

News and had also founded the thoroughly scatological biker magazine *FTW* ("Fuck the World"). Bitchin's novel involved a small
band of bikers on the run from Los Angeles riding chopper Harleys.
The story offers great insight into the code of the outlaw biker, noting that "no matter what the biker has done, as long as he hasn't
cheated a brother or broken any of the bikers' rules, he is accepted,
especially if he is running from the police." Much of the story involves a polemic against helmet laws, which Bitchin vehemently
opposed. He was instrumental in organizing antihelmet rallies
around the nation, many of which saw thousands of bikers sur-
round state capitols and successfully frighten lawmakers into eas-
ing the regulations.

But Bitchin's central theme was an intense sense of clan-
nish belonging centered around a strange and brutish machine
that appeared on the verge of disappearing from the market. His
book, plus the plethora of hard-core biker magazines, newsletters,
weekly papers, posters, and after-market accessories, did not go
unnoticed in Milwaukee. These wild men, these hard riders, these
last cowboys on their mechanical broncos — like it or not —
formed the heart and soul, the very essence of the Harley mystique. Take your squeaky-clean, primrose-perfect rice burners,
your Jap scrap that started every time, ran like a fine watch,
and were so fast they'd scare you witless; you take those vapid,
soulless techno-wonders and stick 'em! The Harley, the true
symbol of human frailty and audacity, was to be honored and
revered, not for its utility or its sheer excellence, but for its
god-awful, all-American, in-your-face, hog-stomping, ball-busting,
real-life representation of man's own imperfections. If this rebelliousness, this sheer vitality and off-the-wall lust for the elemental life could somehow be tapped to offset the seamless onslaught

of the Japanese, perhaps, just maybe, Harley-Davidson could survive.

The vividness of the brand's image notwithstanding, 1981 was a terrible time to attempt a leveraged buyout of a struggling motorcycle company. The western world was in a major recession, still staggering from an inflationary spiral in the late 1970s that saw interest rates edge near 20 percent. By mid-1981, the new management team was in place. Beals was board chairman, with Charles Thompson serving as president. They now faced the reality of more than 6,000 unsold motorcycles languishing in warehouses, each suffering from mediocre quality and antiquated design, plus an empty till for operating capital. To exacerbate matters, Honda and Yamaha were engaged in an all-out war for worldwide motorcycle domination. While this fight did not directly involve Harley-Davidson, the struggle between the two giants was bound to kick dirt in the faces of their smaller rivals. As both Honda and Yamaha relentlessly slashed prices and poured flashy new models onto the market, Harley-Davidson's chances of increasing sales fell to near zero.

The entire American automobile and motorcycle industry was in a state of chaos. The Japanese controlled almost half the bellwether California car market, and their national share edged toward 25 percent. Fearing massive tariff reprisals, the Japanese imposed voluntary quotas of 2.2 million vehicles entering the United States, an action clearly taken to sidetrack formal legislation by an increasingly angry Congress. As Ronald Reagan entered office, unemployment rose to 10.8 percent, and car and motorcycle sales took an alarming downturn. The timing for the buyout of Harley-Davidson could not have been worse, but Beals and company struggled onward. The NOVA project with Porsche was reluctantly canceled, although a design for an overhead camshaft version of a V-4 was on the drawing board. The engine was a modular design, capable of being built in displacements ranging between 500 and 1,000 cc's. But there simply weren't sufficient funds for such an ambitious redesign, although plans for the revised and updated V-2 Evolution engine were pushed forward on a shoestring.

Beals fought back with two strategies. An extensive study of the Japanese motorcycle industry was undertaken, and yet another formal complaint was entered against Harley-Davidson's rivals — in this case citing Section 201 of the 1974 Trade Act — which claimed that Japan, Inc., was engaging in unfair competition by dumping motorcycles on the market and overtly copying Harley designs. Both charges were true, although the issue was complicated by the fact that Honda and Kawasaki were building motorcycles in their own American factories, which, in a broad sense, made them domestic products.

Study of Japanese manufacturing techniques — which became a mini-industry for industrial consultants, economists, and university think tanks in the 1980s — revealed three major differences between the Japanese and the Yankee ways of doing business. Employee involvement by the Japanese was vastly greater than in American factories; the workforce was valued not only for its manual skills but for its mental energy. Secondly, the control of inventory through a "just in time" arrangement with suppliers reduced overhead costs and increased flexibility. The third difference was — to the universal frustration of everyone probing the Japanese way of doing business — American in origin. Two brilliant manufacturing experts, W. Edwards Deming and Joseph Juran, had been consulting for the Japanese since the end of World War II, teaching them sophisticated but universal truths about statistical process controls that elevated manufacturing efficiencies to stratospheric levels compared to obsolete American techniques. While Deming and Juran were treated as prophets in Japan, they had been largely ignored in their homeland. But by the mid-1980s, hundreds of American businesses, including Harley-Davidson, would embrace their policies as part of a broad campaign to counter the Japanese invasion.

As Harley-Davidson struggled into the early 1980s, pinching pennies and trying to bail out its badly leaking business by relying on Willie G. Davidson's brilliance to restyle and revamp old motorcycles into flashy new models, a strange alteration in the national mood was playing to the benighted company's advantage. As Jimmy Carter moped out of office, grumping about the malaise of the population, an ebullient and optimistic Ronald Reagan stormed into the White House, bringing with him a crooked smile that concealed a rock-hard intent to face down the Soviet Union and to revive the national spirit. The long-term results of his policies would be debated, with critics citing his massive buildup of the national debt and encouragement of a predatory economic system unseen since the 1920s. Supporters would cheer his challenge of the Soviet Union and credit him with its collapse in an economic war it could not win. Either way, the national mood changed radically in the eighties, with pride and optimism rising significantly as Reagan alternately smiled and hard-knuckled his adversaries into line. The first to fall were the air controllers, who, through their union, PATCO, defied the government by striking for higher wages in 1981. Reagan summarily fired them and hired replacements, thereby becoming the first postwar president to face down a powerful union. A year later, he dedicated the Vietnam memorial, which helped temper the bitterness and hatred that had poisoned the national psyche for a decade. Poll after poll revealed a radical rise in the nation's mood, which was further enhanced by Reagan's assault on the corrupt but sentimentalized Sandinista regime in Nicaragua and a brief but decisive invasion of Grenada.

The surly self-loathing of the sixties and seventies was being replaced by a new national pride and what might be called a revival of the old gunfighter mentality. Reagan called forth the imagery of the great western frontier and the spiritual power of the prototypical American cowboy. Since the days of historian Frederick Jackson Turner, who in 1893 proposed his seminal thesis on the significance of the American frontier, the notion that the American character had been formed by the independence and aggressiveness inherent in the westward agrarian movement of the nineteenth century had been widely accepted. Theodore Roosevelt expanded on Turner's observations, claiming that the entrepreneurial spirit embodied in the exploitation of minerals and ranch lands in the great West embodied the very essence of the American persona. John F. Kennedy also employed this theme, using the frontier as a metaphor for his presidential campaign and for his policies relating to Vietnam, where *cowboys* and *Indians* were commonly used terms for the American troops and the Vietcong. The ironies of an eastern brahmin exploiting the imagery of the great West in his "New Frontier" notwithstanding, the position contained powerful medicine. In accepting the 1960 Democratic presidential nomination, Kennedy artfully employed the romance of the western frontier: "I stand here tonight," he said, "facing west on what was the last frontier. From the lands that stretch three thousand miles behind me, the pioneers of old gave up their safety, their comfort and sometimes their lives to build a new world here in the West. . . . We stand on the edge of a new frontier — the frontier of the 1960s, a frontier of unknown opportunities and paths."

It was a powerful and resonant message, calling forth the heroic imagery of the nation's most legendary characters: the Bridgers, the Hickocks, the Earps, the Custers, the Houstons, the gunfighters, Indian scouts and warriors, trappers, miners, prospectors, and freebooters who, through sheer audacity and daredevilry, tamed the continent.

After nearly two decades of self-flagellation and pointless navel examination by legions of Cassandras, counterculture mountebanks, and political criminals in the highest offices, it was Reagan, the tall man in the saddle from California, who would enhance and exploit this imagery like no other president. Never mind that his only feats on horseback had come in front of a movie camera or that his war record was restricted to Hollywood training films, Reagan was to become a symbol around the world as the Cowboy President. With him would rise a new era of national pride and optimism.

Inherent in the frontier mentality was an embracing of honest, real-man, red-meat realities, as opposed to the fancy footwork embodied in the androgynous new world. It was not a coincidence that within the framework of Reaganism came a revival of old-time Pentecostal religion and a throwback to old fashions and technologies. Back to the basics was the cry, including a reversion to good old Yankee big-stick diplomacy and quick-draw foreign policy. The circumspect banalities of prior administrations regarding the Soviet Union were replaced by Reagan's bold descriptions of it as an "evil empire" and calls to Premier Gorbachev to tear down the Berlin Wall. The American military roared into action in Grenada, over the skies of Tripoli, in Panama, and covertly in Nicaragua. *Rambo* replaced the pitiful victims of *The Deer Hunter* and *Apocalypse Now*, while Reagan cozied up to such movie tough guys as Clint Eastwood ("Make my day") and John Wayne, whose words introduced Reagan's biographical film at the 1984 Republican convention. In a broad sense, it was the "Duke" who represented the brand of patriotism espoused by Reagan in his most passionate public moments — and by the most vocal Harley-Davidson aficionados. (Although biographers have revealed that Wayne, the prototypical American GI in such classics as *The Sands of Iwo Jima* and *Back to Bataan*, was in fact a draft dodger in World War II, choosing to stick it out in Hollywood while older actors like Jimmy Stewart and Clark Gable volunteered for combat duty. Even Reagan, though he was semiblind without his contacts, joined up and thereby ruined the prime years of his career.) While Wayne's involvement with Harley-Davidson was nonexistent, he stands with the motorcycle as part of the great American myth, an atavistic hero figure whose persona gained strength from his playacting, much as some Harley riders absorb potency from a machine that in reality serves as little more than a theatrical prop.

Somehow the emergence of Ronald Reagan and his feel-good themes built on timeless Yankee homilies triggered a slowdown in the public surge toward high technology. This was symbolized by such subtleties as the rejection of digital watches in favor of old-fashioned analogue types like the Rolex — the ultimate status-icon jewelry of the 1980s. Automobiles with onboard recorded messages ("Your door is ajar," "Please fasten your seatbelt") were openly disdained. Wonder fibers were abhorred in favor of honest cotton and wool, while western wear — cowboy boots, hand-tooled belts, and Levi's — enjoyed massive popularity.

Riding on this surge of jingoism and the revival of the cowboy mythology came Harley-Davidson, staggering back to life as Reagan re-energized the American spirit. What better symbol for this than a small motorcycle company producing a quintessentially honest and traditional American product, being attacked by yes, say it, slant-eyed little harbor bombers who killed our men and raped our women only forty years ago? To the ramparts! The yellow hordes are upon us!

Even as Harley-Davidson was awash in sympathy — much of it self-serving and self-generated — as the beleaguered little guy about to be overwhelmed by overseas predators, the Japanese motorcycle manufacturers were far from interested in driving the company out of business. Sensitive as they were to the grumblings of Congress about their incursions into the automobile market, Honda executives in particular were concerned that a failure by Harley-Davidson would only bring the wrath of Congress upon them, with egregious tariffs and other trade reprisals. Much as General Motors — when it controlled nearly 60 percent of the domestic automobile market in the late 1950s — had been terrified that the Sherman Anti-Trust Act would be invoked against it, Honda and the other Japanese motorcycle manufacturers considered it essential that Harley-Davidson remain in business, if for no other reason than to defuse the protectionists in Congress.

This would not be easy, due to a collapsing market caused by the recession and the dynamism of the Japanese and their fleets of excellent bikes. By 1982, Citicorp was threatening to pull the plug on Harley-Davidson as sales slipped from 53,000 units to a mere 35,000 and layoffs slashed the workforce from 4,000 in 1980 to a skeletal 2,200. Once again the company was on the brink, although a year later the Reagan administration acted decisively in its favor. Tariffs totaling 45 percent were slapped on all imported Japanese motorcycles over 700 cc, seemingly giving Harley-Davidson a pricing edge in the large cruiser market. The tariffs were to remain in place for five years, dropping to 10 percent in the final three years, to give the Milwaukee firm a chance to regain its market position.

The tariff was for the most part symbolic posturing in that the Hondas and Kawasakis being produced in the United States were exempt. Moreover, the Japanese merely readjusted their product lines to offer 699 cc models with essentially the same performance capabilities as the larger Harleys. But the very act of retaliation, the first response from the American government, which had remained largely impassive since the Japanese car and motorcycle assault had begun in the early 1960s, caused a tremendous burst of enthusiasm among Harley owners and within the company.

In June of 1983, Willie G. Davidson led a band of corporate types and enthusiast customers on a ride from the York, Pennsylvania, assembly plant to the home base in Milwaukee. The theme of the trip was "The eagle flies alone," a clear reference to the end of the AMF connection and the company's stand-alone battle against the Japanese. The eagle was but one of several brilliant logo configurations that were to serve Harley-Davidson so well in ensuing years. The patriotic connotations were obvious; an artful melding of the bird with the black and orange corporate colors (first used by the factory racing team in the 1960s) created a powerful image of defiant independence, of the outsider battling an amorphous but powerful establishment. Slowly, Harley-Davidson was discovering that its market growth would come from the inside out, from a small but fanatic band of outlaws and quasi outlaws who radiated its appeal into the general population. No more would the company shun the bad guys; instead it would rely on their reputation of veiled menace to establish a marketing niche like no other.

Although Beals and company encountered a small but nasty dealer revolt when markup margins were cut by 5 percent and pres-

sure exerted to improve the sales and service environment in the
dumpier outlets, a major breakthrough came in 1983, when marketing director Clyde Fessler created the company-owned-and-
operated Harley Owners Group, or HOG. It was formed in part to
counteract the dissident Harley-Davidson Owners Association and
in part to coalesce new customers (who automatically gained membership) into tightly controlled regional chapters.

For the first time in its history, the company reached out to its
owner body in a fashion far transcending the old *Enthusiast* magazine. HOG members were contacted regularly through an artfully
produced *HOG Tales* newsletter outlining a myriad of social gatherings, rallies, races, charity rides, picnics, and bike shows, all
sanctioned and promoted by the company. This involved a radical
turnabout in policy in that the heretofore pejorative "hog" was embraced as a self-effacing, irreverent corporate nickname — a daring act akin to Rolls-Royce referring to its automobiles as "Rollers"
or Mercedes-Benz as "Mercs." Harley-Davidson set about trade-
marking "HOG," which led to several protracted but ultimately
unsuccessful lawsuits with independent repair shops and Harley
customizers who had been using the term for years.

The imagery of the outsider and the dissident outcast dove-
tailed perfectly with that of the Harley-Davidson customer, who
considered himself a defender of the faith. At the very core of this
mind-set were the Hells Angels, the ultimate outsiders and the truly
anointed. While it was impossible for a reputable, old-line company
beholden to Wall Street bankers for its very existence to openly
cozy up to a gang of grubby outlaws, Harley-Davidson masterfully
mixed the bad-guy image of the biker gangs with that of the independent, free-thinking, patriotic American cowboy, unfettered by
convention yet totally loyal to the nation's core traditions.

Perhaps the first openly commercial attempt to connect with the outlaws had come in 1980, with the introduction of the FXDB Sturgis model, yet another artful rehash of existing bits and pieces (with the exception of a new belt drive developed with Gates Rubber Corporation that was to become standard issue on most Harley models). Developed by a talented young engineer named Erik Buell in company with Willie G. Davidson, marketing director Clyde Fessler, and racing boss Dick O'Brien (this quartet was the major creative force within the company during its revival), the Sturgis was named for perhaps the rowdiest motorcycle rally of them all. The Black Hills town of Sturgis, South Dakota (population five thousand), is synonymous with bad-ass biker conclaves. Since its prewar beginnings as a simple weekend cookout and rally, Sturgis had grown by the 1980s into an annual blowout for biker gangs from around the nation. The outlaw clans swarmed into the town each summer to fight each other, ogle their mamas in wet T-shirt contests, drink themselves goofy, and consume enough drugs to render the entire population of a small city insensate for a decade. Sturgis was the real thing, a gathering of truly righteous brothers, not some faux dress-up party where bozos and wanna-bes played games. For decades it had retained its purity, attracting perhaps two to three thousand legitimate bikers. In later years that number would swell twentyfold, as the biker lifestyle entered the mainstream and began to attract the trend surfers. But when Davidson and company decided to reach out to the pure souls with the Sturgis model, it was a supremely ballsy move, as if Colt had created a Dillinger or Ford had introduced a sedan named the Bonnie and Clyde. With the FXDB Sturgis, the company openly acknowledged its roots in the biker culture. Surely previous models introduced in the late 1970s, like the FSX Low Rider and the FXEF Fat Boy, had paid homage to the custom motorcycle trend and thereby given a casual nod to the bikers, but the ominous orange-and-black Sturgis, along with its sister ship, the FXWG Wide Glide (a chopper-style machine), signaled a sea change in corporate philosophy. This might best be summed up by the old saw "If you can't beat 'em, join 'em."

The corporation was slowly finding itself during a period when Reaganism was reviving the nation's low self-esteem. While its motorcycle production slowly recovered, thanks to brighter, ballsier models and a restructuring of the manufacturing process based in part on the Japanese model, Harley-Davidson probed ways to expand its marketing base and to thereby blunt Wall Street criticism that it was a one-note Charlie, capable of building only big, unwieldy motorcycles. Several stabs were taken at producing a small, two-seat, three-wheel sports tricycle in the mode of the English Morgan, a three-wheeler built, in various forms, from 1910 to the advent of World War II. Powered by a twin-cylinder British motorcycle engine mounted in the front, the little Morgan provided cheap, sporty transport for Englishmen interested in sidestepping the high taxes levied on four-wheeled vehicles. This same theme was examined by Harley-Davidson in the early 1980s in concert with a Detroit specialty design firm called Cars and Concepts. The project was canceled for funding reasons (although the company briefly marketed a California-built three-wheeler called the Tri-Hawk powered by a small Citroën automobile engine). A former Cars and Concepts employee — now a vice president of Chrysler Corporation — recalls the wild contrast between a pair of Harley-Davidson executives. "When Vaughn Beals showed up at our factory, he was the epitome of corporate elegance: perfectly groomed, three-piece suit, the works. But then Willie G. appeared, looking like a hard-core biker, with the beard, the Levi's, and the leather jacket. Our receptionists were scared to let him in the lobby."

The epicenter of the Harley-Davidson mystique: Sturgis's Main Street at the height of the festivities. (Mark Langello)

Clearly not all Harley-Davidson enthusiasts are outlaws. (Brock Yates)

A classic example of the aesthetics and craftsmanship embodied in a Harley-Davidson custom — one of hundreds lining Sturgis's Main Street. (Brock Yates)

A female Harley-Davidson loyalist tries on for her husband a new set of chaps that she has selected in one of the many makeshift boutiques set up on Sturgis's Main Street during Bike Week. (Brock Yates)

RUBs or the real thing? A pair of True Believers cruise at Sturgis. Note the beeper on the belt of the rearward rider. (Brock Yates)

International publishing executive Masahiro Ishibashi astride his elaborately customized Harley-Davidson in the parking lot of the Tokyo Easyriders club. (Brock Yates)

Sundance: Motorcycle proprietor Takio Shibazaki astride his custom 1930s vintage Knucklehead replica outside his midtown Tokyo shop. (Brock Yates)

Kiminobu Kurokawa, one of the editors of Japan's *Hot Bike* magazine, rejects the home-grown products in favor of his much-modified Harley Davidson. (Brock Yates)

American Andy Sitton (seated) and Singapore Harley-Davidson manager Richard Park (center) endure egregious government regulations and controls to ride, sell, and service their rare and expensive imports from Milwaukee. (Brock Yates)

A new Heritage Softail sits proudly among the clutter of merchandise in Athens's crowded, madcap Monastiraki thieves' market.

(Brock Yates)

Custom Harley-Davidsons are seen worldwide. This one was found sitting in Vince Vito's Harley-Davidson dealership in Nice, France. (Brock Yates)

Stephen Peroutka (left) and Bobo Faehndrich run Bobo's Chopper Corner in Munich, much like hundreds of Harley-Davidson dealerships in the United States. (Brock Yates)

Only in America? Not quite. These Harley-Davidson loyalists were sighted on a busy Italian autostrada heading toward Milan on a cool spring night. (Brock Yates)

The prototypical Harley rider. Punkers, preppies, and pretty boys need not apply.

(Mark Langello)

Led by the likes of Davidson, the company was now exploiting its real persona. Corporate executives, including Beals, Bleustein, and others, began making regular appearances among the great unwashed, riding in HOG rallies, hanging out at the major biker gatherings at Laconia, Daytona Beach, and Sturgis, and working hard to upgrade and modernize the dealer outlets and the product line. "The eagle" was truly beginning to fly alone, energizing owners who had long felt isolated and ignored, not only by the world in general, but by the company that produced the very source of their identity. The world was shocked by the power and energy of these enthusiasts, rising as they did out of seamy suburbs and working-class neighborhoods to trumpet the pride inherent in the awakening giant. Honda, like other Japanese manufacturers, tried to respond, organizing a HOG-like owner group, but to no avail. Like most Japanese products, Honda motorcycles offered perfect function but no passion.

It might be speculated that most popular trends begin either at the top of the social order or at the bottom, but never in the middle. Foreign cars, Scandinavian furniture, organic foods and other health fads, for example, began among the affluent. Conversely, rock 'n' roll, country-and-western music, pickup trucks, Mexican food, and ghetto fashions were first popularized among the proletariat. At the very bottom were the most dispossessed of them all, the biker gangs, who formed the nexus of the new Harley-Davidson religion, an imagery so intensely vivid that it defied imitation by anyone else, much less a Japanese rival.

Observes Bob Bitchin about the mind-set of the day:

Sure, the rice rockets were perfect. They were faster than the fastest Harley and they ran all day. But believe it or not, the fact that Harleys broke a lot was an asset. You'd be parked at the side of the road, working on a busted chain or bad coil, and sure enough, another biker would stop and help. You'd meet all kinds of good friends that way. It was a brotherhood built around a machine that wasn't perfect, just like the people who rode them.

Reviled by the establishment and the subject of contempt from the riders of superior Japanese motorcycles, the Harley-Davidson underclass, fiercely proud as only the socially outcast can be, began to sense a new prominence. The keepers of the true faith, the marginalized cultists, had never flagged in their loyalty to the marque despite the best efforts of the corporate types during the AMF years to sanitize the image and reach out to mainstream riders. This did not work, in the main because Harley-Davidson ownership demanded a great commitment to the quirky machine and an empathy with the lifestyle surrounding it. It was not enough in the 1960s and 1970s to merely ride a hog. There was more to it, a mystique involving the essence of the motorcycle and the outsider image it embodied. The complexity and orneriness of the machine were components of its appeal. The ability to tear it down like an infantryman fieldstripping his M16 marked one's passage into the brotherhood. A hands-on relationship with a Harley-Davidson established one as a true believer, and the more basic the relationship, the deeper the involvement in the lifestyle. To the pure outlaw biker—the paradigm of the entire phenomenon — his Harley-Davidson was his single most important possession, much like a cowboy's horse. He bridged Robert Pirsig's gap between the classical and the romantic, thereby establishing an existential connection between himself and his Harley that defies description. The mind-set is perhaps best expressed by a saying often found on patches worn by hard-core bikers: "If I have to explain, don't bother asking."

Because breakdowns, oil leaks, chain ruptures, electrical failures, bearing burnouts, leaky head gaskets, fried valves, and other roadside emergencies were not only accepted but perversely desired as tests of skill and resourcefulness, old-line bikers viewed the introduction of the Evolution engine in 1983 with limited enthusiasm. To be sure, it retained the classic Harley-Davidson forty-five-degree V-twin layout and its ancient, oddball firing order with its lumpy, guttural exhaust bark. But its enhanced sophistication in design and computerized ignition were viewed by the hard core as a betrayal of the Harley engine's essential purity. Worse yet, it opened the door to even more tyros and wanna-bes with no mechanical knowledge who could now elbow into the scene. Like it or not, the new Evolution was a smoother, more reliable variation on the old Harley theme, and it surely contributed to the boom that was to follow. But in many ways it marked the end of the outlaws who had created the mystique in the first place. Had they had their way, all Harley-Davidsons would be Panheads and Shovelheads with kick starters and elemental coil and condenser ignitions that demand constant attention. The arrival of smooth-edged technical perfection would in the end lead to their co-option by the interlopers — the hated and ridiculed RUBs, or "Rich Urban Bikers" — and the real bikers' marginalization, much as barbed wire had doomed the open-range cowpoke.

The $15 million expended by the cash-strapped company to develop the Evolution engine was well spent. It was a vast improvement, offering better cooling, more power (by 15 percent — or about fifty-five horsepower, although the company never releases horsepower figures). The FXRS Sport Glide and other models with the new engine were well received by the motorcycle press, although critics noted that the bulk of the new cruisers was edging past 700 pounds.

In a purely isolated business sense, it can be claimed that such advances as the new engine in updated models manufactured and marketed by a management team in tune with late-industrial age techniques were the keys to Harley-Davidson's recovery. Additional credit might be given to the Reagan administration's tariff on large Japanese motorcycles and to the infusion of cash by Citicorp. But all that might have been irrelevant had not the time frame centered on the madcap 1980s. It was then that Michael Milken, Ivan Boesky, and others discovered the wonders of junk bonds, and Reagan's Rambo-like strikes at Libya and Grenada energized a lethargic and moribund public. The endemic American mythology embodied in the dime novels and the great West, built on themes of resolve and independent thinking, gained new credibility, inspired by the old actor in the White House.

Reagan's parallels with Teddy Roosevelt in terms of public policy are limited, but his often bombastic style of governance was similar to that of the fabled Rough Rider. And what better example of American virility than a roaring, home-built motorcycle that thumbed its nose at the effete and the postmodern world? It is hardly a coincidence that the revival of Harley-Davidson took place during the 1980s, when national morale was at its highest since the end of World War II and when the hand-wringing angst of the 1970s seemed forever discredited. With this new consciousness came the destruction of the youth culture within the world of motorcycling. Unlike the prototypical participants in other forms of recreation, the hard-core biker was no kid. The classic biker was called a graybeard; he was a grizzled road warrior, scarred and wind buffed, a flinty veteran whose wisdom about life's elemental values and Harley-Davidson motorcycles established him as the strongest, toughest lion in the pride. This veneration of age and seniority formed the heart and soul of the Harley culture. Age was a patina that could not be duplicated, and as the poseurs appeared, they were forced to value the seniors, as opposed to the agile, smart-ass youngsters who set the fashion in other trendy recreations like skiing, surfing, and rock climbing.

Even today, the prototypical biker, the essential personality who stands at the center of the entire Harley-Davidson world whether anybody likes it or not, is the patriarch of one of the powerful internationally based clubs like the Angels or the Pagans. He will be in his forties or fifties, perhaps even older, still longhaired and full bearded, his face sunbaked and furrowed, his gunfighter's eyes steady, his expression always taciturn and laconic. He carries some tattoos on his beefy, well-muscled body, but hardly at the level of the ridiculous decorations exhibited by body-art fetishists at various biker rallies. This graybeard, this grizzled veteran of the great cause, hazy and unformed as it might be, stands at the very pinnacle of the movement, both feared and respected by all participants as they desperately ape his fashions.

The notion of the four Harley-Davidson founders that their motorcycles would somehow rival the automobile as workaday, pillar-to-post transportation devices had long since been made obsolete, first by the sports riders, then by the outlaws. The Harley-Davidson was no longer a simple machine, but a transcendental totem serving a hazy culture of fantasized mobility, personal freedom, and control.

It is to the eternal credit of the progressives within the new Harley-Davidson management that they were to so masterfully exploit that odd marketing advantage. A gaping pothole on the road to recovery was avoided in 1985, when Citicorp threatened to withdraw financing and the company briefly faced the prospect of declaring Chapter Eleven bankruptcy. This dilemma was solved by representatives of Dean Witter Reynolds, who created a public stock offering that was made through the American Stock Exchange in early 1986. The ensuing capitalization permitted the purchase of Holiday Rambler recreation vehicles for $155 million, thereby silencing Wall Street critics who claimed that the company's singular production of motorcycles was too vertical for long-term growth. It was an arduous period of big-money tightroping as Beals attempted to shake off the musty remnants of the old culture while repositioning the company as the premier maker of heavyweight, cruiser-style motorcycles in the world.

With its debt restructured and its quality levels improving, the company steadily moved toward profit. The hours to assemble a motorcycle had been reduced by a third, with fewer defects. Its product line, in the main masterfully restyled machines built from existing components and the new engine, was increased from three basic models to nearly two dozen, ranging from the agile 883 Sportsters to the leviathan Super Glides intended to battle Honda in the big, over-the-road cruiser segment. Harley-Davidson's share of that lucrative market had risen from a low of 23 percent during the dark days of 1983 to more than 40 percent as the company entered 1987.

It was in March of that year that Harley-Davidson stunned the nation by calling for an early cancellation of the Japanese tariff. This announcement, essentially a public relations coup, served as a clarion call to American industry that a domestic manufacturer could survive the onslaught from the East, albeit with a little government help and some serious internal reforms. Suddenly the two-wheeled David had slain Goliath in a slugfest that had appeared impossible for him to win. The cowboys had again beaten the Indians, eliciting a spasm of pride that continues to this day. Harley-Davidson was celebrated from coast to coast on T-shirts braying such chauvinism as "Harley-Davidson: The last great American," and calling upon the Book of Isaiah to pronounce, "They shall mount up with wings as eagles." It was during this period that the company turned up the wick on merchandise sales, licensing nearly one hundred after-market firms to employ the black-and-orange corporate logo — an aspect of the business that would become an enormous profit center in its own right.

Two months later, in May of 1987, the Old Cowboy himself, Ronald Reagan, helicoptered up from Washington to the York, Pennsylvania, assembly plant to celebrate the tariff lifting. It was a shining moment, with legions of Harley-Davidson employees gathered around, many of them waving small American flags as Reagan said in his traditionally reassuring tones, "All of you . . . from the board room to the factory floor, were involved. So when I was told you needed a little more time to train, I said yes, kick on the engine, Harley, and turn on your thunder."

Drowning in the cheers and foot stomping, the Old Cowboy then ambled to a spanking new Sportster parked nearby and threw a leg over the saddle. As strobe lights pierced the gloom and television cameras chewed miles of tape, the president reached for the starter button and the big engine barked its presence. Smiling and waving at the throngs, he whispered to a Harley official standing nearby, "Hey, this thing won't take off on me, will it?"

The cheers were still echoing between York and Milwaukee on July 1 of that year, when the corporate elite — Beals, Bleustein, Willie G., etc. — punched the throttles on their new Harleys in front of the New York Harley-Davidson dealership in Long Island City, Queens. With them was a gaggle of Harley dealers and leather-clad enthusiasts, all of whom had gathered for a ride across the Fifty-ninth Street Bridge, down Second Avenue to Wall Street. With the big hogs rumbling and spitting, the caravan, led by New York cops on similar machines, rolled out. The Huns had arrived! They picked up riders as they rattled southbound on Second Avenue, and curious New Yorkers lined the sidewalks, gaping at the spectacle of monster motorcycles briefly displacing the fleets of yawping cabs and fuming buses.

Beals and his bad-boy legions eased to a stop in front of the hallowed New York Stock Exchange, where they were met by its president, John Phelan, who broke ancient precedent by formally welcoming Harley-Davidson into the stock exchange on the Wall Street sidewalk. On display in the lobby was a sparkling new Heritage Softail, but the actual anointing, the transference of Harley-Davidson trading from the American Exchange to the haughty precincts of the New York mart, took place outside, where hundreds of razor-cut, Armani-suited, gold-Rolexed, wing-tipped hotshot traders and brokers swore on the spot that to hell with environmentally correct ten-speeds and Range Rovers for ski trips to Sugar Bush, their next toy would be a god-awful, hellfire Harley-Davidson.

Step back, Harley-Davidson was on its way to the suburbs, where the thunder would reach ear-shattering levels.

PART THREE · THE GREAT REVIVAL

8 · THE CHARGE OF THE ROLEX BRIGADES

Shortly after Vaughn Beals's romping Harley exhaust stopped echoing through the concrete canyons of Wall Street, a lightbulb went on in the brains of several million male boomers. They were seized with a single, crazed goal: *"I've got to own a Harley-Davidson motorcycle!"* Everywhere, from Fairfield County to Fairfax, Virginia, from Marin County to Malibu, forty-two-year-old divorced orthodontists, pasty-faced bond traders, thin-armed producers, Woodstock-refugee, Madison Avenue account executives, Washington political flunkies, and tort lawyers who hadn't ridden anything since a ten-speed in Harvard Square, were shucking their Armanis, their Turnbulls and Assers and their clodhopper wing tips, their tasseled Cole Haans and their Guccis and suiting up in black leather jackets and engineer's boots. Off went the eighty-dollar Versace ties, to be replaced by real-guy workman's bandannas as they poured into Harley-Davidson stores, scooping up Heritage Softails and Road Kings and Electra Glides in a frenzy of classic status slavery.

Here were these multitudes of boomers who'd dodged Vietnam in graduate school protractions, who'd considered high-risk living to involve the fat content in pasta, who were haunted by the threats of asbestos, holes in the ozone layer, and the weak door latches in their minivans, suddenly pitching away their Perriers and their Birkenstocks and heading for the mad adventure of the open road. Freedom. Emancipation from middle-class guilt. Shredding convention! By God, here come the yuppie outlaws!

By 1990, the whole complexion of the Harley-Davidson market had been radically altered by this surge of new-wave buyers. The traditional Harley set — the longtime loyalists, the HOG members, the fatso cruiser types, the Sportster customizers, and the mandarins of the whole movement, the outlaw bikers — were being elbowed aside as the grand old machine became a favorite of upscale trendies, whom the true believers denounced as RUBs, or Rubies, which stood for "Rich Urban Bikers." Other fringe players appeared, to be described by some purists as Sewers ("Suburban Weekend Riders"), Riots ("Retired Idiots on Tour"), Ahabs ("Aspiring Hard-ass Bikers"), Bastards ("Bought a Sportster, Therefore a Radical Dude"), Igloos ("I Got the Look, Will Own One Soon"), and Hoots ("Have One Ordered; True Story").

Slowly, the Harley-Davidson customer base was splintering into widely diverse groups. In addition to the newcomers, who had spiked the demographics upward (from 1983 to 1991, personal household income for the big cruiser customers jumped from $35,700 to $67,000, and the percentage of college graduates more than doubled), the middle ground was occupied by the established, longtime HOG members, the workaday stiffs, family guys, and decent folk who centered their social agenda around the rallies, weekend rides, cookouts, endless charity runs, and other organizational events energized by the same internal political machinations as those of any social organization. Beyond them lay thousands of even more casual enthusiasts, the weekend wannabes, the collectors and restorers of classic Harley-Davidsons, and those attracted to the machines as pieces of kinetic art. On the outer fringes were the Christians and the Antichrists: the outlaw bands — the Hells Angels, Satan's Slaves, Pagans, etc. — on one side, countered by religious riders prowling the highways for converts under the colors of the Christian Motorcyclists Association, the Tribe of Judah Motorcycle Ministries, Bikers for Christ, Christ's Disciples, Heaven's Saints, and the Gospel Riders on the other side. Based primarily in the hard-shell Bible Belt of the South, the religious riders operated in a parallel universe from that of the outlaws, curiously bound to them by a single icon.

While a vast percentage of Harley-Davidson customers (96 to 98 percent, depending on the model), were males, women played roles as more than baubles ornamentally perched on the rear seat. The best-known group was San Francisco's Dykes on Bikes, a leather-tough collection of butch riders who were a local attraction in that vast theater of the absurd known as San Francisco. Eastern counterparts were New York's Sirens and Boston's Moving Violations, both lesbian riding clubs formed up to advance the cause of their members' lifestyle in such outré events as Manhattan's Gay Pride parade. Beyond them, literally thousands of straight young women took to Harleys, learning to ride with the best of men and even engaging in road racing and flat-track competition.

As a spin-off of HOG, the company formed the Ladies of Harley, with a membership of about thirty thousand. It was by far the largest and most active of the female organizations, to be joined by such international clubs as Women on Wheels and Women in the Wind. Smaller regional groups included the Missouri-based JUGGS (Just Us Girls Gettin' Scooters), Leather and Lace, Canada's Medusa's Maidens, and the all-black Ebony Queens of Flint, Michigan, to name but a few of the more than twenty all-female riding clubs. One magazine, *American Woman Motorscene*, is devoted to female riders, although it deals with rival brands, including BMW and the big four Japanese. Ann Ferrar's 1996 book, *Hear Me Roar: Women, Motorcycles, and the Rapture of the Road*, celebrated the riding exploits of female riders over the years, neatly bridging the gap between establishment feminism and the boy-toy sexuality implicit in the sensuous, leather-clad foxes who decorate the big bike rallies — especially aboard Harley-Davidsons — where raw sex openly mingles with the exhaust fumes.

But at the core of the whole scene, male and female, acting as a nugget of truth, lurks the image of the outlaws. In terms of style and behavior, the ringmasters remain the Angels and their rivals. They govern the fashions, the attitude, and the public demeanor of the Harley-Davidson mind-set. Leather and denim, tattoos — fake or real — headbands, beards, and mustaches are the amulets of membership, regardless of the affiliation. "Colors" — the sacred embroidered brand of the true outlaw over which deadly battles have often been fought — are now co-opted by pallid weekenders, who feebly try to emulate the righteous brothers of the true faith. But while imitation colors are employed by all manner of Harley-Davidson enthusiast groups, they remain potent symbols among the outlaws. Throughout the nation, bars, topless clubs, dealerships, custom shops, accessory stores, etc., exhibit signs proclaiming "No Colors." This ban is intended to prevent ugly battles that are bound to erupt when rival members meet on neutral turf — especially turf involving women, booze, and Harley-Davidsons. Such is the rigid, deadly serious convention surrounding these badges of membership, traceable back to the origins of the movement in the early 1950s.

The outlaw clubs, formed around rigid codes and elemental ethics centered on group loyalty and survival, are dadaists, committed not only to their intensely unconventional lifestyle of menace and outrage, but to a certain exhibitionism designed to shock and infuriate the squares. A sense of showmanship permeates all Harley-Davidson riders, who assume an attitude of bloated potence and importance embodied in the motorcycle itself. The Harley rider, be he a Pagan member, a Gospel Rider, or a costumed RUB, becomes something of a showman once on board. The furious rattle of his exhaust is at the heart of it, an ingredient so essential to the mystique that in the mid-1990s the company began proceedings to trademark the unique cadenced thump of their world-famous engines.

Regardless of their particular affiliation within the cult, Harley riders radiate an authority beyond their normal demeanor when suited up and aboard their bikes. Noisily costumed, they become public theater, demanding attention as they sweep down the highway, either in the two-by-two cavalry formation adopted by the outlaws in the early fifties, or in the single, lone-rider style. Garbed in leather, they stomp into barrooms in ten-league boots, exuding potency and peril rooted in the ancient perceived imagery of Hollister.

The mind-set of the Harley-Davidson rider was examined by two young Oregon professors named John Schouten and James

McAlexander, who purchased Harleys and spent several years touring and carousing with various biker types. Their study, published
in the June 1995 issue of *Journal of Consumer Research*, is an intense examination of the Harley-Davidson experience. They observed that "riding a Harley can be regarded as performing for an
audience," and noted the extent to which riders "seek, monitor and
respond to the audience."

Like all researchers studying the phenomenon, Schouten, an
assistant professor of marketing at the University of Oregon, and
McAlexander, who holds a similar position at Oregon State University, zeroed in on the heart of the culture, the annual Black Hills
Motorcycle Classic at Sturgis, South Dakota. Here the subcult is in
full bloom, a wooly Woodstock on wheels with a patina and tradition unmatched in the world of pop culture. The great gathering,
known simply as "Sturgis," traces its roots to the summer of 1938,
when the local Indian motorcycle dealer, J. C. "Pappy" Hoel, and
his wife, Pearl, prompted a local motorcycle club, the Jackpine
Gypsies, to organize a two-day rally and race for area enthusiasts. It
was not unlike hundreds of similar events being held around the
nation, and any notion of its gaining national prominence, based on
the skimpy, Depression-worn population around Sturgis, Dead-
wood, and Rapid City, never entered the Hoels' minds. For the first
few years, the event consisted of little more than innocent camping
in Pappy and Pearl's Junction Street backyard, some rides through
the stunning Black Hills, and informal races at the local horse
track.

Somehow, for reasons lost to history and the booze-addled
brains of the oldest bikers, Sturgis became a magnet for hard-core
outlaws in the middle 1950s. The clubs were coalescing, first in California, then in the smoky industrial towns of the Northeast. Stur-

gis, being roughly in the center of the nation (Los Angeles, 1,363 miles; New York, 1,722 miles), began to serve as a common meeting ground each August, much as the fertile valleys of Colorado along the Green River served as the sites of annual blowouts for the legendary mountain men trappers 150 years earlier.

Ray Allen Billington, the noted western historian, describes the mountain men arriving at the rendezvous, "yelling like demons . . . then the flasks were tapped. . . . Eventually both the alcohol and the Mountain Men were exhausted. Those who had gambled away their guns and horses purged the next year's catch for new supplies, and all stumbled away into the wilderness, the year's earnings squandered in a few days of barbaric dissipation." So too for Sturgis, where the toughest of the bikers, the legitimate bearers of the title, bear a notable resemblance to their forebears. David Mann, a Kansas City–born artist laureate of the movement, has produced a body of romantic paintings depicting grizzled bikers, always heavily bearded, always graying and grim faced, riding across the western landscape on their high-barred choppers, with the ghostlike images of mountain men, Sioux warriors, pony express riders, even buffalo, in spiritual company. Identification with the great western frontier and its wild, freebooting independence is never far from the bikers' self-perception. From it has arisen a certain note of self-pity and misplaced martyrdom, as if they, as the last generation of real Americans, are being herded into oblivion as surely as the railroad magnates, the hustle-buck merchants, and the land grabbers crushed the mountain men. Like all fanatics, they revel not only in their uniqueness, but in their constant threat from the hated establishment. To their credit, they withstood the collapse of the sixties while their brief comrades-in-arms, the hippies and counterculturists, the poseur Marxists and Maoists, the Weathermen and the draft-card burners, silently and meekly dispersed to split-levels in the suburbs, only now to reappear, suited up in thousand-dollar leathers and custom Harleys, on Sturgis's exhaust-shrouded Main Street.

The pilgrimage to this nondescript mecca, a featureless burg of five thousand souls surrounded by craggy, pine-topped ridges and scrubby open range, began to gain national prominence in the 1960s, as the biker movement broke away from the counterculture and formed its own core identity. Every August, Sturgis's Main Street was slowly taken over by the bikers, who turned it into a long parking lot for hard-ridden choppers and Harley customs. The true believers spread out into campgrounds on the edge of town and drank, screwed, and freaked out on every chemical known to man while staging informal races and tours on local roads. It was hard partying, and veteran local cops recall knifings, shootings, and bloody slugfests between various gangs as they dueled over women, territory, and arcane slights. Sturgis was home base, hallowed ground; nirvana for the anointed. For the entire week of the rally, automobiles — called "cages" or "coffins" by the righteous brothers — were ruled off Sturgis's downtown streets. The "citizens" — biker jargon for real-world residents — began to leave Sturgis for the week of the festivities, many of them renting their Main Street businesses and even their homes to be transformed into temporary Harley accessory shops, tattoo parlors, and T-shirt emporiums.

For much of August the interstates of Wyoming and the Dakotas swarmed with Harleys, most of them snorting choppers ridden by authentic bikers, the One Percenters, their bedrolls and sometimes their old ladies (riding "sissy") mounted behind them. Sturgis was the real thing, legitimized and commercialized by the appearance of corporate types like Willie G. Davidson and the use of the Sturgis name for the all-black (with orange-and-chrome trim), belt-drive FXDB in 1980. This machine flirted with the chopper styling, as did the Wide Glide and the earlier Low Rider and Fat Boy, long favored by the outlaw bikers. The Sturgis served as open acknowledgment by the company that customizers outside the realm of the establishment had stolen the march in exploiting motorcycle trends and tastes. But with fame came compromise and co-option by the new breed of faux bikers, the hated and reviled RUBs, who elbowed onto the scene as shameless phonies, suiting up in leather and fake tattoos to role-play a faintly sadomasochistic lifestyle that in reality terrified and revolted them.

By the time Sturgis celebrated its fiftieth anniversary in August 1988, the gathering had reached immense proportions, attracting perhaps a quarter-million bikers, RUBs, and trendsurfers automatically lured to major happenings. The clash of cultures seemed to set everyone off balance, and by the time the merchants, homeowners, and Meade County ranchers reoccupied their little city, a melee outside a bar called Gunner's had left two members of the Sons of Silence club stabbed and an Outlaw club member shot. An Australian biker, crazed on drugs, had attacked people and motorcycles with a knife before being gunned down by police. He was one of nine celebrants to return home in boxes in 1988. The rest, save one who suffocated in a tent, died in the more gruesome of the 113 reported traffic accidents that injured another 78 riders. A total of 202 were jailed for drunk riding, and 73 more were charged with illegal drug possession.

Tamer bikers who arrived in recent years have significantly diminished the Sturgis street action. It has become more a massive fashion show than a legitimate biker conclave. For every One Percenter in Sturgis, for every Hells Angel, Pagan, Satan's Sinner, or ancient, graybeard Booze Fighter, there are a hundred poseurs vamping and styling up and down Main Street on their $30,000 Arlen Ness–inspired customs, towing their incredible blond ladies in show-me-some-tits leather and glue-on tattoos. They shamelessly imitate the outlaw bikers, laments Bob Bitchin, who has left the life to publish a monthly magazine on long-range sailboat cruising. "Hell, the real bikers are blue-collar guys, working day jobs and scrimping to keep their scooters running. They can't afford a new Harley and all the fancy stuff that goes with it. Now the chrome has replaced the grease." The Black Hills Motorcycle Classic has become a multimillion-dollar annual tourism event for the entire area. The traditional punch-outs, shoot-ups, and drunken campground blasts remain in small measure, as do members of the Jackpine Gypsies, who still help organize the monster event. But both have taken a subordinate role to the legions of vendors who rent the stores on Main Street to hustle engine parts, chrome bits, custom seats, knives, silver jewelry, leathers, tattoos, Nazi and devil-worship symbols, and enough T-shirts to clothe the entire population of South Dakota for the next ten generations. For every shirt touting Sturgis and the glories of Harley-Davidson, dozens can be found carrying a variety of messages designed to infuriate straights. This is a social structure where the sexes are identified on the most basic terms and women serve only as baubles, in total defiance of conventional feminist doctrine and current political correctness. Among the T-shirts to be found on parade at Sturgis are such unliberated tweakers as "Never trust anything that bleeds for five days and doesn't die," "My other toy has tits," "Rape: The ultimate compliment," and "I'd rather see my sister in a whorehouse than my brother on a Honda." Others celebrate the over-the-top perception of the biker's life by proclaiming, "If it can't kill you, it ain't sport," and "If you're not living on the edge, you're taking up too much space." The balls-out partying at Sturgis and within the biker world in general is affirmed by such advertisements as "Party till you puke," "Ride naked," "I've spent 90% of my life chasing fast bikes, hot women and good parties. The other 10% was wasted," and "Smoke, drink, fuck and ride." The elemental class warfare embodied by the cult is expressed by such messages as "Places to go, people to annoy," "Be unpredictable, be spontaneous, be outrageous, be American," "Loud and proud," and, simply, "Eat the rich."

The latter is surely a snide reference to the swarms of RUBs who arrive at Sturgis (and Daytona and the third great conclave held annually in Laconia, New Hampshire) on Harleys that have been trailered to the edge of town and then ridden into the festivities. For the authentic bikers, who have thrashed their way to South Dakota from tough towns like San Pedro and Pittsburgh, the notion of rich guys loading up their pristine, chrome-embellished customs in Wells Cargo and Pace American trailers and hauling them behind expensive RVs to Sturgis borders on blasphemy. But as the nineties unfolded, the Harley-Davidson craze had multiplied the RUBs and the Rolex riders a hundredfold, driving sales past the 150,000 mark and recapturing over half the big cruiser market from the Japanese — while marginalizing the authentic possessors of the holy grail.

Slowly, the old debauches at traditional campgrounds like Buffalo Chip, Bull Dog, Day's End, and Hog Heaven, the sheer, hellfire good times, gave way to slickly organized tours to scenic spots like Devils Tower and Mount Rushmore, concerts featuring big-name acts like Steppenwolf, and seamless, expensively produced manufacturers shows and expos.

Sturgis's Main Street, mobbed with thousands of motorcycles, almost all of which are Harleys, has become a French Quarter in leather, where seminaked broads and fake outlaws from Beverly Hills posture for the gaping throngs. Mad, dadaist variations of leather and pierced and tattooed bodies replace the dim traditions of freewheeling outlaw blowouts at places like Hollister and Laconia as hollow paraders play a superficial weekend game. Yet the core of the Harley culture still stands, the tiny, embattled, eternally imitated but essentially marginalized Hells Angels.

Even those who tried to maintain the essence of the lifestyle have given way to temptation. *Easyriders*, the once-pure bible of the biker, has grown fat and four-colored, with flashy nudes as professionally air-brushed as those in *Playboy* sprawled across fifty-thousand-dollar custom Harleys. Its creator, Keith Ball, and friend Joe Teresi (a Minnesota native and former biker), are rich men, presiding over an empire of eleven magazines, including the PG-rated *VQ*, and nearly forty franchised Easyriders emporiums, featuring food, rock 'n' roll, and their own line of biker clothing that rivals that of Harley-Davidson in style and expense.

While the Easyriders leadership operates outside the company orbit, the Harley-Davidson serves as the centerpiece of their business. They are not authorized dealers, nor are they totally accepted, selling as they do rival lines of clothing and accessories as well as Harley-Davidson clones like the U.S.-built Big Dog and the Titan. Both are expensive V-twin knockoffs of the mother machine, two of several being built in the U.S.A. to serve the growing market. Nonetheless, the booming Easyriders outlets, reaching from Tokyo to Helsinki, play a critical supporting role in expanding and exploiting the Harley-Davidson mystique. In reflecting on the twenty-fifth birthday of *Easyriders*, magazine contributor Tex Campbell mused about the success of a publication "devoted to men, women and machines the average citizen regarded with fear and loathing . . . identifying with loners and outcasts and celebrating sex and drugs as undeniable facts of life . . . while tirelessly fighting the misguided and malign efforts of bureaucrats, eggheads, candyasses and do-gooders to erode personal freedoms." Campbell's defense of out-law motorcycles aside, there is no debating that Ball, Teresi, and company touched the mother lode of American motorcycling. All of the palliative advertising and promotion, all of the woozy talk about the pure fun of it all notwithstanding, riding a motorcycle — whether for a Harley-Davidson bagger with his old lady perched on the back, her boobs waving in the wind, or a nineteen-year-old rich kid from Darien on his tiny, high-winding Kawasaki rice burner — is haul-ass adventure, laden with danger and smacking of dark sin. Schouten and McAlexander describe some of it as "a transcenden-tal departure from the mundane," and sociologist Norman Land-quist wrote in 1987 that riding a Harley-Davidson is a modern-day equivalent of the "shamanic experience of magical flight." The om-nipresence of swastikas, iron crosses, and symbols of devil wor-ship like death's heads and occult amulets on bikers' costumes is in part rooted in a perverse amusement gained in outraging the straights, but the darker, cultic aspects of the Antichrist are never far below the surface.

Much has been done to sanitize the sport for public consump-tion, but at the core lies the renegade lifestyle. It is the biker who forms the bedrock, the base element, of this subculture from which radiates the sense of uniqueness that Ball, Teresi, and others so art-fully tap. Harley-Davidson executives hated them and their tawdry rags for nearly two decades, refusing to accept the reality that *Easyriders* was speaking to the true believers. It was only after Willie G. Davidson and others within the company reached out to this crowd of Campbell's "loners and outcasts" in arm's-length company with Ball and Teresi that they were co-opted into a well-structured commercial market.

By the mid-1990s, millions were in the game, deluding themselves that they were freethinkers because they chose black leather costumes, mouthed tough-guy banalities and slogans, rode Harleys, and hung out at scenes like Sturgis and Daytona Beach. Like the hippies and other subcults before them — the beats and the bohemians — they enslaved themselves in a mindless cult with the same insufferable rules of conformity as the so-called straight society they so feverishly denounced. In 1996, humorist Dave Barry mused about Harley riders being "rebels, lone wolves, guys who do it Their Way, guys who do not follow the crowd. You can tell because they were wearing the same jeans, jackets, boots, bandannas, sunglasses, belt buckles, tattoos and (presumably) underwear worn by roughly 28 million other lone wolf Harley guys." Based on Barry's trenchant observations, the ultimate statement of independence and a fuck-the-world attitude might be for the Hells Angels or any other bad-ass bikers to appear on Sturgis's Main Street wearing Armani suits. What better way to shuck the aged conventions that imprison free souls? Sadly, such contradictions escape true believers, and outlaws are said to content themselves with exhibitions of prodigious drug consumption, employing such mind-blowing concoctions as "speedshakes" (speed and LSD brewed up in Thunderbird wine) and party games like "the grab bag," wherein players grab a fistful of pills — reds, yellowjackets, mescaline, uppers, downers, tranks (tranquilizers), and acid — and slug them down with a beer chaser. A wobbly ride on their scooters with a pack of equally messed-up pals might follow. As with all outrider cults, outraging and infuriating the straight establishment is part of the fun. Example: A gaggle of bikers has been known to hang out in a local bar waiting for proper citizens, preferably women, to stroll by. Two of the scruffiest clubbers then rush outside to engage in hopelessly sloppy French kisses. But seldom, unless openly challenged by a bellicose "citizen," do the Angels or members of any other biker club assault anyone outside their immediate rivals. While imposing and fearsome to the general public, motorcycle club members pose little or no threat to those who do not challenge them directly. They operate in a separate universe based on different, more intense codes. Average folks are in no more danger around them than they might be in a Las Vegas casino with mob connections or in a Chinese restaurant owned by a Far Eastern drug cartel.

Regardless of the elemental role the Harley-Davidson plays in outlaw biker culture, it might be suggested that the machine wins its inclusion among the cultists by default. After all, it is the only established, well-known American-made motorcycle, and traditionally patriotic bikers, many of them disenfranchised veterans, have been left with no choice but to embrace the Harley. Indians, gone from the marketplace since 1953, are still accepted among the clans, but their availability is nil, and therefore the Harley is the sole choice. It is in the bylaws of several of the larger and more notorious outlaw clubs that ownership of a Harley-Davidson of more than 750 cc (which includes virtually all American-made Harleys) is required for members in good standing. Can reverence for its hairy exhaust sound, its primeval mechanics, and its tradition-bound image be traced to the early gangs of the late forties, or did it arrive as an afterthought? The use of a Triumph by Brando in *The Wild One* and the presence of numerous English motorcycles at Hollister and other early biker gatherings imply the latter. Still, after nearly a hundred years, it persists as an honest machine — albeit in a different state of reality than that envisioned by the four founders.

At its core it is simple, blunt, and guileless; open and uncomplicated, like the nation that produces and embraces it. With its ancient, molar-shaking engine and its unseemly bulk, it is, compared to the best of the Japanese bikes, a technological joke. Its giant power plant generates a paltry fifty-two to fifty-five horsepower, while some Japanese bikes, with half the displacement, belch out twice that much with ease. Until recently, when the factory began building special racing machines and designer Erik Buell's neat little Harley-Davidson subsidiary began offering lightweight, high-performance road-racing bikes in the European and Japanese mode, Harleys were a travesty in international competition, restricted to American dirt tracks, where AMA rules gave them de facto exclusivity. At Daytona Beach, Harleys until recently were so outclassed that they had to be given a special race — to be cheered by the true believers in a rowdy grandstand on the back straight of the Daytona International Speedway called Hog Heaven. But so what? Speed is no more an element in the Harley's appeal than the paint content of a Rembrandt or Michael Jordan's shoe size. The Harley-Davidson transcends its mechanical parts and capabilities, becoming a strangely organic component of its owner's life.

This aliveness is not present in any other machine. Even the most fanatic BMW motorcycle enthusiast — in a sense as devoted as his Harley counterparts — or the Porsche or Ferrari car nut, does not perceive his machine to be anything more than a technological wonder worthy of endless surgical ministrations. A living, breathing thing? Never. But in the minds of many Harley-Davidson owners, this device lives and breathes, operating with the same haughty independence as a cowboy's horse. For the most part it is loyal and docile, but, at its own whim, it can be cranky and even lethally treacherous. It is a friend that demands respect.

Sophisticated foreigners are perpetually confused by this purely American combination: open gregariousness and a bumpkinish naïveté that conceal an inner toughness, resolve, and even ruthlessness. Americans, like their only real motorcycle, are infinitely adaptable, able to make and remake themselves according to immediate demands. The poor Japanese, geniuses at production and mechanical nuance but straitjacketed culturally, cannot compete on this level. It borders on the hilarious to watch them, in a mad game of technological pyrotechnics, trying to build better Harley-Davidsons, all the while missing the point.

Stephen E. Ambrose, in his wonderful examination of the American GI in the European theater during World War II titled *Citizen Soldiers*, notes that the Wehrmacht had better tanks and small arms than the Americans and an elite force of battlefield-trained noncoms and junior officers facing farm boys and fresh-faced city kids. Yet these striplings, bogged down behind Normandy's hedgerows, improvised in the heat of battle a ground-to-air communications linkup that created fiendishly complex and effective close-in air bombardments and troop strafings that had never occurred to the Germans during six years of war on three continents! A rigidity of culture unknown to the gum-chewing, irreverent, faintly anarchistic Yankees would be the ultimate downfall of the vaunted Wehrmacht, as it has been in so many tightly focused attacks on American interests of all kinds.

"The Japanese just don't understand Americans," says a respected motorcycle magazine editor (who asks for anonymity because the magazine he works for depends heavily on Japanese motorcycle manufacturer advertising).

They keep beating their heads against the wall, trying to figure out why this old slug of a Harley, which is bog slow, noisy, and has poor handling, keeps murdering them in the marketplace. You take a Harley out on a really difficult stretch of road, like California's Ortega Highway or over the Angeles Crest, and a Harley-Davidson is a nightmare compared to a quick, nimble Jap bike. But that's irrelevant. The average Harley biker, excluding the real hard-core guys that everybody tries to ape, is, excuse the expression, born to be *mild*. He's not a serious rider. Sure, he and his pals suit up every Sunday morning and ride up to the Rock Store [a favored restaurant on Mulholland Drive northwest of Los Angeles] or to Alice's Restaurant over in Woodside and slug down some eggs benedict and cappuccino and maybe get a look at Arnold Schwarzenegger or Sly Stallone or Mickey Rourke or some other Hollywood stud, but is he going to strap on a bedroll and haul six hundred miles a day to get to Sturgis? Not bloody likely.

To the RUB rider, his Harley-Davidson is a piece of jewelry, to be worn on special occasions, like a good suit or a Rolex. It makes a social statement, adding an element of macho to his otherwise safe and sterile life. This makes the Japanese crazy, because in their society technology is status. The guy with the hottest computer, the latest camera, the trickiest crotch-rocket or "zoomsplat," is king. To serve this need, the Hondas, Sonys, and Yamahas make the best stuff. If tomorrow God totally eliminated motorcycles from human consciousness, the day after Honda would be producing the world's most perfect refrigerators.

In the machine age, the Japanese are flawless makers of machines. But there is more to the equation. To watch the rider of a Japanese superbike is to see a linkage of human and machine. Hunched over the fuel tank, his face out of the airstream behind a tiny aerodynamic windscreen, he becomes a component of the motorcycle. He has subordinated himself to the machine. By contrast, the rider of a Harley-Davidson remains upright, sitting atop his steed as if he were riding a horse. He and his Harley remain separate entities, independent of each other, but interdependent in terms of the mission at hand.

It is this elevation of the individual over the machine that separates the Harley-Davidson rider from the rest. Constant of purpose for more than sixty years, since the seminal EL model was introduced, yet infinitely alterable to the owner's individual aesthetic needs, a Harley can be chopped and cobbed, painted and repainted, butchered and battered, Panheaded, Shovelheaded, sissy-barred, bagged and unbagged, chromed, dechromed, injected, raked, flaked, and air-brushed, but it remains a Harley-Davidson. This urge to modify and improvise is purely and totally American. The Harley-Davidson is as implicitly irreverent, churlish, impudent, imprudent, proud, audacious, subliminally sexual, and overtly lethal as that other great projection of the American persona, the Colt .45. It is not coincidental that among the most popular American offerings to populations around the world are the Harley-Davidson, the Zippo lighter, the Gibson guitar, the Stetson hat, and Justin cowboy boots. Couple those with even more universal American icons like Coca-Cola and Disney's characters, and you have a collection of *antiques*. Most date to the beginnings of the twentieth century, with the most recent — the Zippo and Disney's mice, et al. — relative newcomers from the early 1930s. Shuck all the Microsoft miracles, the wonder drugs, the Boeing 777s, the digitized Silicone Valley breakthroughs, and the Hollywood bonanzas of the hour, and the most enduring, most universal, most purely American exports are as aged and venerable as the unique national traits first identified by de Tocqueville nearly two hundred years ago.

By the middle 1990s, Harley-Davidson's image had come 180

degrees from the days it was considered at best a day laborer's Cadillac and at the worst a fiendish, apocalyptic horse of the new Mongol hordes. Gone were the days when that quintessential hippie psychopath, Charles Manson, preached to his pitiful little "family" that his great revolution would be led by legions of raging maniacs on Harleys. Gone too were the days when outlaw biker clubs like the Hells Angels were viewed simply as groups of wild degenerates seeking their own special version of the counterculture. Fame and Sonny Barger's brilliant manipulations of the press had forced them and their rival clubs into more desperate acts, both to maintain their reputation and to fuel ever-more exotic tastes for drugs, booze, weapons, and motorcycles. Some clubs became crime families, pure and simple, operating with a code of ethics as complex and perverse as the Mafia's. Drunken brawls and barroom slugfests with rival clubs gave way to sophisticated drug dealing, organized prostitution rings, hijacking, dealing in stolen Harleys and parts, and other felonies, often concealed behind legitimate saloon and strip club businesses. This expansion of their original scatological but irrelevant antics into the world of organized crime brought new riches and also the attention of serious law-enforcement agencies. Being essentially white male–dominated organizations (although black and Hispanic biker gangs exist and thrive in the ghettos), the biker clubs, like the Mafia, have been relatively easy to infiltrate and wiretap. The expansion of the clubs into big-time crime has been interdicted, not only by increased anticrime activities, but by the encroachment of new ethnic crime families — Jamaicans, Vietnamese, Cambodians, Russians, and Chinese — whose members are easily as ruthless and aggressive as the toughest Angel or Pagan. These forces, the law on one side, the new minority gangs on the other, tend to keep the biker gangs in check, forcing them overseas, especially into the Scandinavian countries, and into internecine warfare with their own kind. While strong at the core and suprisingly resilient, they have dropped out of the news as a major criminal element. Aside from local headlines generated by interclub shootings, riots, and murders, they remain little more than fashion prototypes for the new class of gentleman Harley riders. The Hells Angels and other mighty biker clubs can now be found at biker rallies like Sturgis and Laconia hawking T-shirts and other souvenir wares while doing their share to contribute to a unique aspect of the new biker culture, the charity ride.

When sociologists muse over why a thirty-eight-year-old bond trader from Greenwich will suit up on summer weekends like a semiliterate high-school dropout with a police record and hang out at the Marcus Dairy in Darien with what appears to be every Harley-Davidson rider east of the Mississippi, they often miss the point that there is a highly altruistic component to the entire movement. That is the charity ride, wherein all manner of biker organizations, including HOG chapters, Easyriders stores, the Bros club, and hundreds of Harley dealerships, organize annual rides to benefit all manner of needy causes. Over the years, millions of dollars have been generated by such nationally famous and celebrated efforts as the Love Ride, sponsored each November by Harley-Davidson of Glendale owner Oliver Shokouh to benefit the Muscular Dystrophy Association and involving almost 25,000 riders, or the Georgia-based Ride for Kids, a series of events staged to benefit the Pediatric Brain Tumor Foundation. The Memorial Day Rolling Thunder ride to Washington, D.C., honors Vietnam war dead and POW/MIAs, and such rides as the Christmas-season Toys for Tots ride organized by the Independent Bikers of Queens are duplicated hundreds of times over by riders (including BMW clubs and others) across the nation.

These rides are not crafty public-relations ploys to soften the image of the biker culture or a scheme conceived by Harley-Davidson's marketing department to sell more motorcycles, but sincere, grass-roots efforts intended to contribute to the public welfare. While good burghers everywhere still harbor the same kind of reflexive fear of bikers as they do for black teenagers in white neighborhoods, the image continues to soften, in part because many of their sons and daughters — the architects, the doctors, the psychiatrists, the lawyers — have expressed a desire to own a Harley-Davidson. They have no intention of going native and joining the Gypsy Jokers, but the sheer romance of the machine, its patina, its bellowing exhaust, its beckoning toward the open road, its aura of danger, and the faint chance it offers to recover the aromatic romance of the lost frontier, is difficult to resist.

Harley-Davidson has thundered out of the rundown back streets of Fontana into such mainstream locations as Manhattan's Avenue of the Americas, where the chichi Harley-Davidson Café sits within throwing distance of CBS's Black Rock headquarters, the Time Life building, and the New York Hilton. Opened in 1993 under license from the company to Motorcycle Equities, Inc., the Harley-Davidson Café instantly became a hangout for the local glitterati, who dined on ten-dollar designer hamburgers and purchased fifty-dollar souvenir sweatshirts from the boutique featuring all manner of licensed Harley-Davidson clothing and jewelry. There is serious RUB activity in status-enslaved Manhattan, the most culturally and geographically hostile location for personal mechanized transportation in North America. Yet any number of other bars and restaurants, including Hogs and Heifers, Red Rock West, and Amer-

ican Trash are must-stop destinations for show-offs who have discovered the Harley-Davidson to be the perfect social amulet for
frustrated alpha males. Barricaded on an island of concrete and
chained to a computer terminal for most of one's life, what better
way to express repressed maleness than to rumble out onto the
frontier (limited, sadly, to Gotham's great avenues and cross
streets) on a big-banger Harley? The success of the café, which on
weekends attracts the ultimate New York Rolex riders, prompted
MEI, Inc., to open a second operation in that ultimate showcase of
poseurs and nouveau show-offs, Las Vegas.

From nowhere thoroughfares like the main streets of Sturgis
and Daytona Beach and hard-ass beer joints like Gunner's and the
Boot Hill Saloon, to midtown Manhattan and Glitter Gulch. Truly,
the long ride of Harley-Davidson into the mainstream is over, and
perhaps the end of the great frontier is in sight.

9 · THE DAYTONA SYNDROME

They opened the drawbridges. By noon, Daytona Beach had become so clogged with motorcycles that city officials raised the three main spans over the Halifax River Intercoastal Waterway, thereby essentially cutting off what is touted as "The World's Most Famous Beach" from the mainland. Too many motorcycles. Too many thumping up and down the sandy expanses of the beach itself from the Ponce Inlet to the Granada Bridge at Ormond Beach. Too many cramming Main Street around the Boot Hill Saloon and Froggy's and the Easyriders store; too many in and around the vast Ocean Center and the Ocean Pier; too many on the main thoroughfares of Peninsula and A1A; too many crowding every parking lot, sidewalk, and alleyway, every motel and hotel driveway; too many in backyards, on front porches, in garages, basements, attics, and broom closets, to a point where the place was encrusted with motorcycles swarming over the beach town like mechanical locusts. There were choppers and baggers, Pans and Shovels, customs and Springers and Softails and Knuckles; every possible permutation of Harley-Davidson imaginable numbering — who knew? — perhaps five hundred thousand, overwhelming the place during that annual springtime fertility rite, beer blast, and nutball rider roundup known as "Bike Week."

With the beach (known locally as the "peninsula") temporarily cut off by the moatlike Halifax, the action simply swirled elsewhere, from Art's Place in DeLeon Springs and the Iron Horse and Jackson Hole saloons in Ormond Beach. To the south, there was the Ringside and the Shark Lounge and the Last Resort and the Squeeze Inn Pub planted among the sand dunes, the Palmettos and the scruffy condos and motels in South Daytona, while a short ride farther on were Sopotnick's Cabbage Patch and Gilly's Pub 44 in New Smyrna Beach.

In the city proper, out on International Speedway Boulevard, in the shadow of the enormous Daytona track complex, exhibitors, vendors, hustlers, and traveling bunco artists set up shop on every square inch of vacant property, transforming the town into a wacky thieves' market of motorcycle gadgetry. A few miles to the west toward De Land, carved out of the swampy scrub, lay the Volusia County Fairgrounds, where a swap meet blanketed several hundred acres with motorcycles and parts of every description. Another was held at the Daytona Flea Market, and a third, at local Stetson University's field house, was considered prime territory for collectors and restorers seeking rare bits for ancient Harleys and BMWs.

Perhaps well over three-quarters of the half-million or so bikers who jammed the interstates from Orlando to Jacksonville and over-

whelmed Daytona and Ormond Beaches were on Harleys. The
Japanese manufacturers, as well as the Italian Ducati firm, imported giant racing teams to contest for the top spot in the championship 200-mile race on the fabled speedway's high banks and
infield road course. Racing also took place on the dirt oval inside
the Daytona Municipal Stadium and on other area short tracks,
where the Harleys showed their muscle.

Like Sturgis, Daytona's annual Bike Week is a traditional event
that *demands* attendance, not only for serious bikers of all stripes
and intensities, but for manufacturers, who annually employ the
weeklong March event as a powerful tool to introduce new products at endless special events held at venues like Mark Martin's
Klassix Auto Museum on ISC (International Speedway Corporation) Boulevard and at the American Motorcycle Institute, the local
technical school devoted to training motorcycle mechanics. But it
is on the beach at the huge Ocean Center convention facility that
truly outré motorcycle styling can be seen. The Ocean Center Custom Show and the popular Rat's Hole counterpart held in its parking lot show off the prime efforts of the most famous customizers
and stylists, who each year offer up more and more amazing examples of kinetic art built around modified Harleys. It is the Harley
that forms the base, the Carrara marble, from which the master-
pieces are sculpted. The odd BMW or Honda might be seen in
wildly customized form, but for the true bike artist, the aesthetics
of the Harley V-twin and its attendant mechanical bits are so visual,
so traditional, so emotionally charged, that no other choice is either reasonable or possible.

If there is one man among the multitudes who appreciates and
inspires this level of aesthetics, it is the most famous, most popular,
most respected biker of all, Willie G. Davidson. He appeared at a re-

cent Bike Week having ridden down from Milwaukee on back roads with a group of close friends aboard his subtly customized black-on-black Road King. Whenever he stepped into public view at the company's elaborate dealership on South Beach Street or at any of the shows or exhibits, Willie G. was swarmed with autograph hunters. Always affable, always smiling, always accessible, Davidson is a corporate public-relations dream: a gregarious executive who can easily relate to his customers in terms of lifestyle and enthusiasm for the product. To the multitudes, Willie G. Davidson is the consummate biker, a man in leather and silver who can ride with the best while preserving the true faith in the corporate suites. He has no counterpart in the business world — a celebrity executive capable of hanging with the Bros during the annual Boot Hill Saloon Big Belly contest or Gilly's Club 44 Ladies' Arm-Wrestling Championship or the Bikers Ball, which annually generates nearly $100,000 for the Boys and Girls Clubs of America. Daytona Beach Bike Week is showtime for Harley-Davidson, and its megastar is Willie G., the slight, gray-bearded superbiker who, more than any other Harley-Davidson personality, represents royalty in this intense little kingdom.

While the local blue-hairs, AARP mall rats, and tourists who flock to this place, sometimes called the Redneck Riviera, flee town during the annual invasion or wait out the madness behind locked condo and trailer doors, their jalousie windows nailed down, Bike Week has never been confused with the sack of Rome. Local officials note that not only are the bikers about as well behaved as the similarly sized crowd that appears for the February stock-car racing "Speed Weeks," but they are Angelic compared to the college students who infest the town during the April spring break. While the local police forces keep busy writing tickets for illegal parking, speeding, public intoxication, and the brawling that is bound to break out in any crowd of this size, even if it were there for a Scrabble tournament, there is generally little for the news media to report in terms of lurid crimes or public outrage. In 1998, the cops wrote a mere forty-seven speeding tickets and investigated the thefts of only forty-five motorcycles, all Harleys. One murder — of a vendor as he slept in his motor home — was a rare capital crime and was considered to be unrelated to the festivities.

Bike Week involves a strange set of unwritten rules and customs. A longtime attendee notes:

> Nobody touches anybody else. Even in the madness around Main Street, people are constantly avoiding each other and saying "Excuse me." This may arise more out of fear than respect, but it's a fact. There is *no* touching. Moreover, you never touch anybody else's motorcycle. Never. It is a mortal sin. Even if the owner isn't around, warnings will issue out of the crowd to anyone suspected of laying on an unauthorized hand.

Some estimate that as many as half the Harleys in Daytona Beach include guns as part of their standard inventory. A grizzled woman who runs a local leather-repair shop is so experienced in stitching concealed pistol holsters into various makes of Harley saddles that she can instantly determine whether a Colt Python, a Smith & Wesson model 657, or a Beretta model 92 will fit into a given space. Most of this armament remains concealed and unused, thanks in part to the ubiquitous presence of police, many of whom come in from all parts of the nation to work as deputized auxiliaries for the Daytona Beach regulars. "They cut the bikers a lot of slack," says a local resident. "They'll let 'em run loud pipes — the louder the better — and they can party in the street and have a good time. But the cops have lines in the sand. You cross 'em and you're in deep shit. They are tough but fair, and you don't mess with 'em. And believe me, even the most badass biker on Main Street never forgets that Florida has the death penalty."

A visitor to Bike Week might conclude that this is a lily white crowd. There are no blacks and no Hispanics, no minorities of any kind. The only colors to be seen on the sun-drenched, sand-blown peninsula are painted on the luridly hued machines. The riders seem a supremacist's dream team. Yet nearby, in a sixteen-square-block section of the city well away from the peninsula, around Bethune-Cookman College, an informal Black Bike Week is held concurrently. Black bikers ride and party among themselves in this ghetto, amplifying the harsh fact that for all the trappings of brotherhood and good-time motorcycle frolics, the racial divide is as sharp among bikers as it is in the rest of society.

Amid this sea of black leather and tattoos and body jewelry that ebbs and flows around Main Street and environs, it is difficult to identify the players. A senior executive of a Fortune 500 company might be confused with a recently paroled, thoroughly sociopathic member of one of the major biker clubs. A housewife who spends her time riding a Hoover upright in a Mansfield, Ohio, split-level might be a biker's old lady who went to the finals in Sopotnick's coleslaw wrestling contest (nudity on the field of combat brings disqualification, but it is welcomed in the grandstands). Sopotnick's also features a Jap Bike Blowup, wherein a popular, high-revving Honda, Kawasaki, Suzuki, or Yamaha is cabled to a crane and yanked high above the crowd of Harley fans. Its fuel tank charged with nitro and other explosives, the bike's engine is then buzzed to insane rpm's until it explodes in a giant blossom of fire and flying parts to the accompaniment of crazed cheers.

Much like the great pre-Lenten bacchanals at the Mardi Gras or Rio's Carnival, Bike Week provides the power of anonymity, concealing true identity in a costume, merely exchanging the masks and lurid getups seen in the French Quarter for outfits featuring black leather and chains. All are sexually provocative and enormously potent, especially for those threatened by a society moving steadily toward androgyny in fashion and in the workplace. The disguise, be it leather or lace, not only distorts the identity of the wearer, but radically amplifies his or her sexuality, which is repressed or totally nullified in normal daily life. As the centerpiece of the biker's costume, the Harley-Davidson has transcended its simple role as a wind-in-the-face freedom machine and has become a twentieth-century sexual totem, projecting sexual potency beyond the tiresome cant that it serves merely as a penis extension between a man's thighs. The power of the engine and the rhythmic thump of its exhaust can lead to all manner of pop-psychological interpretation, but suffice to say that at places like Daytona Beach and Sturgis, the sexuality — pure, tear-up-the-bedsheets, hump-the-Harley-bitch sexuality — is openly flaunted in public exhibitions that energize the tribal, hedonistic scene. It is vivid, provocative, and ragingly heterosexual.

Threatened with emasculation and haunted by their repressed libidos, many men have found the Harley-Davidson to be a powerful sexual talisman, enhancing their lost maleness much as do hang gliding, spelunking, white-water kayaking, skydiving, snowboarding, and car racing. As the modern male's role as sexual predator and food gatherer is being eliminated, tempered, or feminized, he becomes unruly, obscene, and risk prone in part to reestablish identity. So the Fairfield County stockbroker, perhaps a member of the exclusive, motorcycle-oriented Greenwich Riding Club — after a proper dose of conventional wisdom from the Sunday *Times* and *Meet the Press* — hauls out his Harley and thumps over to the Marcus Dairy or annually trailers his bike to the Ritz-Carlton on Amelia Island, where, supermanlike, he changes into his leathers and rides to Bike Week. There he spits and scratches his balls in public, revs his engine, swills beer, and tells horribly sexist jokes in an elemental, lowlife act of male bonding that is the antithesis of the caring, drum-thumping campfire confessionals of the "Iron Johns" briefly popular in the early 1990s.

This may be evidence of what is fashionably called "defining deviancy downward," but the actions of the hordes at Bike Week, ogling the topless chicks at New Smyrna Beach's Bottoms Up Club and Molly Brown's or slugging back brews while witnessing the Boot Hill Big Belly contest, are no less profane, no more disgusting, no more antisocial than those of the endless chain of rockers and rappers who screech rebellion and nihilism at the nation's youth on MTV or the megarich jocks who beat up their women, pack their noses with cocaine, and attack their coaches while being cheered by an adoring public. At least within the biker cult there is a basic if ill-formed and ill-defined ethic involving mutual respect and a strange code of the West surrounding one's possessions (i.e., one's horse substitute and one's woman). Crude and primitive, perhaps. But in the sense that it requires loyalty and a level of personal courage that has disappeared in most other aspects of modern society, it is not to be entirely discounted.

The vividly sexual leather dress-up that pervades the streets of Daytona Beach becomes as much a statement for the age-old sexual realities as it does for a frolic on the sunny beaches. It is in many cases pure theater — "Halloween for old guys," as one veteran observer puts it. But who is wearing the costumes and who is going to find out?

A large, muscular man veered into a Daytona Beach gas station during a recent Bike Week on his noisy custom Harley. He was flinty eyed and angry. He reached into his saddlebag. Would he pull out a .45 automatic and start blazing away? The bystanders backed off. Out came his cell phone. Yanking off a glove, he pounded on the tiny keys, then jabbed the unit against his ear. "Jennifer, you know your bedtime. Do what the baby-sitter says!" he growled ominously.

Who was this rider whose anger was directed not at a rival gang member but at his small daughter and her *baby-sitter?* Was he an authentic Harley-Davidson rider or a so-called soft man of the nineties in the trappings of roguishness on a weekend of motorized slumming? Why was he there? To simply drink, party, and ride in the sunshine, then return home, his masculinity somehow replenished? The gathering of the great clan, the security of the sheer numbers, lent a protective coloration to him, permitting a brief transformation and possibly an affirmation that regardless of fantasies about a postmodern, amorphous, kinder, gentler world, aboard his Harley-Davidson he was once again a man.

Perhaps the popularity of an elemental machine like a Harley-Davidson motorcycle and the cultlike gatherings at places like Daytona Beach and Sturgis reflects a more desperate purpose than mere drunken debauchery and middle-class minirebellion for an otherwise constricted society. Yes, there is the simpleminded, sybaritic component of inhibitions lost, but if that is the sole intent of such gatherings, why the need for a loud, blowsy motorcycle as part of the party gear? Why not simply have a beer blast, like the collegiate spring-breakers, and forget the complexity and the in-convenience of riding, dragging, or shipping a giant Harley to the affair? Why? Because the Harley-Davidson is the linchpin, the so-cial amulet, the secret handshake, the unspoken password for ad-mission. Without it, one is a mere "citizen," a pitiful bystander. For the true believer, this machine is an expression of personal power in a world where power is increasingly diffused and fragmented. During a brief, sweet moment in Daytona Beach, even the most be-nighted, browbeaten victim of circumstance can blip the throttle of his monster Harley and feel the power, taste the potency, and toss away the fear. Such is the transcendental muscle packed in this unique and venerable machine.

The Harley-Davidson emits an aura of danger. The very act of balancing a 700-pound motor vehicle between one's legs at eighty miles per hour is reasonably hazardous and in a small way affirms the personal courage of the person who does it. This is a society in which daily risk has been almost totally eliminated. Americans are free of war and pestilence. They live longer and healthier lives than at any time in history. They live in a period of protracted peace and prosperity, yet the nation is stiff with fear. Each night the evening news reports the potential, often luridly overblown agonies of new diseases, new predators, new financial scams, and new environ-mental threats, each of which seems poised to shatter the tranquil-lity. In a society where virtually every aspect of an unusually safe and serene daily life *seems* potentially lethal, riding a motor-cycle — and a Harley-Davidson in particular — becomes a form of fantasy risk, an act of defiance among a population that has come to engage death and violence primarily as abstractions on illumi-nated screens.

Economists refer to a phenomenon called "risk homeostasis,"

which involves a compulsion by litigators, do-gooders, and bureaucrats to multiply the safety factors in society on an ever-accelerating basis, so as life becomes safer, the rules get more stringent. A counterreaction then occurs wherein some members of the culture seek extra risk, either with overt acts like skydiving and motorcycle riding, or passive gambling and investment forays — anything to wriggle free of the oppression of the nanny state.

There being no new frontiers to conquer, no new continents to explore, and precious few crannies of the globe that haven't been examined at least by remote cameras, seismographs, or human beings in all manner of submersibles, man is being forced inward. Several decades ago, Arthur C. Clark made a frightening observation: We may be stuck on this little orb in a corner of the universe. Fantasies of conquering outer space *Star Trek* style may be impossible, he said, leaving us isolated and alone, with no chance of heading out on another great adventure. West is now east. The twain have met. Nothing exists for us beyond the wild blue yonder except more wild blue yonder. The notion of a few astronauts huddled in some artificial life pod on the moon or Mars is a feeble substitute for the great historical exoduses. Where the most daring and audacious of past generations had the opportunity to search and explore, to conquer and civilize, we are left to climb rocks, scuba dive, and ride motorcycles, if in fact most of us have not already become so passive that all adventure necessary can be obtained via a computer mouse.

The end of the geographic frontier has driven many people to seek new horizons in cyberspace and in New Age spiritualism, holistic nostrums, UFO fascinations, and mysticism of all kinds. To counterbalance this rush toward inner space comes a groping for fundamental verities. The miracle of the personal computer seems to have stabilized at about 35 percent of all American households, with the rest either too poor, too stupid, or perhaps too busy and preoccupied with real life to subordinate themselves to a machine. The revival of old-time hellfire religion continues. The collection of antiques of all kinds, from books, to furniture, to autographs, to automobiles, thrives as people seek tangible links with the past. Hard evidence exists that the population is moving away from urban areas, seeking the solace of the country. Between 1990 and 1994, the population in rural areas of America grew 74 percent; during the prior decade, the hinterlands lost population. This attempted escape from urban sprawl and search for community and a sense of place has been caused by, according to James Howard Kunstler in the *Atlantic Monthly*, a reaction against city life that has become "socially devastating and spiritually degrading." This has produced a move away from what Thomas Jefferson called "the mobs of great cities" to quieter, simpler living in small towns from rural Ohio to the Rockies. This shift has in part been facilitated by the information revolution, which permits at-home work on a large scale, but there is a downside to this paradise, as described by Andrew Peyton Thomas, who warned in a recent issue of the *Weekly Standard* that the telecommunications revolution might destroy rather than enhance a sense of community. "The Internet, virtual reality and other devices vitiate the need for human contact," he writes. "The potential for a mass surrender to a narcissistic fantasy world at the expense of family and civic ties is real and obvious."

This loss of feel, sound, touch, and smell — the tactile evidence of living — is in part due to the rise of the computer, an utterly soulless machine with no response mechanism other than its graphic screen presentation and artificial sound reproduction. So too for much of modern living that, save for the everpresent din of background music or the chatter of television, people live in an increasingly nonmechanical world. The great factories of yore, with their grinding, clanking machinery and their noontime steam whistles, are gone, as is the sound of clacking typewriters in offices, replaced by the inert, essentially silent operation of the computer.

This nostalgia for things that can be felt and heard relates to the appeal of the vibrating, wobbly, deafening Harley-Davidson, which transmits so many appealing tactile messages. The sound emitted from a Harley-Davidson V-twin engine, which has been employed without essential change since 1909, is so special that it is the subject of a patent application. The oddly cadenced exhaust note cannot be duplicated by the Japanese — despite their feverish attempts — unless they employ single-crankpin layouts with the same narrow-angle V-twin cylinder architecture as the Harley-Davidson. A number of variations on the same basic engine theme have also been patented by the motor company in a wide-ranging attempt to block the Japanese from copying one of the most unique and distinctive sounds of the twentieth century.

Surely this search for elemental qualities and what some describe as simpler truths comes in reaction to the clutter and ennui of our brave new world. Some critics dismiss all this as a temporary infatuation of the elite, who have periodically embraced Thoreau-like links with nature and a modified Ludditism. The overwhelming flow of information, the degradation of the environment, the urban glut, the unraveling of social mores and manners, etc., have all served as triggering mechanisms. But as one critic observes, this neo-Shakerism has its limits. Peter Kiviston, a sociology professor at Augustana College, noted in a *USA Today* story on the trendiness of the simple life, "The Amish live a very simple life. But I don't see anybody else desiring to get rid of electricity."

Only the most lunatic Ted Kaczynskis choose to live in the dark Montana woods, but there is little question that a certain disquiet exists among the populations of modern industrial societies about the future. As superficially tranquil and comfortable as it seems, an awful angst pervades the land. Perhaps this is what some social critics cite as a manifestation of our impending fin de siècle, noting that at the end of the nineteenth century, the frontier had been conquered and the world appeared to be embarking on a decade of unprecedented prosperity and technological revolution. As this century ends and the third millennium begins, many people face a seamless, silent, insidious sense of isolation and loss of individual control that has powerful Orwellian overtones. There is no escape, no privacy, no dodging an all-pervasive intrusion via a myriad of data banks poking into the deepest and most intimate aspects of daily life. Perhaps in this atmosphere elemental machines like a Harley-Davidson motorcycle serve as small gestures of rebellion and affirmations of — dare one employ the shopworn cliché? — personal freedom.

Will the much-celebrated arrival of the information age save us? Will mass communication via the Internet, cell phones, satellite systems, CNN, talk radio, E-mail, fax, etc., transform our world into the grand panacea of a global village populated by the "family of man"? So far there are unsettling hints of the law of unintended consequences. In his recent book *Data Smog*, journalist David Shenk points out, with other social critics, that the communications revolution has fragmented, not expanded, society. The Internet, he notes, "encourages a cultural splintering that can render physical communities less relevant and frees people from having to climb outside their own biases, assumptions and inherited ways of thought." He charges that cyberspace "promotes a highly decentralized, deregulated community with little common discourse and minimal public infrastructure." Race and ethnicity, political loyalty, gender, age, geographical location, even sports team affiliation, are the source of more conflict, not less. If the information age has not heightened tensions in the Middle East, the fragmented Soviet Union, Northern Ireland, Korea, and the Balkans, and between the Muslims and Jews, Protestants and Catholics, and Indians and Pakistanis, it has certainly not tempered them.

It has also led to all levels of cultism in America, ranging from paranoid isolationists hiding out in the Idaho mountains awaiting an assault from squadrons of black helicopters led by Hillary Rodham Clinton, to more benign manifestations like rabid sports team fans, Deadheads, fundamentalist religious groups, and yes, the Harley-Davidson aficionados, all of whom are united around a single obsession that provides protective coloration and a sense of uniqueness and individual control. In a world where control over one's daily life has become increasingly blurred and amorphous, salvation can come within the confines of a group offering true faith.

If there is a single source of this reactive and restless search for independence embodied in the Harley-Davidson true faith, it lies on the northern edges of Milwaukee, where Capitol Drive splits off from the four-lane heading to Fond du Lac and where the heart of the machine — the fabled V-twin and its attendant transmission — is manufactured before being shipped to either York or Kansas City for final assembly in completed motorcycles. The factory dates to World War II, when A. O. Smith Co. constructed it to make aircraft propellers for the military. It was purchased in 1948 and was the subject of a well-remembered "mystery tour" when company president William H. Davidson loaded a group of key dealers aboard a train at the Juneau Avenue factory siding and transported them to the new site, where a $3.5-million initial investment would produce major dividends in the years to come. Behind the main plant complex lay an extra fifty acres, where in 1995–96 a massive new product development center was constructed in contemporary brushed aluminum and glass, its arched edifice vaguely reminiscent of the airport hangars dating to the early part of the century. The building was named for its most famous and revered occupant and the company's creative energy source, the legendary Willie G. Davidson. It is inside this space-age edifice — in a sense the stylistic antithesis of the machine being designed within — that Davidson and his small team of engineers, designers, and artists work in splendid isolation.

Willie G. remains a larger-than-life fountainhead of motorcycle wisdom and ethics. One expects a burly, bombastic tough guy, a bigmouthed know-it-all who revels in his notoriety. But he is in fact a modest, almost self-effacing man, smaller in stature than implied by his endless appearances in the dozens of publications and books devoted to Harley-Davidson. A close-cropped gray beard surrounds a toothy, everpresent smile, and his eyes, sharp and intense behind steel-rimmed glasses, brighten with artistic intensity when he speaks of form and function as they relate to modern motorcycles and automobiles. While he is a credentialed and widely recognized designer, it is Davidson's link to the very beginnings of the company that gives robust dimension and flavor to his life. He muses about visiting his grandfather's mansion on Milwaukee's Lake Michigan "gold coast" as a little boy and dabbing at balls on the immense pool table. He recalls that his great aunt Mamie volunteered to pinstripe gas tanks during the grinding Depression years of the early 1930s — years when the true artistry and aesthetics of the product first manifested themselves.

Mounted on a wall behind him in a softly lit conference room is a V-2 Evolution engine, the pure heart of the entire Harley-Davidson empire. "The V-twin is who we are," he says.

> Its architecture is perfect in the way it fits a motorcycle frame. It's our equivalent to the Mercedes-Benz star or the Chevrolet bow tie. For us to abandon the forty-five-degree V-twin would be a disaster, and it has never been seriously considered, even during the NOVA project with Porsche. [That relationship has recently been revived, but there is little question that it will involve refinements to the V-twin and no radical new engine layouts.] Our V-twin embodies so much tradition that it is the company charter. It's our golden goose. Its aesthetics are as important to us as its performance.
>
> You've got to remember Indian. Their big Chief had a fine flathead V-twin, but when they began to feel the competition from Triumph and other English bikes after the war, they tried to respond with a vertical twin that wasn't properly developed and tested. It helped break the company. We won't make the same mistake.

Davidson, always the designer, speaks constantly in terms of forms and shapes, understanding that his primary goal is to create contemporary motorcycles with powerful links to tradition and the corporate past. His most recent masterpiece, the Heritage Springer, is a classic bike, featuring exposed coil springs mounted on its front forks, a component abandoned in the product line in 1949 with the introduction of the Hydra Glide suspension system. He muses over this constancy of design and his unique opportunity to revive and refine classic components, noting that buried in the massive Harley-Davidson parts catalog are numbers sequentially dating from 1915. "We have to retain the sound, the feel, and the visual impact of our traditional product," he says, emphasizing that the entire company, including its bar-and-shield logo — which dates from 1910 — is steeped in history and possesses a priceless patina. He is close friends with Chrysler Corporation's Tom Gale, recognized as the most creative of the Detroit designers and the man who developed such daring products as the Dodge Viper sports car and the Plymouth Prowler retro hot rod. "Like our motorcycles, those cars aren't re-creations of antiques but the employment of shapes that have permanent appeal," says Davidson. "And within that whole context, you have to be a bit controversial."

It was Davidson's seminal Super Glide of 1971 that broke the barrier between the standard-issue Harley-Davidson and the daring shapes of the California choppers and bobbers. It was a breakthrough product that set the company on the road to prosperity, led in no small way by Willie G.'s reach toward the One Percenters' radical machinery. He holds the famed independent customizers like Arlen Ness in great regard, noting that he first met him at Sturgis in the mid-1970s. "It was a tight little group then, maybe no more than five thousand hard-core bikers. The whole scene was really laid back — pretty cool," he says softly, implying that his bond with the outlaw bikers, at least in terms of design creativity and energy, remains strong.

The vivid stylishness of the bikers' customs is apparent not only in many of Willie G.'s nuances of motorcycle design — including the nearly two dozen ever-changing custom fuel tank designs and paintwork, some of which are dazzling in lavish layout and detail — but in the vast line of Harley-Davidson Motor clothes created by a separate division headed by his daughter, Karen (two of Willie

G.'s sons also work for the company; William is in the marketing department, and Michael is a consultant in dealer store design). The impressive lineup of high-quality clothes and accessories created by Karen Davidson and her staff generates nearly $100 million of the company's annual gross sales of nearly $2 billion. They are sold not only through the franchised dealerships but in a growing network of what the company calls AROs, or alternate retail outlets, devoted exclusively to clothing, including $500 leather jackets, jewelry, and a myriad of officially licensed products ranging from biker Barbie dolls to Department 56 collectible Christmas ornaments.

This gold mine of imagery and romance borders on impossible to duplicate, although more and more manufacturers are trying to elbow into the market. Not only do the Japanese struggle to manufacture fleets of seamless fake Heritages, Road Kings, etc., but a group of new domestic challengers has also arrived on the scene. Most are tiny players, like Wichita's Big Dog, which produces about 300 bikes a year, all costing upwards of $22,000. But a recent entry from Polaris, a $1.2-billion maker of snowmobiles, jet skis, and all-terrain vehicles, could nibble at the outer edges of the Harley kingdom. The Polaris Victory V92 is yet another V-twin knockoff, despite corporate denials, and is intended to reach the market at a lower price than comparable Harleys (a ploy with dubious potential, considering the failure of the Japanese to sell their phony Harleys for considerably less money). Another entry, the Belle Plaine, Minnesota–based Excelsior-Henderson company, is a publicly financed project to revive two famed pioneer brands in the industry, but considering that the original Excelsior company went out of business in 1931, when some of the current customer's great-grandfathers were riding motorcycles, the potential for widespread nostalgia purchases may be limited.

Willie G., perhaps more than anyone on earth, is aware of these interlopers, as he is of the steady stream of V-twin clones issuing from the Japanese. Many of them are excellent machines by his own admission, and some are nearly half as expensive as a full-dress Road King bagger. It is his responsibility to keep the flame alive. Behind the closed doors of his design studio, his little team labors on a new generation of engines code-named P22 and introduced to the public in late 1998 as the Twin Cam 88. True to Davidson's credo, the traditional forty-five-degree V-twin air-cooled architecture has been retained, although the Twin Cam 88 offers a fresh new twin-cam design and eight extra cubic inches (from eighty to eighty-eight, hence the designation), plus advanced, computer-managed fuel injection. The result is improved performance, reduced emissions, *and* the venerated Harley-Davidson rumble. Some enthusiasts have already labeled the new engine the Fat Head.

Says an observer about Willie G. Davidson and his staff:

Outsiders think he and the entire motor company design staff are hidebound and conservative. They have the impression that Willie G. is some kind of demigod whose word is law. They're wrong on both counts. Harley-Davidson is endlessly looking at all kinds of new designs, from inside and outside the design center. They'll try anything, provided it works with the V-twin design. That is not to say that there aren't factions within the company that would like to move on to more contemporary engines, but Willie G. holds the line on that front. But even the most progressive engineers in the company don't fear him or hesitate to advance their theories, no matter how revolu-

tionary. In that sense, Willie G. Davidson is as open-minded as anybody in the business.

Home base for what is reverentially called "the motor company" lies at the end of a working-class street called Juneau Avenue
in western Milwaukee. There stands the original vast brick edifice,
a classic, broad-shouldered structure dating to before World War I
and now registered as a historic landmark. Actual manufacture has
long since been transferred to more modern operations at the Capitol Drive facility and a new plant on Pilgrim Road a few miles away
and in York, Pennsylvania. Another 330,000-square-foot Kansas City
plant is now on line as part of the company's plan to produce
200,000 motorcycles by its one hundredth anniversary in 2003.
Most of the old Juneau Avenue facility, standing in the shadow of
the immense Miller Brewing Company's main brewery, has been
converted to administration space for the growing operation,
which in the past decade has more than doubled production to
about 150,000 bikes a year. At the front of the main building is a
small parking lot exclusively for motorcycles, guarded by a sign
warning "No cages" — although adjacent lots are crammed with
the dreaded four-wheelers. The reception area features what is
known in the company as "the lobby bike," a spindly Harley-
Davidson that company historians and restorers have officially
designated number one. After extensive research, it was deter-
mined that its single-cylinder engine was stamped "Number One,"
positively dating it to late 1903 or early 1904. However, the frame
is a 1905½ model — the first truly sophisticated version to be
offered by the fledgling company. It is believed that the hybrid
machine was modified for display at the Pan-Pacific Exposition
in San Francisco in 1915, then fell into forgotten disrepair in a cor-

ner of the factory until a botched attempt at restoration was made during the AMF reign. A total ground-up disassembly and reconstruction was then undertaken by company archivist Martin Jack Rosenblum and local expert Harley-Davidson craftsmen Ray Schlee and John Rank. The result is the rarest and most cherished motorcycle in the world, the Harley-Davidson with the oldest engine and frame, dating to the tentative and fragile origins of the company. Today it stands proudly, its white balloon tires contrasting vividly with its jet black frame, a prime example of the continuity and pride that energize the company nearly a century later.

In the hushed precincts of the top floor, where sixty years ago hard-handed Germans and Swedes labored in the din to build hulking Knuckleheads, a labyrinth of paneled workspace leads to the modest corner office of president and CEO Jeff Bleustein. He is bespectacled and contemplative, which befits his impressive academic credentials and defies the notion that a man who builds tough-guy motorcycles for a living might radiate more swagger befitting his product. But he has been through the wars, watching his company plunge to near destruction more than once during the 1980s, then, with chairman Richard Teerlink, along with now-retired Vaughn Beals, Willie G. Davidson, and a small team of visionaries, yanking Harley-Davidson from the fire and creating its phoenixlike recovery.

"We're still a drop in the bucket," he muses.

There will never come a day when there'll be a motorcycle in every garage, so we have to keep our business in perspective. We'll try to expand to meet the demand, but we can never, ever forget the special relationship we have with our customers. We have a unique covenant with them, which makes this more than a business. In many ways they think they own us. We can never ignore the loyalty or abuse it. During the boom years of the early nineties, demand was so strong that we could easily have tacked another thousand dollars on the price. That's another one hundred million in raw profit without lifting a finger. We would have been heroes on Wall Street, but we chose to leave it on the table. To have exploited that advantage short-term would have damaged that covenant and frankly, it was never seriously considered.

Bleustein, like other senior executives, spends an inordinate amount of the time mingling with Harley loyalists around the world, having recently returned from a Japanese HOG rally at Yonogo, a resort town near Osaka. "There were four thousand riders, and the streets were lined with Japanese and American flags," he says. "It's hard to think of many products around which the Japanese would tolerate flying the American flag. But that's what the Harley-Davidson is all about. It's not so much that it's American, but that it is *Americana*. There's a big difference."

Deep in the bowels of the South Building, erected in the immediate post–World War I years, a rattling freight elevator rises to the fourth floor. Once admitted through a locked steel door, one enters the bailiwick of Dr. Martin Jack Rosenblum, the company historian, archivist, and "purveyor of motorcycle culture." A slight man with a receding hairline, intense eyes, and a flowing salt-and-pepper beard that makes him appear more like a Talmudic scholar than a devotee of motorcycles, Rosenblum is a former professor of English literature at the University of Wisconsin, blues singer, gun collector, hard-core motorcycle rider, and the author of *The Holy Ranger*, a collection of blank verse espousing the spiritual side of motorcycle riding. In the foreword to the thin volume, Rosenblum equates riding his Harley Sportster with a Japanese tea ceremony. "When you pour the tea, you are really pouring it, and you don't spill a drop. This is my understanding of what meditation is. I probably meditate more in a twenty-four-hour period than most holy men do. I just do it on a Harley."

The central poem of the collection is "The Holy Ranger As Avenging Angel." Its theme is a memorial to the loss of freedom in the modern state and a call for the Holy Ranger, i.e., the independent man of resolve, to follow the dictum of Walt Whitman and "Resist much, obey little." His snakeskin boots propped on a desk surrounded by stacks of books and documents, Rosenblum is a fountainhead of company lore, defending the legend but only within the limits of scholarship and historical accuracy.

He speaks of the motorcycle as a practical art object, noting that "we live in a world of virtual experience. The Harley-Davidson is one of those objects that has stood the test of time. Not a lot is genuine anymore. Very little is truly emotional, and that is why it — the motorcycle — remains one of the most sought-after symbols in the world. It represents, within the collective unconscious, something genuine, something emotional, something powerful. *It's the last horse on the frontier.*"

Tugging occasionally at the thicket of his beard, adjusting a hand-wrought silver bracelet on his thin wrist, Rosenblum rhapsodizes about the outlaw image and the One Percenters, whom he equates with the Cole Youngers and the Jesse Jameses of yore, links with great American frontier talismans like the Colt .45 Frontier revolver and the Gibson guitar, created in Kalamazoo, Michigan, in the 1850s and still revered as the Stradivarius of folk music. His voice is deep, reverential, and resounds through his poetry:

> *Handling a Harley around a corner when blacktop*
> *immediately turns to gravel, a foot down won't save it*
> *gives an awful strength to the Heart and your hands hang on*
> *to mindful courage all*
> *the time with graceful force and power*
> *rises from history that will not be toppled by fashionable*
> *modern laws.*

Rosenblum works and writes in his cluttered office next to a world-class collection of Harley-Davidsons from every era, including early Silent Gray Fellows and three of the ill-fated, Porsche-built NOVA project V-4s, looking pudgy and ungainly among the leaner, later production models. Rosenblum, the poet laureate and folk bard of Harley-Davidson, spends his days probing his massive archives, still on a mission of discovery. Nearby, among the motorcycles themselves, master craftsman Ray Schlee continues the laborious, exacting task of restoration and renovation of the priceless collection. These two men serve as keepers of the flame.

The Harley-Davidson motorcycle touches nerves unreachable by all but a handful of brands in the entire world. For a relatively small company, its imagery and scope of social influence reach into every nook and cranny of modern society. In the words of Willie G. Davidson, "It is more than a machine," much like a Rolex is more than a watch, the Zippo is more than a lighter, and the Colt Frontier is more than a pistol. They, like a select group of other products, pack extrasocial value, a mass of imagery and mystique that cannot be duplicated or imitated. A few other vehicles — including the Porsche and the Ferrari — enjoy similar heritages, but the Harley-Davidson is unique in that it exudes a raffish reputation for lawlessness and independence that transcends responsible behavior and conventional status. It says something about its owner that moves him toward the edge, implying a sense of iconoclasm, independence, and personal courage. Perhaps if the State of New Hampshire had not used it first, the company's motto might be "Live free or die." Such is the dynamic of the fabled machine and the people who ride it.

EPILOGUE · COWBOYS AROUND THE WORLD

There is a corn-fed folksiness about Harley-Davidson that blurs the fact that since the 1920s, this heartland product from Milwaukee has been an international presence. Big and raucous, the uniquely American V-twin motorcycle enjoyed an intense loyalty in England, France, and Germany during the decade following World War I despite heavy taxation and a limited dealer network. Enthusiasts who wanted more power and speed than offered by the small, lightweight, fuel-efficient domestic products were attracted to Harleys not only for their performance but for their frowzy American personality. Dealerships like Warr's of London, which began the exclusive sale of Harley-Davidsons in 1924, have prevailed to this day thanks to a small contingent of hard-core riders who found that the thumping monsters offered tactile sensations radically more vivid and exhilarating than the tamer local machinery.

Today, Harley-Davidson sells almost 30 percent of its 150,000 annual production overseas, reaching into markets where Japanese and Italian sport bikes — powerful, featherweight machines twenty to fifty miles per hour faster than the big Harleys — dominate sales. While Harley-Davidson holds nearly 50 percent of the market for big cruiser-style motorcycles in the United States, its share in Europe is less than 8 percent. There, its sheer bulk, its high cost, and its low-tech image mitigate against its becoming anything more than an exclusive status symbol among trendies bent on producing mild shock and outrage among their peers. As a practical transportation module, the Harley-Davidson makes no sense outside the vast acreage of North America. In the narrow, labyrinthine streets of ancient European cities, maneuvering a big Harley is akin to docking an aircraft carrier. Worse yet, Harleys have been less reliable than their Japanese and German rivals. They demand constant fiddling and tuning as opposed to the endless, humdrum constancy of operation offered by the average Honda, Suzuki, or BMW.

Yet the fierce loyalty prevails. Clyde Fessler, who originated the HOG membership concept and who now runs Harley's European marketing operations, concentrates on exploiting the intense cohesion of the Harley-Davidson owner body. He and his staff recently organized a HOG rally at Austria's Faaker See to celebrate the firm's ninety-fifth anniversary. More than ten thousand HOG members from all over Europe appeared for the festivities. The same enthusiasm thrives in other parts of the world, from South America to the Far East, where HOG chapters exist in the unlikeliest places and where the Harley-Davidson culture is as vibrant and totally American as the height of Daytona Beach Bike Week.

I puzzled over this phenomenon. What was it about this purely American motorcycle that gave it a worldwide export market? It seemed to probe into every nationality and culture, from Old Blighty to the inscrutable East. There seemed to be only one way to fathom the situation. In the spring of 1997, my wife, Pamela, and I set off for a round-the-world trip to examine the Harley-Davidson culture firsthand. I wish I could say that I made the tour on my Heritage Softail, a repeat of one of Dave Barr's epic rides, but the strictures of time and limitations of budget demanded otherwise. Many circumnavigations of the globe have been made on motorcycles, but ours was made via commercial airliner and the much-reviled "cage" (in this case an Audi A6 sedan used in Europe). Working west to east, we made our way first to the place where, seemingly, the Harley-Davidson would be most out of its element: the epicenter of motorcycle manufacturing, a nation that prides itself as the source of the finest internal combustion technology on the planet — Japan.

The Tokyo Easyriders Club occupies an innocuous building buried in the sprawl of the great city's Shibuya district, one of thousands of buildings planted among a rat's nest of zigzagging streets and elevated four-lane toll roads. To the westerner, Tokyo is a staggering, strangely silent stew pot of humanity quietly and earnestly bustling about in swarms of Nissans, Hondas, and Toyotas amid towers of steel and concrete, a postmodern city of indecipherable ancient traditions artfully integrated into a contemporary cyberworld powered by microchips and illuminated by neon and argon. To the occupants of the endless streams of tiny sedans and chuffing Hino and Isuzu trucks trundling past, Easyriders is all but invisible, one more two-story Bauhaus box in a sea of cement. Yet to men like Masahiro Ishibashi, Easyriders represents a small, diamond-hard life source of reality.

He rides into its cramped parking lot aboard a spectacular custom Harley-Davidson, styled on Peter Fonda's Captain America but more elaborate, with gold-leaf scrolling on its tank and flawlessly burnished bits of chrome on its engine. Ishibashi is dressed in a set of magnificent, glove-soft, fawn-colored leathers, complete with sleeve and leg fringe. His helmet is custom painted to match the motorcycle, and heads turn as he pulls it away to reveal his chiseled, high-cheekboned features. As he strides inside, his bike is left in a place of honor among the rabble of choppers and customs in the parking lot.

Sitting in the club's second-floor restaurant, which is decorated in rough-hewn timbers and wrought iron like a Dodge City saloon, Masahiro Ishibashi is clearly a rich and powerful man. He is the president of the Japanese division of a giant worldwide publishing empire, making it more logical that his primary mode of transport would be a shimmering black Lexus Celsior or a Nissan President limousine driven by a white-gloved chauffeur. "My family was traditional," he says in flawless English.

I was taught that bad boys rode motorcycles, and my youth was spent with sports cars — for the most part European Mercedes, Alfas, and BMWs. But as I grew older, I felt that I owed myself a small gift, like a motorcycle. I looked around at the little Japanese motorcycles, the fifty and one hundred twenty-five cc Hondas and such, but they meant nothing. Then I came here and saw my first Harley-Davidson. It was beautiful, and I had to have one.

I ordered a Heritage Softail. It cost me a million yen, over eighteen thousand dollars, and when it arrived, I realized one thing: I couldn't ride a motorcycle. I had never been on one. I arranged for it to be transported from the dealer to my home, where it sat in the garage until one night. It was time. Convincing myself that it was nothing more than a big bicycle with an engine, I rolled it out and carefully rode it one hundred meters to a stoplight. Trying to maintain my balance and drenched in sweat, I rode up onto the Shuto Kousoku freeway and got into the Roppongi district. It was after midnight, and the place was swarming with kids, rock and roll music, fast cars, and hundreds of bikes — ridden mostly by what we call "bad boys." It was madness. I could barely control the big machine, but somehow I managed to get back home. My wife was waiting outside. She waved to me as I approached, but I couldn't respond. I didn't dare take my hands off the handlebar even for a second.

That was eight years and several motorcycles ago, leading to Ishibashi's exquisite custom parked outside. "Now I ride every weekend as a sort of Sunday morning ritual," he says. "For me there's no other motorcycle except the Harley-Davidson. It's alive. It's my friend. It's not perfect. You have to take care of it, like a person. Yes, it's my friend."

Ishibashi is a maverick, a loner who operates outside the packs of young Ginza cruisers and the so-called fashion riders who rattle around the trendy Roppongi district clubs in southwest Tokyo. Nor is he part of the so-called police types, a collection of older Harleyists who dress up like cops and ride in two-by-two formation in a bizarre Far Eastern imitation of the California Highway Patrol. He is a casual member of HOG, among nearly ten thousand Japanese Harley-Davidson owners, but his social position, his status in a powerful hierarchical culture, sets him apart from the other, normally middle-class, Harley customers. Such is the loneliness of the man in the lush leathers aboard a dazzling custom Harley-Davidson. "For most people a vehicle, be it an automobile or a motorcycle, is a pure transportation device, a thing merely to carry one's body from point A to B," he says. "But for me, my Harley-Davidson has a more elemental mission: to carry me from point A back to point A. Nothing more, nothing less."

Across the great city, in a cluttered residential district, three more keepers of the flame operate in a one-room office in the basement of a small apartment house. Shin Ukeda, a slight, intense man in his late twenties, is the editor of *Hot Bike*, a magazine devoted to Harley-Davidsons. He speaks English well and brags that he rode from Los Angeles to Milwaukee to take part in the immense 1993 celebration of the ninetieth birthday of the company, a mass pilgrimage that saw an estimated 170,000 loyalists descend on the city and triggered traffic jams across southern Wisconsin and northern Illinois. Seated with him among the litter of old magazines, Harley parts, and stacks of paper, are his fellow staffers, the prematurely balding Shigeki Yuzawa and Kiminobu Kurokawa, a rangy, dark-featured youth with ink black shoulder-length hair. Behind them, spread across a wall above bulging filing cabinets, is a poster of an erotically chopped custom Harley autographed by the legendary California master customizer Arlen Ness.

Outside, crammed fork to tail, is a cluster of Harleys, most of them grimy and roughly maintained, representations of ownership by enthusiasts with minuscule resources compared to those of the powerful publishing mogul. Shin Ukeda pulls a tattered snapshot from his wallet and displays a faded picture of his grandfather astride a Japanese Rikuo Type 97 Knucklehead during the Second World War, one of thousands of Japanese-built Harley clones manufactured for the Imperial Army. "After the war, the old Rikuos and Harley-Davidsons brought over by the Americans became favorites," he explains. "Many have been restored and are still ridden, although Harley riders in Japan can be broken into two main groups. The old ones are the police types. They ride in formation and try to imitate American CHiPs. They look a bit silly." He sniffs. "The others, who read our magazine and another called *Vibes*, are younger. Some of them are what Americans call rich urban bikers, or Rubes. Others are what we call 'fashion riders.' They try to look like Hells Angels, but they don't fight. They act nasty and cruise the Ginza and Roppongi, but they are harmless. Just looking bad."

When the subject of Japanese-built motorcycles is raised, Kiminobu Kurokawa shakes his mane of hair and shrugs. "They are high tech. Japanese people are fascinated with high tech, but our own V-twins built like a Harley-Davidson are fakes. They are imitations. We don't like imitations, and Honda and Yamaha make poor imitation Harley-Davidsons."

"They don't understand," adds Shigeki Yuzawa. "A Harley-Davidson is special. It is like no other machine. It makes *hot* noise. It's like an *animal*."

In a nation obsessed with high technology, where computer sales boom and where super-definition television is already in use and most new cars come with Sony RGB 680 GPS digital mapping systems to facilitate navigating the insane maze of streets in a city of nine million, this retrogression into the ancient and venerable world of Harley-Davidson can reach extreme levels. Sundance Motorcycles, located in a small storefront, restores old Harleys, builds complete, brand-new 1936-vintage Knucklehead engines, and offers a wide list of parts for the sixty-year-old designs. The young men in the shop agree about the Harley mystique. "Japanese motorcycles have no passion," says the owner, a compact, intense man in his early thirties named Takio Shibazaki. He stands astride one of his Sundance replicas, an artfully styled machine containing his firm's custom version of a Knucklehead engine. "You can ride one three hundred kilometers [180 miles] an hour and not even feel the engine. But with a Harley you feel it at forty kilometers [24 mph]. It has a heartbeat."

A burly American with graying hair rides up and parks a giant black Honda Valkyrie along the row of Harleys lining the sidewalk. Jack Beasely, a Californian, has worked in Tokyo as a photographer for thirteen years and notes that it took him eleven tries to pass his motorcycle test, although he was an experienced rider in the United States. Small motorcycles with engine sizes under 400 cc are considered utilitarian by the government and sufficiently underpowered that average citizens can ride them safely. But for larger machines — including the Harleys and the fabled home-built superbikes, which can approach 200 miles per hour in stock form — the standards are higher. Only 10 percent of the applicants pass the rigid test. Beasely owns a Harley Super Glide, delivered after a nine-month wait from one of the nearly one hundred Japanese dealers (which include the giant Parco department store chain whose stores dot the trendier sections of Japan's major cities).

Beasely regards the Honda for a moment. It is a cruiser type, intended to rival the Harley-Davidson, although unlike some Japanese models that shamelessly imitate the Harley V-twin design, the Valkyrie is powered by a sophisticated opposed six-cylinder, water-cooled engine developed for the GoldWing line. "You know," he muses, "this thing is perfect. It has gobs of smooth power. It is perfectly balanced. It handles great, and it'll stop on a dime — if we had dimes here in Japan. But . . . so *what?* Some day, the whole world is going to wake up and say 'Fuck technology. Give me the real thing.' There's a saying here that the Japanese produce scholars but no geniuses. In its own way, the Harley-Davidson is an expression of perverse genius: a machine so old that it's new, so steeped in tradition that it's trendy. Yes. The *real thing*. That's why it works in a nation so fixated with acquired western tastes."

Americans, isolated behind two vast oceans, naively refer to this phenomenon as "globalization." But the rest of the world calls it "Americanization": a fascinating, forbidden shot of hard cultural liquor that, while eroding national customs and values, smacks of the anarchy and independence of the great western frontier. Much of the world seems to embrace these values, while in the nation that produced them they are denounced as obsolete and counterproductive.

Citizens of the Pacific Rim seem to be seeking the real thing, not of their own making but in the faux-American style that permeates every form of life. Yankee culture is everywhere, from the Manhattan-like skyscrapers that dot the urban centers, to the McDonald's, the Gaps, the Eddie Bauers, and the Levi's stores, to the ever-present Marlboro billboards. Tokyo, excluding the serene enclave surrounding the Imperial Palace, might be downtown Pittsburgh. The lobby of the famed Imperial Hotel, once a centerpiece of the empire (although the original was designed by Frank Lloyd Wright), is a swirl of western high fashion, save for the occasional Japanese woman in her traditional kimono. So too is Hong Kong, with its audacious picket of towering office buildings; everything is western, save for the sea of Chinese faces and the endless, crazed blur of glyphed signage. As they did in various guises in the last century, the westerners are invading, this time not with gunboats, cannons, or Bibles, but with burgers and ATM machines and styling tips issuing not from the Central Committee for Cultural Correctness but from Disney and Warner Brothers. Amid the cacophony of this sociological Waring blender rolls the occasional Harley-Davidson, representing the essential American as rebel, which by its aura of anarchy threatens every establishment, no matter how well-founded.

If there is one social system that demands order above all else, it is that of Singapore, that island citadel of police-state mercantilism that has organized itself like a nineteenth-century English public school. Within this totally structured system, there is little room for a tatty, unruly machine like the Harley-Davidson, yet it thrives among a small but intensely enthusiastic coterie. Despite the sluggish economy and the near collapse of the Far Eastern economic miracle, Harleys remain steady sellers in Singapore, defying extreme measures by the government to control not only the motorcycle population, but that of all motor vehicles in the pristine, gardenlike environs of the former crown colony now disguised as a republic and controlled by a shadowy expatriate Chinese elite.

Whereas the streets of Jakarta, Bangkok, and Kuala Lumpur are clogged with swarming, honking, fuming cars, trucks, and motorcycles of all sizes and shapes, the city of Singapore's perfectly manicured boulevards and avenues are serenely free of traffic, even during rush hours. This is due to government policies that make ownership not only an exclusive privilege but egregiously expensive. Private cars and motorcycles can only be purchased after a "certificate of entitlement" is issued and a whopping check is written, which in the case of expensive motorcycles like a BMW or a Harley-Davidson, can total as much as $3,000. Add that to a 12 percent customs duty and a 15 percent registration fee, and the final price of a Harley can easily soar past $35,000. The rider is then able to use his motorcycle, provided he can pass a stringent Class Three test required to ride all bikes over 400 cc and never breaks the maximum speed limit of eighty kilometers (forty-eight miles) per hour.

If this isn't enough to deter ownership, the government forbids any alteration to the original stock machine, including custom paintwork, wheels, exhaust pipes, and other modifications. The regulation is enforced by an official photograph taken when the motorcycle or car is registered. The photo is checked when the owner pays the $336 annual motorcycle road tax. Considering that this island paradise is a place where chewing gum is outlawed (an errant hunk having jammed a subway door a decade ago), and fines, floggings, and jail sentences can be handed down for jaywalking, littering, and other public displays of sloppiness, there is little wonder that the small band of Harley-Davidson enthusiasts does most of its riding in the wild acreage of Malaysia to the north. A short hop over the bridge to the mainland at Johor Baharu, and ahead lies more than a thousand miles of open roads to Bangkok and beyond. A few intrepid riders have pushed deep into Burma to the east and even into the wooly, untamed hinterlands of Laos and Cambodia, although Malaysia offers excellent riding, in part because the Sultan of Johor, a son of the former king, owns six Harley-Davidsons. Therefore, when not puttering around chic Orchard Road or the fashionable Singapore shopping areas of Takashima, Sun-Tec, and the Tampines estate, where the Gucci, Vuitton, Chanel, Cartier, Hermès, and Bally boutiques seem as ubiquitous as Wal-Marts and Targets in Des Moines, the local band of Harley owners, numbering perhaps a thousand, can be found on the weekends north of the border, thundering through the Malaysian rubber plantations and highlands. The old machine remains strong social medicine in the tightly constricted Singapore society, which, once past the niggling intrusions by the government on daily life, offers one of the highest standards of living on earth. Writing in the widely read *Strait Times* daily paper, local sports star Muhamad Hosni Muhamad commented, "It's exotic. A Harley is to bikes what Ferrari is to cars. I encountered my first Harley in Australia in 1992. I heard this sound coming. I thought it was an army tank. Imagine my surprise when a bike came around the corner. Its rumble is a very attractive sound."

The epicenter of Harley-Davidson activity in Singapore is the company's only authorized dealership, on Alexandra Road, a small-ish, rather modest shop obscured between two sprawling factories. Richard Park, the beefy Malaysian manager, has, like so many of his overseas counterparts, been to the mountain. He has traveled to Milwaukee on several occasions and has participated in massive gatherings of the clan at Sturgis and Daytona Beach. His dealership serves as a meeting place for the local HOG chapter, where director Andy Sitton, a sandy-haired, middle-aged transplanted American oil executive, presides over the intensely loyal membership. The group is a diverse and friendly mixture of Singapore natives, westerners like Sitton and Englishman Tony Goldman, a managing director of the Scott Vickers Group, and assorted pals from all over the world. A serious commitment is required, owing to the high initial cost of the motorcycle and the complexity of adhering to the myriad laws of ownership. But as is the case in other major cities across the re-gion, it is the sheer, bald-faced audacity of the machine and its unique exhaust that are at the heart of its appeal in Singapore.

The sound. Everywhere across the great Far East this raucous, purely American thunder packs powerful status. In teeming Jakarta, the capital of the polyglot island nation of Indonesia, the Harley-Davidson remains a toy of the very rich, even as the nation's econ-omy has collapsed. Its roughly two thousand Harley owners come from the ruling elite, gathering on the weekends at a club south of the city called the Eagle's Nest, from there to embark on orderly, police-escorted rides through the rice paddies that spread across Java. The Harley-Davidson name is so potent that even its $80,000 cost, including massive taxes, have not deterred the privileged classes from ownership. A special law was passed to exclude Harley-Davidsons from a ban on imported motorcycles of over 250 cc, and Robby Djohan, a retired bank president, arranged a licensing agreement with Harley-Davidson to assemble their motorcycles in Jakarta under the name Jatayu (a popular eagle character in Indonesian puppet shows). The first model, appropriately enough, was presented to the nation's all-powerful, seventy-five-year-old president-cum-dictator, Suharto, before he was deposed during the 1998 economic crisis.

Despite the orderly, sanitizing effects of rigid central governments, the raffish, faintly anarchistic aura of the Harley-Davidson persists in the Far and Middle East, from Hong Kong to Dubai — where a huge dealership caters to the local princes. The riders are for the most part wealthy businessmen, playboys, and royals who can afford the expense and possess the influence to navigate the labyrinth of regulations to gain ownership. Yet the bad guys lurk in the background, offering dimension and verisimilitude to the basic image. Rumors abound that the Hells Angels are part owners of a hotel complex in Thailand, and gangs known as the Headhunters, the Immortals, and the Jesters operate in the major cities.

To many members of the eastern upper classes, often raised within the strictures of Islam or ancient social customs, the Harley-Davidson offers a relatively harmless form of rebellion. It serves as the symbol of suggested anarchy, a subtle weapon against convention that separates its owner from his class on an incremental basis, an essentially innocent gap that labels him as an adventurous soul without shredding his basic cultural bonds. Therefore, when the loyalists gather each April for a Pacific Rim version of the Sturgis bike bash on the island of Phuket off the western coast of Malaysia, it is a tame version of the Black Hills bacchanal, with little more than modest wet T-shirt contests and drag races to enliven the festivities. Members of the various HOG chapters must conceal their club patches on Phuket because references of all kinds to pork in the Muslim nation are illegal. Laws forbidding loud exhaust pipes and requiring low speeds, rigid social and religious conventions, and bank-breaking taxes and import duties all conspire against the Harley-Davidson owner in one form or another across the Middle and Far East, from the steamy, sandy shores of the Persian Gulf to the teeming huddle of Tokyo. Yet the mad old machine, this archaic symbol of American independence and mobility, prevails, a rare and prized talisman of the mysterious, distant culture of the tall, uncourtly men called Yankees.

Compared to Athens, Singapore is an Eden of serenity, a garden that happens to encompass a city. Athens is a shabby madhouse that happens to encompass the cradle of western civilization. Bedlam among the ruins. Save for its glittering monuments, topped by the humbling majesty of the Acropolis, Athens is a grimy, deafening sprawl of twentieth-century tastelessness. Mile upon mile of blocky poured-concrete offices and apartment houses line its soot-stained streets. Mobs of tiny scooters and small, dirty, dented sedans create an endless hurricane of sound. Each stoplight becomes the starting line for a scooter drag race, in which hundreds of men of all ages, their dark eyes burning with competitive zeal, launch their screaming 50 cc Vespas, Hondas, and Piaggios like dervishes toward the next intersection. Each seems somehow to believe that by being the fastest, bravest, most audacious rider in his pack, he can somehow revive Greece's long-lost glories, or at the very least strike a blow against the hated Turks.

The First American Motorcycle Store fronts Kailirrois Avenue, a roaring sluiceway of traffic lined with small car repair shops, parts stores, and motorcycle dealerships. Its symbol is a David Mann–inspired graybeard riding a chopper with radical high bars and a swoopy exhaust. Mike Lazarantos, the proprietor, is a powerfully built, chain-smoking, pigtailed man in his late thirties who labors amid a litter of Harley-Davidson parts and semicompleted custom motorcycles. His father was Austrian, his mother Greek, and he loves few people. "Greece is a poor country," he grumbles.

> A rich elite. No middle class. The rest are poor. The Rubes buy all the new Harleys, maybe two hundred or so a year, and they ride 'em around Kolonaki Square with all its fancy bars to get chicks. It's a fashion thing. This is a country of show-offs. Because Greece taxes on the basis of the value of your possessions, not income, most normal guys can't afford a Harley. But among the real riders, old bikes — *real old* Shovelheads and Pans — are the things. I love my old Shovelhead. It's like a tiger in a cage. Think about that engine sound — thump, thump, thump. Like a heartbeat. Like horses' hooves. Like the blades of a big helicopter or an American V-8. There's something about it, but it ain't freedom. *Freedom.* All that crap about freedom on a motorcycle. I'm not free, and because I ride a Harley doesn't mean me or my friends even like Americans. It's us and the Turks. The Americans are in the middle, playing both sides. I bought my daughter a bikini designed like an American flag. She's scared to wear it.

He lights a foul-smelling Greek cigarette and stares at the mobs of scooters screeching past his showroom window. "Greeks are simpleminded. We love American food, American movies and music. American fashions, all that," he says. "We take their tourist dollars and sell 'em souvenir shit and show 'em our monuments, but we don't really like them. Sure, the Harley-Davidson is American, and I love it for its elemental quality. It's real. It's uncomplicated. I can adjust the valves on my old Shovelhead with a pair of pliers. But because it was made in America, so what?"

The disconnect. It is easy to assume that because the Harley-Davidson is purely American, with its eaglelike imagery and its aura of unfettered freedom, that there is an obvious link between the motorcycle and the nation that produces it. Surely among the owners in the United States there exists such a connection. American Harley owners pride themselves as patriots, reveling in the self-delusion that they are keepers of the flame, the last men on the ramparts to preserve the essential freedoms (which in most cases have been distilled to rather simplistic issues involving helmet laws, gun possession, and speed limits). But not so with Mike Lazarantos, who views the Harley-Davidson for what it is, a machine to be cherished regardless of its national origin, who is able to separate its essence from the nation that produced it — much as Americans love French wine but don't especially love Frenchmen, drive German cars but hardly emulate Germans, and wear Swiss watches but can barely locate the tiny country on a map.

The notion that the Harley-Davidson somehow projects international American power is pure delusion. American cultural influence, which Harley-Davidson represents in spades, cannot be confused with American power, either political or military. There was a time, at the end of World War II, when American GIs, with their Hershey bars and their Camels, served as representatives of both power and influence. Now America's ability to extend power globally has diminished, leaving fashionable symbols like the Harley-Davidson in its place. Could it be that future Americans, militarily defanged and marginalized internationally, will fall back on their legendary products as symbols of glory, much like powerless Egyptians, Italians, and Greeks comfort themselves with a delusionary national potency represented only by marble statues and splendid stone ruins? That is not to deny that the Harley-Davidson has become an international symbol of rebellion and antiestablishmentarianism and is a powerful talisman of anarchy in almost every nation on the globe. But that imagery has become internalized by and custom fitted to individual cultures; only in the broadest sense does it relate to American perceptions of its own importance. To the Harley rider vamping around Athens's Constitution Square or to the members of the aged Harley-Davidson Club of Prague, which has remained in operation since 1928 while enduring the gruesome oppressions of both the Nazis and the Communists, the motorcycle has gained a local persona. All generally relate to the booming exhaust, the ride, the sensuous styling, and the endemic aura of potency and power. But the notion that each time the Czech Harley rider, or one of the rare owners among the new Russian rich, climbs aboard his machine, he somehow mumbles a silent prayer to Thomas Jefferson or Abraham Lincoln is nonsense. Like Coca-Cola and Marlboros and other purely American products, Harley-Davidson owes most of its international popularity to the pungent taste it offers, not necessarily to its red, white, and blue pedigree.

This is not to suggest that all Harleys are popular overseas *despite* their Americanism in general and their linkage to the great West and its cowboys in particular. Marlboro plays on its cowboy imagery worldwide, and it is hardly coincidental that many Harley-Davidson dealerships are decorated in western themes. Bobo's Chopper Corner in Munich is a classic example. Bobo Faehndrich, a small, compact man with a scruffy beard and wispy blond hair, has been in business for eighteen years, selling more than one hundred new Harleys a year from his shop in an industrial park managed with typical German cleanliness and efficiency. His store, with its hand-hewn natural wood ceiling and stone floor, is faux frontier, and among the racks of Harley-Davidson fashions — jackets, denim skirts, T-shirts, boots, helmets, gloves, goggles, sunglasses, Harley-labeled Zippo lighters, and jewelry — are American flags and interstate signs, American motorcycle magazines and copies of David Mann's coffee-table book of chopper art.

Bobo's is one of the best known and most prestigious Harley-Davidson dealerships in Germany, which in itself represents the largest overseas market for the company. Its HOG chapters include more than ten thousand members, and between Bobo's and two large Berlin dealerships, Classic Bike and Harley Korso, the brand enjoys tremendous popularity, especially in high-impact locales like the fashionable Schwabing section of Munich. Both Bobo and his manager, Stefan Peroutka, are openly pro-American and have attended numerous Harley gatherings, including Sturgis and Daytona Beach. "Most Germans can't afford them, but everybody wants a Harley," says Peroutka, a slight man wearing a black Harley T-shirt adorned with a fierce air-brushed eagle. "We've even sold two Heritage Softails to guys in Moscow. There's no dealer there, only a boutique where they sell five-hundred-dollar boots and seventy-dollar T-shirts. We did all the business by fax. They cost fifty thousand marks each — well over twenty thousand dollars U.S. — but the money was good. We took the business. Hey, it's the American way, right?" he asks, smiling.

Far to the south, along the Adriatic, lies Rimini, the most popular resort city of eastern Italy, a place where Federico Fellini spent years overeating at his favorite table at the elegant il Grand Hotel di

Rimini, until his death in 1993. It is the same baroque hostelry where Benito Mussolini stashed his mistress, Clara Petacci, during vacations with his family at his nearby seaside villa. Rimini is far away from all things American, save for the occasional peace sign graffito or a sports jacket of famed teams like the Dallas Cowboys, the Chicago Bulls, or the Los Angeles Lakers. The cobbled, tree-lined Via Vespucci is, Italian-fashion, a mad scene of minibikes and scooters — Hondas, Piaggios, and Peugeots by the thousands — all darting and juking among honking, impudent Fiat Pandas, Unos, Puntos, Volkswagen Polos, and Renault Twingos and Clios. Like its neighbors across the Adriatic in Greece, half the population of Italy seems to live astride tiny, buzzing scooters, intent, if nothing else, on driving the other half insane.

In the swarm of Lilliputians stands a Gulliver. On a street corner, a tired and hunched man rents scooters to tourists. But parked in front of his stall on the Paizzale Kennedy is a magnificent, wine red Harley-Davidson Heritage Softail. He has waited months for its delivery from the dealer in Bologna and rolls his eyes to amplify the enormous expense of the beast. "Harley-Davidsons are very popular here," he says. "The young stallions parade them endlessly on summer weekends. There is no better way to find a young girl. As luck would have it, I am too old, too poor, and married. My Harley is just for me," he laments.

Italy is a strong Harley-Davidson market, ranking fourth (behind Germany, the United Kingdom, and Benelux — Belgium, Netherlands, Luxumberg) in ownership and HOG memberships. As in the rest of Europe, the bikes remain expensive, exclusive gas guzzlers, difficult to maneuver in the cramped streets of the ancient cities. Due to their sheer bulk and cost, they are destined to remain baubles for the rich and audacious in a land where the shrewish screech of the scooters will forever drown out the thump of the occasional Harley-Davidson.

Not so in Monaco and along the magical French Riviera, though, where the chiggerlike little scooters are tightly controlled. The streets of such fabled enclaves as Monte Carlo, Antibes, and Cannes remain relatively silent, save for the muffled growl of a Ferrari or Porsche or the mutter of a big BMW or Harley-Davidson. Noise laws are strictly enforced along the Côte d'Azur, and even the richest fool does not tangle with the ever-present gendarmes. Regardless, Harley-Davidsons remain powerful social talismans, always to be seen on warm days proudly parading on the Avenue Albert and around the Place de Casino, where the gawkers, the tourists, the wanna-bes, and the hicks sit by the hour at the Café de Paris in the pitiful hope of spotting a celebrity. So too at stylish Saint-Tropez, a few craggy Mediterranean inlets to the west. Harleys are major showbiz here, gathering up on weekends at the cafés and brasseries, where their owners preen for the gawking masses. Tourists seek a glance at the French superstar singer Johnny Hallyday, who owns several Harleys and therefore lends a near-royal imprimatur to its status.

Vince Vito, owner of Nice's Harley-Davidson dealership on the elegant city's Rue Scaliero, agrees that the Harley's macho image and high-impact trendiness attract customers. Although possessed of the typical French ambivalence toward many things American, he believes that the Yankee heritage of the machine is a positive factor. Vito is a large, mustached man with a head the size and shape of a cannonball. His neat store is laden with American-style clothing, and his radically fashioned custom low rider won fifth place in a national contest sponsored by *Freeway* magazine, a French monthly devoted to the Harley culture. "A lot of Harleys were left over by the GIs when the war ended," he says. "They were converted for civilian use, and that gave Harley a good name." Vito's dealership is but one of thirty authorized outlets spread across France — including three in Paris (as well as two more clothing boutiques on the City of Light's Boulevard Beaumarchais and the Avenue de la Grande Armée). "We sell about sixty bikes a year, which is down from the peak in the early nineties, before our economy got soft. The customers who want them are patient, figuring it's a once-in-a-lifetime purchase," he says.

Like many major foreign dealers, Vince Vito has traveled to the Milwaukee headquarters as well as to Sturgis and Daytona Beach. When asked about the outlaw image, he laughs. "Here they buy Harleys to show off. The local HOG chapter meets at the tennis club. [France has about 3,500 HOG members.] Sure, there are gangs. It's pretty tough up around Dijon, but not here in Provence. The farther north you go, the more of them there are. Like Denmark."

He speaks of an ongoing war in that benign little homeland of Hans Christian Andersen. Danish members of the Bandidos and the Hells Angels have been engaged in deadly combat there for nearly twenty years. The origins of the war are unknown, presumably based on an arcane violation of the code of honor. The Bandidos are affiliated with the Texas-based club and formed in Denmark as an extension of the American club a few years after the Angels did. Both clubs have about eight chapters encompassing all of Scandinavia and Finland, and when not shooting or tossing hand grenades and even aiming shoulder-fired antitank missiles at each other, they beat up on smaller gangs like the Avengers, the Pagans, and the Heathens. Hells Angel Jorn "Jonke" Nielsen has become a celebrity in Denmark, having written a bestselling autobiography after killing a rival gang member in a shootout, fleeing to Canada, then returning to Denmark to enter prison. Three more books followed, all issued from behind bars, and Nielsen became a television talk show celebrity and lecturer. The most recent war, which Nielsen has witnessed from his cell, escalated in 1996, when a Bandido was killed in a parking lot of the Copenhagen airport and another was shot and wounded in Oslo on the same day. Shortly thereafter, a Hells Angels clubhouse was hit by antitank missiles. A hand grenade was then tossed into a low-security prison exercise yard, wounding yet another Bandido. Bomb attacks on the Angels then spread as far away as Finland. Throughout the battle, which does not involve private citizens and centers on the estimated fifty to sixty hard-core members of each club, the Hells Angels souvenir store remains open in Copenhagen. The Harley-Davidson, in ominous chopper form, is a major presence on the Angels T-shirts, jackets, and vests, retaining its primary linkage with the One Percenters around the world.

It is this omnipresent bad-guy imagery that offers such a bizarre marketing opportunity for the company, giving it a reputation for menace and potency and implied residual energy that far transcends the motorcycle itself. Somehow, in the deep recesses of the brain of everyone who ever climbs aboard a Harley-Davidson is the dim assurance that he is empowered with the same invincible lethalness possessed by Jonke Nielsen and his raging band of Danish Angels. Few will admit it, but it is present as surely as the drumbeat cadence of the big twin between his legs.

It is not a coincidence that the Scandinavians have become immersed in the culture of legendary motorcycle clubs like the Angels. There is at the core of them — and of the Harley mind-set in general — a tribal quality strongly relatable to the Nordic myths and the inherent runic powers that predate recorded history. Like the Nazi employment of Aryan mythology during their short-lived and depraved tenure, many of the modern motorcycle clubs deal in a ragged sense of racial purity. While black counterparts exist, most of the major clubs are pure white, with powerful rituals involving membership, weddings, and funerals. Much of their behavior is luridly pagan with even anti-Christian overtones. The death's head, a powerful amulet of the Nazi SS elite, is widely employed among a number of the major motorcycle clubs, in part for its shock value and in part because of strong philosophical links to the heady ritualism of the National Socialists. It is not coincidental that while mostly apolitical, motorcycle gangs have been linked with skinhead groups, rabid antitax and -government organizations, and far-right extremist militia and vigilante bands. While hardly all-pervasive, the heady brews of military structure, discipline, and loyalty can sometimes combine to explode in bloody acts of violence of the kind that rumble across Scandinavia, simultaneously outraging and fascinating the establishment everywhere. In this context, the Harley-Davidson is a mere fashion item, unrelated to the powerful cultism that energizes the lifestyle of the clubs.

This dark world on the fringes of the Harley-Davidson culture and the biker wars it can engender fester in Scandinavia and, closer to home, in the otherwise benign nation of Canada. The Hells Angels now have more than one hundred chapters worldwide, including one in the unlikely location of Manaus, deep in the Brazilian rain forest. But a major center of violence is the Canadian province of Quebec, where a bloody turf war with a local Montreal club, the Rock Machine, has centered on control of the street-level drug trade and a thriving prostitution business built on strip clubs populated by indentured Asian girls. After a brutal and deadly internecine war between rival chapters within the Canadian Angels was settled in the early 1990s, the battle shifted to disposing of the Rock Machine and its allies, the hated Bandidos. More than forty bikers on both sides were killed in a spate of bombings, machine-gunnings, and knifings over a two-year span. The police could do little to stop the carnage until an eleven-year-old boy died in the cross fire. Now special federal laws give the police wide latitude to control the warring factions who battle for control of Canada's drug traffic from Quebec City to Vancouver.

In the United States, the Angels celebrated their fiftieth birthday with what they called World Run '98. The trip began in San Bernardino, the home base of the club, and ran north to Ventura, where the local media fretted that a thousand Visigoths might appear to rape and pillage. In fact, fewer than four hundred members made the trip, and rather than duplicating the Hollister riot that started the whole thing, the Angels were perfect tourists, shopping for souvenirs and posing for a group photo on the steps of San Buenaventura city hall as dozens of baffled cops from around the United States and Canada looked on. At roughly the same time, thirty members of the Pagans, a nationwide club always ready to butt heads with the Angels and other biker groups, were arrested on Long Island for extortion, arson, and weapons possession. These clubs — or gangs, or sophisticated criminal organizations — are essentially unrelated to the Harley-Davidson mystique except in a subliminal sense. While their motorcycles have become less important as they move into a broader world of big-time crime (often in business suits), the pungent, hyperbolic aura of the outlaw and his "chopper," "bobber," or "scoot" permeates the entire Harley-Davidson mind-set, subconsciously representing the essence of rebellious independence and anarchy.

In 1998, the prestigious Guggenheim Museum of Art in New York City attempted to recognize the phenomenon with a much-criticized exhibition titled "The Art of the Motorcycle." Sponsored by BMW, the show traced the history of the machine from a rare 1893 French-built Millet to contemporary bikes from Honda and the host manufacturer, among others. Ten Harley-Davidsons were represented, although the reviewer for the *New York Times* was too aesthetically sensitive to mention them in his critique of the show, sniffing that "muscle bikes are ugly." However, despite the efforts of Guggenheim curator Thomas Krens, who rides a BMW, the link between the high-culture world of the Guggenheim and that of the latently proletarian motorcycle remains tenuous at best. Perhaps that will change based on the popularity of the Guggenheim show, which amazed conventional art lovers and seemed to affirm the widespread fascination and mystique that these machines embody. At the center of the phenomenon lies the Harley-Davidson, the reputation of which has spread across the globe, despite its spurning by the culturati.

If there is a simple reason for the appeal of the Harley-Davidson on a worldwide basis, it lies in its perceived power and its trappings of Yankee insolence. There are any number of nations where the Harley-Davidson is viewed favorably even as American foreign policy, business practices, and even table manners are reviled. The "ugly American" image still pertains, and it is within this context that the Harley derives its appeal. Like the nation that produces it, the venerable machine is an outsized, noisy, cocky, profane, and often ill-mannered country boy with its Huck Finn good nature cloaking a concealed danger. The enduring image of the American cowboy as the freewheeling, always-smiling but lethal gunfighter operating with unfettered independence persists worldwide. The Dallas Cowboys sell their logoed jackets and T-shirts globally, not because a French or a Japanese youth cares a hoot about the team's success on the football field, but for what the team represents in the context of the American myth. So too for Garth Brooks and other country-and-western stars who, through song and lifestyle, carry forth the fading imagery of the great western legends. The same for the Harley-Davidson, a twentieth-century bucking bronco capable of transporting its rider, be he Indonesian or Swede, into the misty realms of yore, when the last cowboys ruled the West.

The company's 1996 annual financial report headlined the following ten words, which summarized its unique philosophy:

HERITAGE

QUALITY

PASSION

LOOK

SOUND

FEEL

RELATIONSHIPS

FREEDOM

INDIVIDUALITY

LIFESTYLE

In a broad and perhaps simplistic sense, this list embodies much of what American culture is all about, that which critics have been denouncing as vapid and superficial, venal and pretentious, bombastic and hollow since its rise to prominence in the early nineteenth century. Henry James, the great novelist and essayist who became so critical of his native land that he spent most of his adult life in England and in fact became a British subject, carried on a correspondence with fellow writer Nathaniel Hawthorne in which James dismissed America as a cultural wasteland:

> No sovereign, no court, no personal loyalty, no aristocracy, no church, no clergy, no army, no diplomatic service, no country gentlemen, no palaces, no castles, nor manors, nor old country houses, nor parsonages, nor thatched cottages, nor Ivied ruins, nor cathedrals, nor abbeys, nor little Norman churches, no great universities, nor public schools, no Oxford or Eaton, nor Harrow, no literature, no novels, no museums, no pictures, no political society, no sporting class — no Epsom or Ascot!

Hawthorne's response was brilliant. He said he delighted in America, which had "no shadow, no antiquity, no mystery, no picturesque and gloomy wrong, nor anything but a commonplace prosperity, in broad and simple daylight."

Some Europeans, led by Count Alexis de Tocqueville, viewed the fresh, vibrant American spirit in a favorable light. De Tocqueville's 1835 treatise *Democracy in America* contains amazing insights into the American character that still pertain as the book nudges toward its two hundredth birthday. The country's brashness, its lack of constricted social mores and stifling class structures, and its bawdy egalitarianism intrigued not only de Tocqueville (while leaving Charles Dickens, after an extended tour, less than enthusiastic), but also the great German poet Johann Goethe, who rejoiced that America had "no ruined castles, no venerable stones, no useless memories, no vain feuds."

It is amazing to American intellectual critics and supporters alike how quickly the nation created its own mythology, its own history, its own sense of self . . . its own "venerable stones and vain feuds." The Revolution — Lexington, Concord, Valley Forge; the western explorations — Lewis and Clark; the agonies of the Civil War and its attendant heroes from Lincoln to Stonewall Jackson; the great frontier, with its legendary Codys, Earps, and Cochises; the victories — Saratoga, the Alamo, Gettysburg, Little Big Horn, San Juan Hill, Belleau Wood, Bataan, Normandy, Iwo Jima; the warriors and the poets, the inventors and the politicians, and the soaring energy of the Plains-born novelists from Cather to Lewis to Hemingway, all conspired and congealed to create within a brief two centuries a deep, rich mixture of heritage and legend that still baffles and troubles the elitists. How can a nation so diverse, so unstructured, so marginally anarchistic, so racially unsettled, so endlessly self-critical, so bombastic and ill-mannered, so erratic and unpredictable, have risen to such power and glory?

And how can it continue? The great frontier and manifest destiny have long ended. All the territory has been conquered and settled. Malibu and Newport Beach are hardly frontier outposts. Now butted up against the great Pacific, the legendary migrations that energized and inspired the nation are over. Yes, the population continues to move, as much as 20 percent each year, swirling into heretofore unlikely spots on the map like hellfire-hot Henderson, Nevada, and wind-and-snow-swept Bozeman, Montana. But we have become flies in a bottle, phototropically seeking open space but trapped on a tiny orb in the outer perimeters of the firmament.

Yet there are pockets of hope. Many are unformed, incoherent, antisocial, irresponsible. They percolate around the edges of society, bubbling for release. They are overly violent, primevally sexual, audacious, and profane. Perhaps they are inverse reactions to the alleged communications revolution, which, rather than increasing human contact, has diminished it or at the very least dehumanized it. A sense of isolation seems to pervade contemporary society, increasing angst and driving people inward to ruminate about their frustrations and failings. They turn to technology as salvation, seeking solace in the miracles of the microchip and the electronic relationships of the Internet, which are at best vacant, hollow, and artificial. Some pessimists fear that a growing dependence on computers can potentially immobilize civilization. A simple satellite failure can now shut down the worldwide paging network and even credit card transactions at locations as mundane as the corner gas station. Teenage hackers have the potential to interdict crucial defense networks. A mathematician at Cambridge has dolefully speculated about a future world in which supercomputers might link up on their own, seizing control of power grids, communications networks, water supply systems, air control hookups, and a myriad of other crucial components of civilization. The computer has been an enormous source of good in the fields of medicine and applied science. Life span and the quality of daily existence have surely been increased due to the microchip. New drugs, new surgical techniques, new methods of diagnosis, etc., would not exist were it not for the microchip. So too for the profusion of convenience items that on the surface offer a level of luxury to the average blue-collar worker unimaginable even to the Rockefellers and the Onassises thirty years ago. Yet the angst increases, seemingly in inverse proportion to the enhancement of the good life. This suggests that without conflict, without challenge, without opposing forces and external threats, man weakens and begins to falter, both individually and collectively.

So what is left? The vacant satisfactions of inner space and the subordination of self to the computer and virtual reality? The docile capitulation to the safety net of the nanny state and the prison ship of political correctness? The mindless goose-step into group-think and New Age frontal lobe massage? Perhaps that is our fate.

But at the end of the bus line, before the last stop on the road to oblivion, lies that crazy, tasteless, violent, bizarre, mongrel horde called Americans with their god-awful music, their horrendous sloppiness and rudeness, and their reservoir of aggravatingly cheerful optimism. At the heart of it is the archaic, throwback Harley-Davidson motorcycle, a dreadful, irresponsible machine with no redeeming social qualities — mechanical pornography to decent folk — that simply won't go away despite the sheer, outrageous blat of its fuming exhaust in the face of seamless technology and the orderly, opulent, but essentially soulless brave new world. But if that rumble, that ungodly roar, that death threat to collectivism and convention dies away, it will be time to turn out the lights.

ABOUT THE AUTHOR

One of the most respected automotive journalists in the country, **Brock Yates** is editor at large for *Car and Driver*, a long-time commentator on both network and cable television, and the author of several books. He has written extensively for a number of magazines, including *Sports Illustrated*, *Life*, *Playboy*, *American Heritage*, and *Reader's Digest*. He lives in Wyoming, New York.